KNACK™
MAKE IT EASY

GROOMING HORSES

KNACK™

GROOMING
HORSES

A Complete Illustrated Guide

JESSIE SHIERS

with contributions by Laura H. Ward,
Associate Professor-Equestrian Studies,
William Woods University

PHOTOGRAPHS BY MOIRA C. HARRIS

Guilford, Connecticut
An imprint of The Globe Pequot Press

Text design by Paul Beatrice

Front and back cover photo credits: Moira C. Harris
All interior photos by Moira C. Harris with the exception of:
Kelly Meadows (p. 47 [right], p. 106, p. 101 [left], p. 114, p. 115, p. 140, p. 141, p. 154, p. 155, p. 178, p. 179 [left], p. 182, p. 183, p. 186, p. 187 [right], p. 188–193, p. 196–205, pp. 209–213); Kathe Dupuis (p. 212 [left]); The Fresian Horse Association (p. 212 [right]); *The Voice Magazine—The Official Breed Journal of The Tennessee Walking Horse*, Lewisburg, Tennessee 931.359.1574 (p. 185 [left]; Jason Smith (pp. 214–215); Stewart Harvey (p. 56 [left])

Library of Congress Cataloging-in-Publication Data is available on file.

ISBN 978-1-59921-390-3

Printed in China
10 9 8 7 6 5 4 3 2 1

Acknowledgments

This book is the result of the input of many different people. There is no way I could have done it on my own. Much appreciation goes first and foremost to Laura Ward of William Woods University for writing the saddle seat chapters, for her expertise in reviewing the entire manuscript, and for organizing the photo shoots at William Woods. Thank you as well to the students at William Woods who served as models and grooms for the photo shoots there. Thanks go to Moira Harris and Kelly Meadows for the photography. Thanks to Sandra Possin and to Susan Doner of Little Bull Run Farm for their input on warmblood breed inspections. And thanks to editors Maureen Graney and Katie Benoit and layout artist Melissa Evarts at The Globe Pequot Press.

CONTENTS

INTRODUCTION

In any discipline, as well as for any proud but non-showing horse owner, the goal of grooming is a beautiful horse. Your horse's appearance is a reflection of yourself and your horsekeeping practices. The object of **Knack Grooming Horses** is to serve as the ultimate guide to grooming, no matter what your skill level. It includes information for the non-showing horse owner as well as detailed instructions for grooming horses for competition in all disciplines—Western, English, and saddle seat alike.

A beautiful horse is one that is in good weight—neither too thin nor too fat—is well conditioned with even development of muscle tone, has healthy skin and a slick, shiny coat, and has strong hooves and a thick, soft mane and tail. When it comes right down to it, the very most important—and effective—aspects of grooming are the two things we do every day: feeding and brushing. The main reason that horses from top show barns look positively iridescent is not a magic bullet. It is simply that they receive optimum quality feed and very thorough daily grooming. Everything else is just details.

Diet and Exercise

Specific needs vary from horse to horse, but some constants remain the same. A balanced diet founded on a base of high-quality hay or pasture is a prerequisite for a beautiful horse. Have your hay analyzed each year, and then choose concentrates, such as grain or vitamin/mineral supplements, as needed based on what nutrients are lacking or out of balance in the hay. Proteins, fats, omega-3 fatty acids, and minerals are all crucial for healthy hair and hoof growth.

While proper nutrients are vital, a healthy lifestyle is not complete without the help of several other factors. For the horse to properly utilize the nutrients you feed him, he must be on a regular deworming program and live a relatively stress-free lifestyle. Horses that are stressed by chronic pain or illness, inadequate turnout and exercise,

isolation, a demanding show schedule, hostile turnout companions, or other factors may have trouble gaining weight and may look rough.

For a show horse, regular healthy exercise is a must to maintain condition and develop proper muscling. Exactly what form this exercise takes will vary according to the discipline and the age and level of training of the horse. An eventer will look his best when he is lean and fit, ready for a hard, fast day on the cross-country course. In comparison, a well-conditioned dressage horse or reining horse may carry more weight and muscle, which he needs to perform the complex movements of his sport. At the far end of the spectrum is the halter Quarter Horse, whose ideal image is muscular and stout. Conditioning programs that lead to these various results should be tailored to the particular horse's needs.

Daily Grooming

After diet, the most important strategy for producing a beautiful horse is thorough daily grooming. A good currying encourages blood flow to the skin, stimulates the skin cells, removes dust, dander, and loose hairs, and distributes the skin's natural oils over the hair coat. After each brushing session, a final ten-minute rubdown with a clean, soft towel or chamois imparts a glowing shine.

In addition, the daily grooming session is an opportunity for the groom or owner to thoroughly inspect every part of the horse, looking for wounds, skin problems, and injuries. Daily hoof care keeps the hooves clean and healthy, preventing problems such as thrush from developing.

Beyond the Basics

Above and beyond the fundamentals of diet, conditioning, and daily brushing, grooming encompasses all skin, coat, and hoof care, including bacterial and fungal skin problems as well as more advanced grooming techniques. The first several chapters of *Knack Grooming*

INTRODUCTION

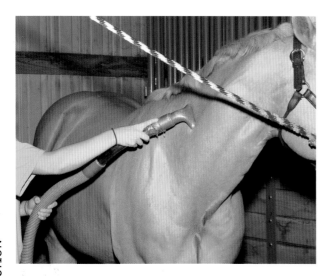

Horses cover these basic aspects of grooming and care for the beginning and intermediate equestrian, from outfitting your grooming kit and creating a safe and functional work area to choosing boots and wraps, and treating common skin and coat ailments. You'll learn how to use a vacuum and clippers, keep a tail long and full, and pull a mane evenly and neatly.

For the more experienced equestrian who is ready to move on to grooming her horse for show, the show preparation chapters explain in detail how to braid, clip, trim, and present a horse for shows. It is important to present the best possible image. It doesn't matter if your horse is a blue-blooded, multi-thousand-dollar animal or an auction rescue—proper grooming and preparation can make him look his best.

Moreover, a well-groomed horse with the traditional braiding or other finishing touches shows respect for your discipline and for the judge. Presenting a horse that is not well groomed is literally an insult to the judge and is indicative of poor horsemanship in general. The knowledge and ability to present a horse well do not require a lot of money or special talents—just time and patience to practice and learn to do the job right.

Different Disciplines

Each show discipline has its own set of standards and styles. Chapters 13 and 14 describe grooming for the English disciplines of hunters and jumpers, dressage, and eventing, using the skills you learned in the earlier chapters on braiding, clipping, and manes and tails. Chapters

Chapter 19 covers some of the more common breeds that are shown in hand at breed shows, including Quarter Horses, Arabians, Morgans, Friesians, and warmbloods. Although it would have been impractical to cover specific grooming practices for every breed, we have included a list of organizations and publications for many breeds in the Resources chapter.

Aside from riding, grooming can be one of the most enjoyable aspects of owning a horse. A beautiful horse is a pleasure to behold. Take your time to perform all of these tasks with pride and attention to detail. The bloom on your horse's coat and the satisfaction of a job well done will be your rewards. Not to mention a possible blue ribbon!

15 and 16 cover all of the Western disciplines for stock horses (such as Quarter Horses, Paints, and Appaloosas) and saddle horses (Morgans, Arabians, and American Saddlebreds). Chapters 17 and 18 focus on the discipline of saddle seat, from Arabians in Country Pleasure to American Saddlebreds in Five-Gaited Performance.

BRUSHES
Every time you groom your horse, you will use a brush or two—or maybe three

Most horsemen have a vast selection of brushes for different applications. Some horses enjoy a good, firm brushing with a stiff-bristled brush. It seems to scratch their itches and produce a sense of calm. Other horses, such as Thoroughbreds and Arabians, have more sensitive skin and require a gentler touch with a softer brush. Your horse will quickly let you know if he doesn't approve of your choice of brush.

Some brushes are made for certain tasks. A stiff and short-bristled brush is good for cleaning dried mud off a horse's legs but leaves the coat looking dusty. A soft, long-bristled brush is best for a final polish of the coat but is useless at breaking up mud clumps. Choose your weapons carefully!

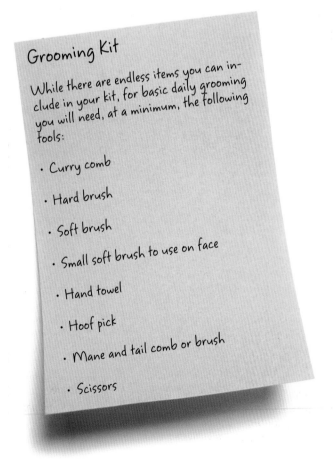

Grooming Kit

While there are endless items you can include in your kit, for basic daily grooming you will need, at a minimum, the following tools:

- Curry comb
- Hard brush
- Soft brush
- Small soft brush to use on face
- Hand towel
- Hoof pick
- Mane and tail comb or brush
- Scissors

Curries

- Hard rubber curries with long teeth are best for mud removal over muscular areas.

- Soft rubber curries with short teeth are good for use over the entire body. Rub firmly over muscular areas and gently over bony ones.

- A jelly scrubber or grooming mitt is a very soft and gentle curry for sensitive horses. It's also a useful bath tool.

- Metal curries are not for use on the horse.

In a boarding, lesson, or training facility with many horses, it is important that each horse have its own grooming kit, with its own brushes and other equipment. A variety of contagious diseases, from skin fungus to strangles, can be spread via contact with an infected grooming tool. Using separate equipment for each horse can help slow the spread of these problems.

Brushes

- Hard brushes (also called body brushes or dandy brushes) have stiff bristles. Use them after the initial currying to brush out the majority of the dirt, using short, brisk strokes.

- Soft brushes, sometimes made of horsehair, are used last, to remove any remaining dust or dander and to lay the coat flat and make it shine.

Mane and Tail Brushes and Combs

- A wide-tined comb can be used gently on the tail, working from bottom to top.

- A mane-pulling comb is part of your braiding kit (see page 92) but can also be used to comb the mane.

- A human hairbrush with plastic bristles makes a serviceable horse hairbrush.

- Combs with movable tines are available and are intended to help prevent hair breakage by being more flexible.

SPRAYS AND OTHER PRODUCTS

A variety of products is available today to help keep your horse shiny and clean

Liniments and braces are liquids or gels that are rubbed briskly into the muscles or tendons and joints of the legs, usually after a hard workout, to reduce inflammation, reduce pain or stiffness, and encourage circulation to the area. A poultice is a thick, sticky, claylike material used for the same purpose.

Shampoos and conditioners are used during a bath. Shampoo contains ingredients that break up the oils and dirt particles in the coat. The lathering action lifts these particles away from the skin and hair, so they can be rinsed away by water. Unfortunately, this same process also removes the natural oils of the skin that serve to protect and

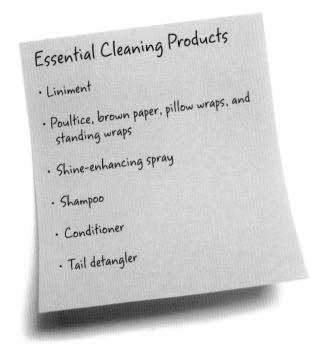

Essential Cleaning Products

- Liniment
- Poultice, brown paper, pillow wraps, and standing wraps
- Shine-enhancing spray
- Shampoo
- Conditioner
- Tail detangler

Liniments, Braces, and Poultices

- Liniment is available in liquid or gel form. Rub it briskly into the skin of the lower legs or large muscles to reduce or prevent soreness and inflammation after a hard ride.

- Add a splash of it to a bucket of water for a bath after a workout.

- Avoid wrapping, as some liniments can cause blistering on sensitive skin.

- Rubbing alcohol can be used as a liniment as well.

- Poultices are used under wraps. See page 64 for more on how and when to use them.

2

soften the hair. Frequent bathing can lead to brittle, dull hair and dry skin. Conditioning products can help counteract this effect.

Equine skin is sensitive. Never bathe a horse with dish detergent, laundry detergent, or car-washing products. Coat-enhancing sprays are generally silicone-based products that are misted onto the horse's coat to create a slippery barrier, which prevents dirt and dust from adhering to the coat and prevents tangles in the tail. These sprays also make the horse's coat shiny and slick.

Shampoos and Conditioners

- Horse shampoo is used for bathing. It cuts grease and entraps small dirt particles so they can be rinsed away with water.

- Conditioner replenishes moisture and oils that may be stripped from the hair by the shampoo, resulting in a softer, shinier coat.

- Always rinse a horse thoroughly with a hose after bathing. Residual products left on the skin can cause itching and dryness.

Shine-Enhancing Sprays

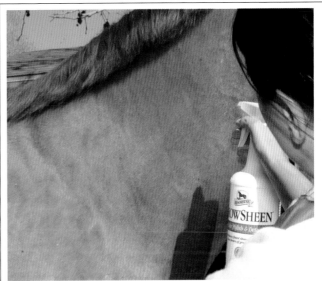

- Finishing sprays and wipes are available for after-bath or daily use to add shine and condition to the coat and to help the hair repel dust and grease so the horse stays cleaner longer.

- These products also serve as detangling agents when used in the mane or tail.

- Silicone is a common ingredient in these products. Some grooms believe that silicone can dry out the hair when used too frequently, so silicone-free products are also available.

HOOF CARE
The most fundamental and vital grooming tool is the humble hoof pick

Use your hoof pick to remove mud, manure, snow, ice, or the occasional stone from the horse's sole. There are several variations on the theme, from picks that fold up to fit in your pocket to picks with brushes on the back to scrub out the clefts of the frog. See page 32 for more on daily hoof care.

In addition, several products can be used on the horse's outer hoof wall and on the sole of the hoof as needed. These products are not necessary for every horse and in some cases may be detrimental. Adding too much water to the hoof wall with a moisturizing product can make the hoof crumbly and soft. Choose these products carefully, according to your horse's needs, and under the advisement of your farrier.

Hoof Care Items

All horse owners need a hoof pick, but not every horse requires every product on this list. Choose products based on your horse's specific problems and environmental conditions.

- Hoof pick with brush

- Hoof conditioner/moisturizer: Adds moisture to dry hooves

- Hoof hardener: Toughens weak hooves

- Hoof sealer: Keeps out excess moisture in wet conditions

- Hoof polish: Use at shows for a finishing touch

- Antibacterial and antifungal thrush treatment: Prevents or treats thrush and other hoof infections

Hoof Pick Assortment

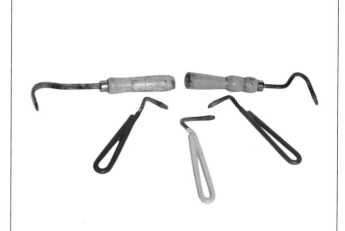

- When it comes to picks, a hard plastic handle with a metal pick and plastic bristle brush is ideal for daily use.

- All-metal picks are better for winter, when frozen ice or mud can bend the pick on a plastic-handled brush.

- Folding pocket hoof picks are usually too awkward for daily use but are easy to carry when traveling or on a trail ride in case a horse picks up a stone.

If a horse has hooves that are chronically weak or shelly, it may indicate a nutritional deficiency. Assess the horse's diet to ensure that he's getting adequate protein. The addition of supplements containing biotin or the amino acids methionine or lysine helps promote healthy hoof growth. It takes from nine months to a year for new hoof growth to reach ground level, so you will not see the effects of a dietary change instantly.

Treatments for the Outer Hoof

- Hardeners and sealants should be applied only to the lower three-quarters of the hoof, never to the coronary band.

- Conditioners and moisturizers, on the other hand, are most effective when rubbed directly into the coronary band.

- For the show-ring shine, wipe off any surface dirt with a clean cloth and apply a coat of polish or oil immediately before the horse enters the ring.

Treatments for the Sole of the Hoof

- Antibacterial or antifungal products are used on the sole of the hoof to prevent or treat thrush and other hoof ailments.

- After thoroughly cleaning the hoof, squirt the product deep into the clefts of the frog, as well as any other affected areas.

- Be careful not to spill any of the "purple stuff" or the "green stuff" onto your skin, clothes, or the horse's hair—the stains are very hard to get out.

FLY CONTROL

Keep your horse happily fly-free with repellents, barriers, and management methods

Whether horses are turned out or being worked, flies and other insects can cause them to be distracted and irritable and can even lead to hoof and leg damage (from stomping) or weight loss (as the horse spends more time avoiding insects than grazing or eating). In addition, some insects can spread infectious diseases, including West Nile virus.

Farm management strategies can minimize the fly population before it becomes a problem. The simplest and most effective strategy is to eliminate potential fly and mosquito breeding environments, keep stalls and paddocks free of manure and old hay, eliminate standing water, and scrub and refill pasture water troughs frequently. In the summer months,

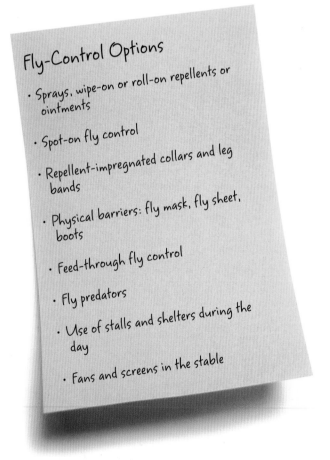

Fly-Control Options

- Sprays, wipe-on or roll-on repellents or ointments

- Spot-on fly control

- Repellent-impregnated collars and leg bands

- Physical barriers: fly mask, fly sheet, boots

- Feed-through fly control

- Fly predators

- Use of stalls and shelters during the day

- Fans and screens in the stable

Sprays and Wipes

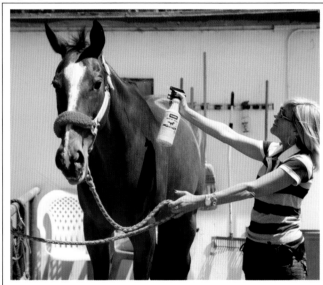

- Commercial fly sprays use a variety of chemicals and natural ingredients to repel or even kill flies and other insects.

- Pyrethrin is a common insecticide found in fly sprays, derived from the oil of the African chrysanthemum flower.

- Citronella is another natural ingredient that repels insects.

- Never spray the product directly onto a horse's face. Instead, spray it onto a cloth or sponge and wipe it onto the skin.

change your turnout schedule so that the horses are in the barn with fans on during the day, and turned out at night.

Fly predators, tiny insects that feed on fly larvae, are a new weapon in the battle against flies. They are extremely effective and available through mail order. Another strategy, feed-through fly control program, uses pelleted products fed to horses daily to prevent the growth of fly larvae in their manure. There are also many products that can be used to make horses more comfortable, ranging from chemical repellents to physical barriers such as masks and sheets.

Ointments and Spot-On Repellents

- Ointments containing fly repellents are great in the summer to prevent flies from irritating and carrying infection to an open wound. After cleaning the wound, wipe on a little of the treated ointment.

- Ointment can also serve as a physical barrier to tiny biting insects. Smear onto vulnerable areas—inside ears, around eyes, around the sheath or teats, and along the midline of the belly.

- Spot-on repellents impregnate the coat with long-lasting insecticides that prevent fly and tick bites.

Masks, Sheets, and Boots

- Fly masks physically prevent flies from landing on and biting the horse and also help to shield the horse's eyes from glaring sun. Masks with ears are the most effective. Some also have an extended nose section to protect the muzzle from insects and sunburn.

- Fly sheets protect from flies while also keeping the horse cooler. Look for a UV-rated sheet to guard against sun bleaching.

- Fly boots can be used on a horse that stomps excessively, but check the horse regularly to be sure the boots don't shift.

CLIPPERS AND VACUUMS
Power tools can provide easier living through technology

Most people will want to invest in a pair of the small clippers available for horses. Whether you need a set of body clippers or a vacuum will depend on the type of horse you have and how you will be using him. See page 70 for more on selecting and using clippers.

Horse vacuums are excellent at speeding up the body grooming process. They take in the dust as well as dirt without drying out the horse's coat (as would a shampoo). Once the horse is used to the vacuum, he usually learns to thoroughly enjoy the process. If you are going to add a vacuum to your grooming area, make sure that you have enough room so that neither the horse nor you will trip over it. See page 42 for more on using a vacuum.

Read through the manual that comes with each tool, which

Clipper Blade Size Chart

- #10 – Against the hair: Trim in cool weather when horse has longer coat including face, ears, and legs

- #10 – With the hair: Blend lines between clipped and unclipped areas or between areas clipped with the body clippers and small clippers

- #15 – Same as #10s with slightly finer cut

- #30 – Same as #40s with slightly coarser cut

- #40 – Against the hair: Trim horse with short coat including the muzzle, inside of ears, and bridle path. This gives the closest trim

- #40 – With the hair: Blend lines between clipped areas

Body Clippers

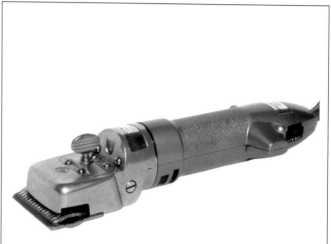

- Body clippers are designed to remove hair over large areas of the horse's body; as a result they have wider blades, which can be changed when they become dull and start leaving streaks as you trim.

- Body clippers come with a storage case and detailed instructions. Proper care extends the life of clippers and makes the job of clipping much more enjoyable.

- Additional items to add to your body clipping kit include: screwdriver, clean rags, soft brush, clipper oil, coolant, blade wash, and heavy duty extension cord.

tells you if there is anything you might need to do before using it for the first time. Also refer back to it for safety tips, extension cord usage, and cleaning.

Detail Clippers

- These clippers go by several different names, including small, detail, or light clippers.

- The most versatile styles have easily removable sets of blades available in different sizes, so they are suitable for all trimming jobs except the major body clips.

- Additional items to add to your small clipping kit include: screwdriver, clean rags, soft brush, clipper oil, coolant, blade wash, and heavy duty extension cord.

Horse Vacuums

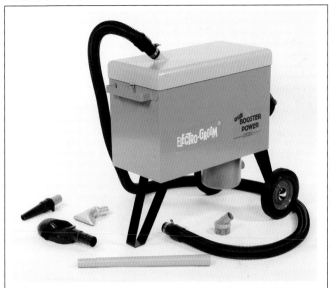

- Horse vacuums range in style from smaller styles designed to be hung over a shoulder to intricate units that are actually attached to a wall in the grooming area. Most common are vacuums that are stand-alone moveable machines.

- There are many types of attachments that can come with or be purchased for a horse vacuum.

- Versatile designs are made to be used as blow dryers and even for bathing the horse using minimal water but producing a deep-down clean.

CLEANING GROOMING EQUIPMENT
Proper care leads to longer-lasting tools and a cleaner horse

Over time, brushes and other grooming tools become coated in dirt and horse hair. This reduces their effectiveness, shortens their lifespan, makes them unpleasant to use, and can make them a breeding ground for bacteria and fungus.

Every couple of weeks, or as needed, depending on how heavily they are used, take ten minutes to clean your brushes. Hot water helps cut grease, as does a gentle dish detergent

or horse shampoo. Adding a splash of bleach to the water will kill bacteria and fungus.

Empty out your grooming tote and throw away any accumulated debris, broken tools, or empty bottles. Scrub out the tote using hot, soapy water, rinse it thoroughly, and let it dry in the sun while you move on to cleaning your brushes.

The instructions below work well for synthetic brushes. If

What You'll Need

- Bucket of hot water

- Dish detergent

- Bleach

- Horse shampoo

- Long, thin implement such as a knitting needle

Soaking

- Put a splash of bleach (not more than a quarter cup), and a generous squirt of mild dish detergent (such as Ivory or Dawn) or horse shampoo into a five-gallon bucket, and fill the bucket with hot water.

- Place brushes into the bucket and soak for several minutes. While you wait, wash out your grooming tote and dry it with a clean cloth.

your brushes have natural bristles, such as horsehair or plant fibers, treat them with a little more caution. Bleach and water can cause natural fibers to deteriorate, so soak them less frequently. Meanwhile, keep all brushes clean as you groom by scraping the bristles against a metal curry comb or stiff-bristled brush every few strokes.

If your brushes have leather backs, don't submerge them in the soapy water—just use enough water to cover the bristles, not the handle. Finish by cleaning and conditioning the handle with leather care products.

Rinsing

- Two at a time, remove brushes from the soaking solution and scrub the bristles against each other. Dunk them into the soaking solution to remove loosened grime.

- If there is matted hair stuck among the bristles, use a long tool such as a knitting needle to slide between the bristles and lift out the hair.

- Rinse the brushes in a bucket of clean water.

Drying

- After rinsing thoroughly, lay the brushes out in the sun to dry. Sunlight helps kill anaerobic bacteria that thrive deep between the bristles.

- If the brushes have plastic handles and nylon bristles, lay them bristles-up to receive the most sunlight.

- If the brushes have wooden handles and natural bristles, lay them bristles-down so the water will not pool at the bases of the bristles and rot the wood.

A SAFE WORK SPACE
A clean, well-lighted place makes grooming easier and safer

The first prerequisite for safe horse handling and grooming is a clean, tidy, and safe working environment. Begin by assessing your own clothing: Wear sturdy, well-fitting clothing, closed-toed shoes, and minimal jewelry, if any. Even a wedding ring can be unsafe, since in the event of a broken or sprained finger, the finger will swell, making the ring impossible to remove.

Next, assess your cross-tying area. It should have a non-slippery floor, even when wet. It should be free of loose objects, such as buckets, pitchforks, shovels, halter, tack, and other items. There should be no sharp protrusions anywhere near the horse. The ceiling should be at least 10 feet high—high enough that a rearing horse won't be in danger of hitting his head—and wide enough to allow horses to comfort-

Clothing

- A safe working environment begins with appropriate clothing and footwear.

- Handlers should wear closed-toed shoes or boots made of a sturdy material, with a non-slip sole. A steel toe is not ideal, since it can bend down and sever a toe under impact.

- Clothing should fit well and should not be baggy. Jeans or other heavy duty pants are best.

- Jewelry should be minimal and should not dangle excessively. Pendulous earrings, necklaces, and bracelets should be removed.

A Tidy Work Space

- The working area should be 10 to 12 feet wide, allowing plenty of room to work around the horse, but not so much room that the cross ties become dangerously long.

- The walls and floor should be tidy and clear of obstacles such as brooms, pitchforks, and buckets.

- Well-placed shelves and hooks are useful for keeping bridles, halters, and other items off the floor.

- Electrical outlets should be equipped with GFCIs and should be covered with plastic caps when not in use.

ably turn around. Easy access to water and electricity sources is convenient.

If your grooming area is outdoors rather than in a barn, there are some special considerations. Shelter from the sun or rain will make your work much more pleasant, not to mention making your farrier and vet happier, too. A safe, solid place to tie the horse is vital.

Non-Slip Floor

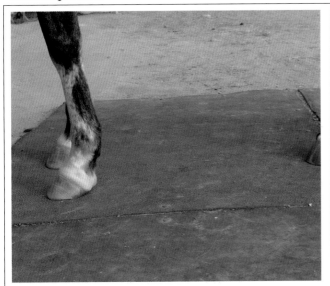

- The floor should be a non-slip, well-draining material.

- Good choices include textured rubber mats, textured concrete, rubber pavers, gravel, or well-packed, non-slippery dirt.

- If the grooming area doubles as a wash stall, the floor should be equipped with a covered drain to allow water to escape.

Outdoor Work Space

- An outdoor work area should be located on level, hard-packed, well-drained ground.

- The work area should include a sturdy tie rail or tie hooks fastened securely to a post. Never tie to a gate or board that could be pulled loose.

- The ideal work area should be covered by a roof overhang for protection from rain, snow, or sun.

HALTERS AND LEADS
The key to communication must fit well and be used properly

When leading, handling the horse from the ground, or tying, the halter is the main tool that's used to control and communicate with horses. Therefore, its fit and suitability are of paramount importance. A halter that is too big won't transmit accurate cues to the horse, can be twisted into his eye, is at risk for catching on objects or even the horse's own hoof, and if it is really too big, could potentially slip off. A halter that is too small is uncomfortable for the horse, can chafe or even cut the skin, and is awkward to put on and take off.

Also consider the material and style of the halter. For regular daily use, the best halter is made of flat leather, which will break under great strain, preventing possible injuries. Nylon halters are fine for leading and handling the horse while he's under supervision, but a horse should not be left

Safe Halter Options

- A safe halter must fit well and must not risk injuring the horse if he should pull back or panic.

- The best halter for tying is a flat leather or nylon halter. If the halter is nylon, it should feature a breakaway safety tab or leather crownpiece that will release the halter in an emergency.

- Rope halters are fine for leading and handling, but they are not safe for tying, since they don't break.

Proper Halter Fit

- The crownpiece of the halter should slide easily over the horse's ears without pinching.

- The noseband should rest approximately two fingers' width below the bottom edge of the horse's cheekbone.

- You should be able to fit three fingers under the noseband, ensuring that it is neither too loose nor too tight.

alone or turned out while wearing a nylon halter in case it becomes snagged. A leather crownpiece is a good addition for increased safety. Many people prefer to use rope halters for groundwork, believing that they allow more precise communication with the horse. They are fine for leading and handling, but a horse should never be cross-tied in a rope halter.

YELLOW LIGHT

When working around legs or sensitive areas, keep one hand on the horse's haunch for early kick detection. You will be able to feel the horse's muscles tense before you see him lift his leg to kick and will have a split second longer either to prevent the kick or to get out of range.

Halter Too Large

- The halter in the photo above is too big for the horse.

- The noseband is too far down on the bridge of the horse's nose and can cause discomfort or even possibly break the small bone at the end of the nose if too much pressure is applied.

- The throatlatch and noseband are too loose, so the halter could become caught on the horse's hoof or another object, causing injury.

Halter Too Small

- The halter in the photo above is too small for the horse.

- The crownpiece is too short, so the handler would have to bend and pinch the horse's ears to put it on.

- The noseband is uncomfortably tight and rests too high up on the horse's face.

- The throatlatch is also too tight, restricting the horse's ability to open his mouth.

TYING

How to secure your horse safely while you groom

Tying is an inevitable and useful part of horse handling. However, there are both safe and unsafe ways to tie. It is unsafe to tie a horse in a place where he can reach objects that can injure him. It is unsafe to tie a horse in an area where there are loose horses. It is unsafe to tie a horse with a lead that is long enough for him to reach the ground with his head, since he could easily step over or on the rope.

The rules for safe tying are simple and may seem like common sense, but they bear repeating. (1) Tie in a safe area. (2) Tie using a breakaway element, such as a double loop of baling twine or a panic snap. (3) Tie only to solid, immovable objects at or above the height of the horse's head when standing at rest. (4) Be sure the horse has been trained to stand tied and will not panic when he feels the

Cross-tying

- Cross ties are the correct length for your horse if they are long enough that he may take a step forward or a step back while tied and not feel trapped.

- In judging the length of your cross ties, they should overlap about 12 to 16 inches. This should give your horse the freedom necessary to be comfortable.

- Cross ties should be equipped with a breakaway snap or attachment in case the horse panics or entangles himself (see Make It Easy sidebar).

Tying to a Wall or Post

- The rule of thumb is to "tie high and short." Always tie to an object that is at least at the level of the horse's withers. Higher is better.

- Be sure the tie rope is short enough that the horse cannot lower his head enough to touch the ground or step on or over the rope.

- Tie using a quick-release knot or panic snap.

- Never tie to a movable object.

restraint. (5) Do not leave a tied horse unsupervised. (6) Tie only in an area that is not full of traffic, so that people and horses will not be constantly passing by the tied horse.

Give the horse lots of praise while training him.

Training the Horse

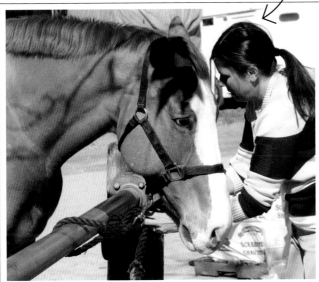

- First make sure the horse knows how to give to pressure.

- Tie the horse to a rubber inner tube that will stretch rather than stopping him short.

- Or, loop the lead rope through a ring or around a bar and hold the other end so you can give when necessary and hold tight when necessary. Wear gloves to protect your hands.

- Praise the horse for standing still. Do not punish or frighten him at any point—you don't want to cause him to panic.

MAKE IT EASY

To make cross ties into breakaway cross ties, cut a length of baling twine 18 inches long. Thread it through the clip on the end of the cross tie, looping it through twice. Tie the ends together securely. Clip a double-ended snap onto the baling twine loop; clip the other end of the snap to the horse's halter. If the horse pulls back, the baling twine breaks, preventing serious injury..

Unsafe Tying

DO NOT TIE A HORSE:

- To an object that can move

- To a solid object using an unbreakable rope and halter

- With a lead chain over his nose or under his chin

- From the bit

- And leave him unattended

- That is not trained to tie

- In a busy place where other horses and people need to constantly get by

17

HANDLING

Work around the horse properly for safer and more pleasant interactions

Any time you are near a horse, there is potential risk of injury to you or to the horse. By staying alert and following some simple protocols, you can minimize those risks.

Know your horse and be aware of what might cause him to spook—a rustling sound, a flash of light, an unfamiliar object. When you pass behind the horse, keep one hand on his body to avoid startling him as you appear on the other side. If the horse has a tendency to kick, avoid injury by staying close to the horse to minimize the force of any potential strike. Keep one eye on the horse's head to assess his attitude—keep an eye out for a raised head, wide eyes, and pricked ears, which can indicate nervousness, or pinned ears, snarly nostrils, and

Leading

- Always lead from the left side, holding the lead rope in your right hand 18 inches or less from the horse's head.

- Coil the end of the rope or reins in your left hand. Never loop a lead rope around your hand or any other body part.

- Do not allow the horse to crowd your space, pull ahead, or lag behind.

- Do not lead a horse under the cross ties of another horse standing in an aisle.

Using a Chain Shank

- If a horse is overly exuber-ant or lacks manners, a chain shank can be a useful safety device.

- Run the chain through the near (left) ring of the halter's noseband from outside to inside, loop it once around the noseband, and run it out through

the off (right) ring of the noseband.

- If it is long enough, clip it to the ring by the throatlatch on the off side. If not, clip it to the ring of the noseband on the off side.

piggy eyes (eyes smaller than normal), which indicate irritation and possibly an impending bite or kick.

It is important to maintain discipline and not allow small infractions to go unchecked. A minor manners problem today can turn into dangerous behavior tomorrow. A horse that is allowed to threaten his handler with a raised hind leg is just one small step away from becoming a kicker.

MAKE IT EASY

To tie an inexperienced horse, start the lesson in an area where the horse is already comfortable, such as in his stall or by his paddock so he can see his pasture mates. Tie enough length that a minor panic doesn't restrict him, leading to a major panic. While you work, loop the lead rope around the bars of the stall so that the horse is not "tied fast." Plan for a number of short, successful lessons rather than one long one.

Chain Attached Incorrectly

- Although some people use a chain under the chin, as shown here, a chain under the chin may cause the horse to throw his head in the air to avoid the pressure.

- Do not pull steadily on the chain. Instead, use short, sharp jerks to correct the horse, and then release the pressure immediately to reward him for compliance.

- Never tie a horse with a chain over its nose, and never let the lead line drag on the ground where the horse could step on it.

Working around the Tied Horse

- Always make sure the horse knows where you are, either by speaking softly to him or by keeping one hand on his body as you walk behind him.

- Stay alert to the horse's body language. Pinned ears may mean the horse is thinking about biting.

- A raised hind leg can be a warning of an impending kick.

- Treat horses with firmness, but do not lose your temper. If you become angry, walk away and calm down before continuing.

19

RESTRAINT

Humane methods for controlling the horse in an emergency situation

Ideally, all horses would be well-trained to stand calmly under all circumstances. However, horses are living creatures who can have negative reactions to things that frighten them. When a horse feels threatened or pressured, he may bite, strike, kick, or dance about, making it difficult or even dangerous to perform some grooming and veterinary tasks.

There are times when a job needs to get done and there is no time to train the horse to stand patiently. Moreover, some horses will not tolerate certain procedures, no matter how carefully and slowly they're introduced. Such procedures may include bandaging or wrapping, clipping, sheath cleaning, mane pulling, or giving injections.

Nose Twitch

- A twitch is made of a short rope or chain attached to a wooden rod. Also available is the "humane" twitch (shown above), made of two shaped metal rods with a joint at the end.

- Loop the rope or chain around the horse's upper lip and twist the rod until the loop tightens.

- CAUTION: To avoid permanent damage, do not over-tighten and do not leave the twitch in place for more than fifteen minutes at a time.

Holding the Lip

- A temporary substitute for an actual twitch is to grab the horse's upper lip between palm and fingertips, as shown in this photograph, and hold tightly.

- This action will restrain a horse for a short period of time, but it is not ideal for longer procedures, since the horse can easily pull away, and the handler's muscles may tire quickly.

In such cases, there is a variety of restraint methods available that are humane for the horse and make the human handler's job much easier and safer. The most commonly known is the nose twitch, which activates a pressure point in the horse's muzzle, causing him to become relatively immobile and distracting him from a painful or unpleasant procedure until the twitch is released. A variation on the nose twitch is to grasp the upper lip in your hand. Holding up a leg and applying the shoulder roll technique are also useful methods for restraining the horse under certain conditions.

Holding Up a Leg

- Holding up one leg is a simple and painless way to prevent a relatively calm horse from moving his other legs.

- Have a partner hold up a horse's opposite leg if you need to tend to a wound on a leg, apply a bandage, or clip a leg.

- This method is not safe to use on panicky or unpredictable horses, who may still try to move and may cause themselves or their handlers to fall down.

Shoulder Roll

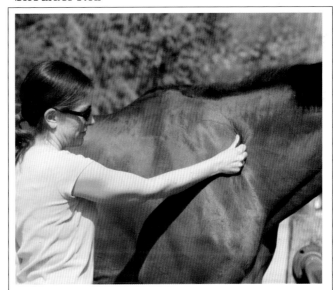

- Horses can also be immobilized by using the shoulder roll. While not as effective as a nose twitch, it is also less complicated and less bothersome to the horse.

- Grab a fold of skin on the horse's lower neck in front of the shoulder and twist it forward. Apply more pressure as needed, or release the pressure if the horse stands quietly.

GROOMING WITH CHILDREN
Fun and educational grooming activities to teach little riders

Young riders should learn not only how to walk, trot, steer, and stop, but also how to handle, lead, groom, and tack up a horse. Lessons should include information on horses' anatomy, health, care, behavior, and safety. Instructors and parents should place as much emphasis on good horsemanship as on good equitation.

Children should be taught safe, correct procedures for leading and handling the horse during their first lessons. They also need to be told exactly how to behave and what not to do around horses. There are many things that experienced adults take for granted that are not obvious to young children, such as the fact that it is unsafe to duck under the horse's belly to get to the other side or to hang from the horse's tail.

Leading

- Teach the child to walk at the horse's left shoulder. Do not let the horse get ahead of her or behind her.

- Do not at any time allow a child to loop or tie the horse's lead to her wrist, waist, or belt. This is very dangerous and leads to getting hurt.

Safety around the Horse

- Teach the child how to read the horse's mood and notice if he is angry, nervous, or frightened. Show her how to look at his ears and eyes to read his emotions.

- Remind the child never to run, scream, or act up around horses. They are easily startled.

- Encourage the child not to go underneath the horse's neck or belly and to be sure to stay clear of his hooves at all times.

- Some children may need to be taught not to antagonize the horse by pulling on his tail, poking his face, or hitting him.

As long as the horse or pony is an appropriate size, a child should be capable of grooming and tacking up on her own (with supervision). Use first grooming lessons as an opportunity to teach anatomy, pointing out all the different body parts as the child brushes each one. Emphasize the importance of understanding horse behavior so the child can recognize when the horse is angry or in pain.

RED●LIGHT

Remind children not to duck under their horse's head or belly to get from one side to another. He cannot see the child under his neck, and when she suddenly appears on his other side he may spook. Ducking under the belly is very dangerous, but inexperienced children often make this mistake.

Grooming

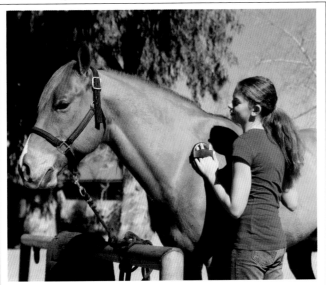

- Small children may need a stool or a lift from a parent in order to reach the tall parts of the horse.

- Teach children to curry, hard brush, and soft brush before every ride.

- Be sure they understand the importance of grooming. Help them recognize any small problems, such as wounds or bug bites.

Tacking

- The child can set the saddle pad and saddle high up on the withers and then slide them gently back into place to make sure the hair lies flat.

- Help the child with more difficult tasks such as girth tightening and getting the bit into the horse's mouth.

Then stand back and let her do up the bridle buckles so she feels a sense of accomplishment.

- Make sure children understand how each piece of equipment works, and always double check the tack and boots before the child mounts.

BRUSHING: WHAT TO DO FIRST
The daily grooming session is an important ritual

GROOMING HORSES

Not only does grooming keep the horse clean, but also it has many other benefits: bonding between owner and horse; ground-training and manners refreshers for the horse as needed; an opportunity to check the horse for physical problems such as injuries, swellings, skin problems, weight loss or gain, or behavioral changes; bringing circulation to the skin; lightly massaging the muscles; and distributing the skin's natural oils throughout the coat.

To begin, the basic routine is as follows: First, pick the horse's hooves (see page 32). Next, using a curry in one hand and a stiff-bristled body brush in the other, knock off any dried clumps of mud. Wet mud is more difficult to remove. It's best

Currying

- The first step in the grooming session is currying. Don't use the curry on bony parts such as the face or legs, as it may be uncomfortable for the horse.

- Sensitive horses may object to hard plastic curries. Try a brush made of a softer material to make grooming a pleasant experience for everyone.

- Currying has the added benefits of increasing circulation to the skin and lightly massaging and warming the superficial muscles.

Body Brushing

- Next, use a hard brush (also known as a body brush or dandy brush) in short, firm strokes in the direction of hair growth.

- Use a flicking motion to whisk dirt and hair away from the horse's skin.

- Use the hard brush firmly on the muscular parts of the horse and gently on the legs. Do not use it on the face.

to either hose it off or wait for it to dry, and then brush it off.

Use the curry firmly in small, circular motions over the muscular parts of the horse's body (neck, chest, shoulders, barrel, and haunches). The curry brings to the surface dirt, dry skin, and loose hairs that will later be brushed away. Currying takes "elbow grease," meaning you need to groom with energy to pull up the dirt.

Allow wet legs to dry first for easier mud removal.

Brushing Legs

- Use the body brush on the horse's legs in a downward motion to remove mud and dirt. If the horse has just come in from a wet environment, allowing the legs to dry before grooming them makes mud removal easier.

- Work carefully around the pasterns and hoof bulbs to clear away any caked-on mud or manure that could lead to skin irritation.

- If needed, a rubber curry can be used lightly on the legs to break up mud.

Soft Brushing

- The soft brush is used last to whisk away dust, polish the coat, and set the hair.

- Use the soft brush in light, short strokes in the direction of hair growth.

- The soft brush may be used over the horse's entire body, including the face and legs.

BASICS

BRUSHING: WHAT TO DO NEXT
The daily grooming session is an important ritual

Once you've finished currying the horse, move on to the brushes. Working from the front of the horse and moving toward the tail, first use a medium-bristled body brush in the direction of hair growth to whisk away the debris loosened by the curry. Also use this brush on the legs and belly.

Switch to a soft-bristled brush to dust off any remaining debris left by the medium brush. Brush the horse's whole body in the direction of hair growth using short, brisk strokes. Use a slightly damp washcloth or small towel to rub the horse's face and ears. Then use your soft brush to set the hair as it dries.

Next, use a different damp cloth or sponge to clean under the horse's tail and between the hind legs as needed. Finger-comb the tail, removing any bits of hay or bedding. Do not brush or comb the tail unless it has just been washed and

Grooming the Face

- If you're unsure how the horse will react to having his face handled, it is safest to unclip the cross ties and hold the horse on a lead line.

- Use a soft brush to gently whisk away dust on the head, under the jaw, and around the ears.

- Use a soft, damp cloth to wipe around the eyes (always wipe downward, never upward, to avoid poking the horse in the eye), inside the nostrils, around the lips, and inside the ears.

- Baby wipes are convenient for quick touch-ups.

Mane

- Comb or brush the mane gently so the hairs all lie flat on the same side.

- If the mane is long, as on an Arabian or Saddlebred, use your fingers instead of a brush to avoid breaking the hairs.

- Check the base of the mane for tick bites, flaky skin, or evidence of rubbing or itching.

- See page 92 for more on care of manes.

conditioned; otherwise you risk breaking the hairs. Comb the mane so that it all hangs on the same side of the neck, and comb the forelock to lie down flat.

After your ride, brush the horse again with the soft brush to remove any arena dust. If he is just a little sweaty, use a medium-bristled brush to brush the sweaty areas (usually under the saddle and girth and on the neck) until the horse is dry. If he's very sweaty, hose or sponge off the sweat.

YELLOW LIGHT

During the summer and fall, look out for bot eggs on your horse's legs and chest. They look like tiny yellow or white specks stuck to the hair. If the horse ingests these eggs, they will hatch and develop into larvae in his intestines. Remove bot eggs with a bot knife, a pumice grooming stone, a disposable razor, or clippers. Steaming the eggs with a hot, damp washcloth makes them easier to remove.

BASICS

Tail

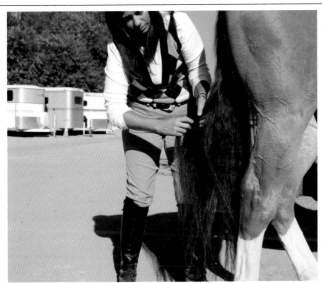

- Remove any shavings, hay, or plant matter in the tail. Inspect the tail for evidence of loose manure, and check the dock for tick bites, flaky skin, or rubbing.

- If desired, apply a detangling spray or liquid (see page 120).

- For show horses, work through the tail by hand to avoid breaking the hairs with a comb or brush.

- If you are not worried about breaking a few hairs, you can use a brush or comb on the tail. Start at the bottom and carefully work your way up, one section at a time.

The Quick Pre-Ride Grooming Session

You may not always have time for a full grooming session. If you're short on time before a ride, be sure to follow this routine:

- Brush saddle and girth area with a hard brush

- Brush mud off legs

- Pick hooves

- Check bridle area and brush if needed

Then just tack up, and you're good to go. Be sure to do a thorough grooming the next day.

BATHING

Scrub and rinse well for a deep-down show-ring cleaning

You will not need to bathe your horse daily, or even weekly. In fact, it is best not to bathe too often, since shampoos can remove beneficial oils from the horse's coat and dry the skin. Nevertheless, it is an important grooming skill. Horses that do not show should be bathed at least a few times a year. Show horses may be bathed before every show.

It is best not to bathe the horse if the ambient temperature is below 60 degrees, as the wet horse can catch a chill. The best day for a bath is a dry, sunny day in the 70s or 80s. In chilly weather, be sure to cover the horse with a cooler after his bath until he is dry. If it is too cold for a full bath, you can use the hot toweling method described on page 31.

After a hot ride in the summer, rinse off the sweaty areas with clear water, using a hose or a sponge and bucket. Add a

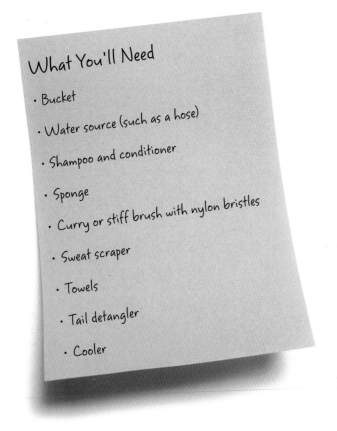

What You'll Need

- Bucket

- Water source (such as a hose)

- Shampoo and conditioner

- Sponge

- Curry or stiff brush with nylon bristles

- Sweat scraper

- Towels

- Tail detangler

- Cooler

Wet the Horse

- Tie or cross-tie the horse in a safe, level, well-drained area with footing that won't become slippery when wet.

- Beginning with the legs to allow the horse to become accustomed to the temperature, soak the horse's coat with clean water from a hose, if available, or a sponge and bucket.

- Do not spray the horse's face with a hose. Use a sponge instead.

capful of liniment to the water to help cut the sweat and cool the horse. Rinse the neck, chest, saddle and girth area, belly, between the hind legs, and head. (Be careful not to get any liniment in the horse's eyes.) Use a sweat scraper to remove as much water as possible, and towel-dry the lower legs.

See the next page for step-by-step bathing instructions.

BASICS

Scrub with Shampoo

- Put a generous squirt of shampoo into a five-gallon bucket and fill it with water. Use warm (not hot) water if it is available.

- Using a sponge or nylon-bristled brush, scrub the horse thoroughly, one section at a time. Begin with the near front half (neck, chest, and shoulder), using plenty of water and suds. Then rinse that section and move to the next.

- Finish by shampooing and rinsing the legs.

Rinse Off Suds

- Using the hose or several buckets of clean water and a clean (non-sudsy) sponge, thoroughly rinse all traces of shampoo from the coat.

- Repeat the process using a coat conditioner if needed. Some conditioners should be rinsed out, while others are meant to be left in.

BATHING (CONTINUED)
Step-by-step instructions for a good bath

For a full bath, the procedure is as follows: First, squirt some horse shampoo into a five-gallon bucket and fill with warm water. Then, soak the horse with a hose. Scrub a quarter of the horse (say, the neck, shoulder, front leg, and barrel on the left side) with the warm, soapy water using a sponge, nylon-bristled brush, or curry.

Rinse thoroughly with the hose, and scrape with a sweat scraper. If any soap bubbles appear, rinse again. Next, move to the hindquarters and back leg on the same side and repeat the scrubbing and rinsing steps.

Repeat these steps on the right front and then right hind. (You may need to change the bath water at some point if the horse is quite dirty.) Next, use a smaller sponge or washcloth to gently bathe the face. Rinse the washcloth in clean water

Washing the Face

- Do not spray the horse's face with the hose. It is unpleasant for the horse and too easy to accidentally direct the stream into his eyes or nostrils.

- Instead, dampen a clean sponge and wipe the horse's face. Shampoo the face with a small amount of horse shampoo, avoiding the eye area.

- Rinse by squeezing clean water over the face with a sponge. Rub gently with a dry towel.

Washing Sensitive Areas

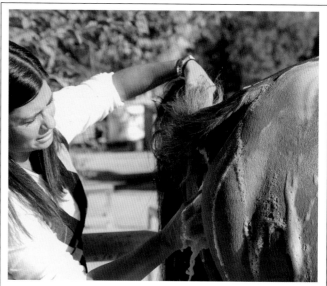

- Use a dedicated sponge for the underside of the dock. This sponge should be labeled with permanent marker.

- Stand to the side of the horse's hindquarters, lift the tail, and gently shampoo this area, cleaning off any manure residue.

- Shampoo between the hind legs as well.

- Rinse with a gentle stream from the hose, always aiming it downward, or sponge with clean water until there is no shampoo left.

and use it to remove the suds. (Do not spray the horse's face.) If he will tolerate it, let the hose water run gently from the top of the head so the water trickles down the face to rinse it.

Lather and rinse the tail, being careful to remove all soap residue to avoid itching. Apply a conditioner to the horse's coat and tail. Some conditioners are meant to be rinsed off, while others are leave-in products. Follow the directions on the bottle. Finally, towel-dry the legs, and in chilly weather cover the horse with a fleece or wool cooler. When the horse is dry, brush him with a clean, soft brush to set the hair.

······· ● ······ GREEN ● LIGHT ·············

When the horse's legs become wet, whether due to a bath, a cold-hosing session, or a swim in a pond, it is important to dry them as thoroughly as possible. First, use your hands to scrape the water off, and then use a clean, dry towel to rub the lower legs. If the legs remain wet, they are susceptible to a variety of fungal infections. In addition, the skin around the pasterns may crack, leading to infection.

Finishing Up

- After bathing, use a scraper in the direction of hair growth over muscular areas to squeegee as much water from the coat as possible. If you see any suds appear while scraping, rinse the horse again with clean water and re-scrape.

- In cold weather, follow up

by rubbing the horse with a clean, dry bath towel.

- While he's still damp, spray with a coat-enhancing product if desired, and brush lightly with a soft brush to set the coat.

- In cold weather, cover the horse with a cooler.

Hot Toweling Method

For winter clean-ups, don't drench the horse and risk a chill. Instead, try hot toweling:

- Cover the horse with a cooler for warmth, and uncover small sections at a time.

- Fill a bucket with hot water. Add a very small amount of shampoo (not enough to cause lather) or baby oil if desired.

- Soak a towel in the hot water, and squeeze it out thoroughly so it is damp and steaming.

- Working on a small area at a time, rub the coat firmly with the hot towel. As the towel becomes soiled, re-fold it so you are using a clean section. Because the water is so hot, it'll evaporate off the coat quickly, avoiding a chill to the horse.

- Replace the towel when it is too dirty or cold. Dump out cool or dirty water and use fresh hot water. You'll go through several towels and several buckets of water.

HOOF CARE

The old saying is as true now as ever: "No hoof, no horse"

Horses' hooves require daily attention. In the case of a shod horse, hoof picking is the one grooming task that should be done every day. While cleaning the hoof, check to be sure the shoe is tight and all nails are in place. A loose shoe can twist, causing the horse to step on a nail or clip, or can be ripped off, damaging the hoof wall. Inspect the sole for rocks, bruises, or signs of abscess. Stay alert for signs of thrush, white line disease, seedy toe, or other problems. Check the outer hoof wall for chips, cracks, and irregularities.

Barefoot horses need less vigilance. There is no risk of a shoe becoming loose or twisted and of the horse picking up a rock. Bare hooves tend to clean themselves out as the horse moves, assuming the environment is relatively dry and clean. Nevertheless, bare hooves should still be checked and

Front Hooves

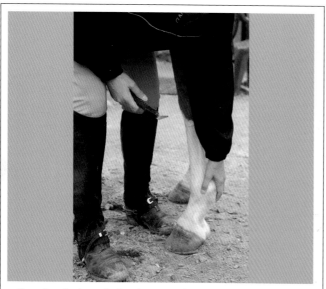

- Stand at the horse's shoulder, facing the rear. Bend over, running your hand down the horse's leg to the fetlock.

- If the horse is well-trained, he should lift his hoof for you. If not, try pinching the tendon or leaning into his shoulder to take the weight off that leg.

- You can also train a horse to respond to a command, such as "give leg."

- Once he lifts the hoof, transfer your grip from the fetlock joint to the hoof for a steadier hold.

Rear Hooves

- Stand at the horse's hip, facing the rear. Bend over, running your hand down the horse's leg to the fetlock.

- Don't startle the horse; stay alert for sudden movements that could forewarn a kick.

- Some horses like to pick the hoof up very high or stretch it out behind them before relaxing. They are only stretching, not preparing to kick, and don't need to be disciplined. Know your horse and what to expect.

- Hold the toe of the hoof while working, keeping your face well out of kicking range.

picked, if needed, every few days. The barefoot horse may also be at increased risk of sole bruising if he lives or works on rocky terrain.

Thrush is a common condition that affects the clefts of the frog. When hooves are not picked regularly or the horse lives in wet or unsanitary conditions, bacteria can infect the soft tissues of the hoof, causing them to deteriorate. When caught early, thrush is easily treated, but if it becomes too advanced it can become chronic, causing lameness. Thrush produces a soft, black substance and a distinctive foul odor.

Prevent or treat it by keeping the horse on dry, clean footing, and picking the hooves daily. Topical application of an anti-thrush product, such as Koppertox or Thrush Buster, can help resolve the problem quickly.

A variety of products may be used on the horse's hoof to increase toughness, moisturize, seal, protect, or disinfect, but be aware that too much moisture can soften the hoof wall. Rub the ointment into the coronary band for the greatest effect because that is where the entire hoof wall grows from.

Picking Hooves

- Use the hoof pick to remove any packed-in matter. If there is a solid mass of material, work the hoof pick under the edge and lift the whole thing out at once, rather than scraping a little bit at a time.

- Always aim the pick toward the toe, not the heel, so that

if the horse suddenly moves you won't risk jabbing the pick into the sensitive tissue.

- Work as quickly and thoroughly as possible to avoid tiring the horse.

- When finished, set the hoof down gently.

Applying Hoof Treatments

- While picking, assess the sole of the hoof for early signs of thrush, sole bruises, tenderness, white line disease, or other problems.

- The outer wall of the hoof should be hard and strong, without evidence of cracks or chipping.

- Apply any needed hoof treatments. See resources for more detailed information on the various products that can be used on hooves.

SHEETS AND BLANKETS
Extra protection to keep horses clean, dry, and warm in bad weather

Not every horse needs a blanket in the winter. Several factors influence the choice of whether or not to blanket: climate, available shelter, breed, age, body condition, the thickness of the natural coat, and whether or not the horse is clipped. An elderly Thoroughbred in poor weight who lives outdoors in Vermont probably needs a blanket. A fat, furry Shetland living in a stable in Virginia probably does not. Any horse that is clipped needs additional protection from the elements, since his natural insulation has been taken away.

There is a variety of different types and weights of blanket. "Denier" refers to the thread count of the outer shell of the blanket. A higher denier generally means a more durable blanket. For turnout blankets, look for a denier of at least 1,200. A stable blanket will have a much lower denier, since

Stable Sheet or Dress Sheet

- A stable sheet or dress sheet is generally made of cotton or fleece and is used when the horse is stalled to keep the coat clean and slick.

- Stable sheets may be used in the trailer to help ward off chills from the wind.

- A dress sheet may be used at a show to keep the horse dry and clean between classes.

- Never turn out a horse in a stable sheet, since it is not waterproof and is likely to tear easily.

Stable Blanket

- Stable blankets are for use when the horse is in a stall in colder weather. They are generally made of nylon or other lightweight material with a layer of insulation (fill) to keep the horse warm, clean, and slick.

- They are not waterproof, so horses should not be turned out in a stable blanket alone, although they are fine if layered under a waterproof turnout sheet or blanket.

it will be used only in the stall and won't be subjected to weather and horseplay. Insulation is measured in grams. A blanket with 100 to 200 grams of fill is a light- or medium-weight blanket adequate for most needs. A heavyweight blanket with more than 300 grams of fill is best for clipped horses in very cold weather.

Turnout Sheet or Turnout Blanket

- Turnout sheets and blankets are waterproof and breathable, which means that although rain and snow cannot seep in, moisture produced by the horse's own body can wick out and away from the blanket, keeping the horse dry and warm underneath.

- Turnouts can lose their waterproofing capabilities over time, so run a hand under the blanket each time you check on the horse in wet weather. If the blanket is leaking, it can be re-waterproofed with a product (usually a spray) designed for that job.

Coolers (Wool, Irish Knit, Fleece)

- When a horse becomes wet in cold weather, due to sweating, bathing, or precipitation, use a cooler to keep him warm while wicking the moisture away from his coat so he dries more quickly.

- On a clipped horse, use a cooler to keep his muscles warm while you warm up before and cool down after a ride.

- Irish knit coolers or anti-sweat sheets don't help keep the horse warm, but they do wick sweat away from the body to keep him dry. They are useful in warmer weather.

NUTRITION FOR A HEALTHY COAT

A diet balanced in vitamins, minerals, fat, and protein results in a beautiful bloom

A healthy coat is the result of good management. A coat or fat supplement alone will not do the trick. Feed the horse quality hay, provide fresh water, deworm bimonthly or as recommended by your veterinarian, groom daily, and maintain a balanced conditioning program. If a horse's coat has a dull, dry appearance, look first to these basics. But assuming that

these conditions have been met, some horses need a little extra nutrition to really bloom.

Often, simply adding a source of fat to the horse's diet can result in a more pleasing appearance and a shinier coat. Ground flax seed, black oil sunflower seeds, rice bran, or corn or other vegetable oils are all concentrated sources of fat that

Nutritional Deficiency

- A rough, dull, washed-out-looking coat can be a sign of nutritional deficiency or worms.

- Assuming the horse is otherwise healthy and is on a good rotating deworming schedule, assess the diet.

- Soil, forage, and hay analysis can help you understand any deficiencies in your pasture or hay, which must be offset by a balanced grain or vitamin/mineral supplement.

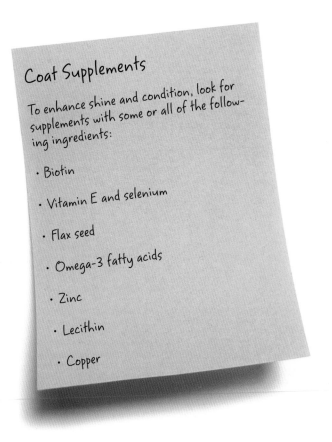

Coat Supplements

To enhance shine and condition, look for supplements with some or all of the following ingredients:

- Biotin

- Vitamin E and selenium

- Flax seed

- Omega-3 fatty acids

- Zinc

- Lecithin

- Copper

help improve coat condition. In other cases, the horse may be lacking in a specific nutrient, such as biotin, selenium, vitamin E, or copper. Ask your vet to assess the horse's diet and determine whether there may be any specific deficiencies. (Use caution when supplementing with selenium, since too much selenium is toxic.)

As simple as it sounds, routine grooming before and after a horse is worked is one of the best things you can do to aid in getting a shine on your horse's coat.

Adding Supplements

- Use caution when introducing any new supplement or grain product to your horse's diet. Begin with a small amount, and gradually increase the quantity over a period of several days until you reach the desired amount. For example, when adding oil, start with two tablespoons, and gradually work up to one cup.

- This will allow the horse to become accustomed to the taste, so that he won't reject the new feed entirely, and also allows his digestive system to acclimate to the new nutrients.

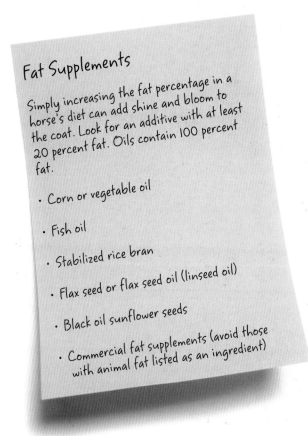

Fat Supplements

Simply increasing the fat percentage in a horse's diet can add shine and bloom to the coat. Look for an additive with at least 20 percent fat. Oils contain 100 percent fat.

- Corn or vegetable oil

- Fish oil

- Stabilized rice bran

- Flax seed or flax seed oil (linseed oil)

- Black oil sunflower seeds

- Commercial fat supplements (avoid those with animal fat listed as an ingredient)

ADVANCED BASICS

SHEATH AND UDDER CLEANING
It's the dirty underbelly of the horsekeeping world—literally

Although unpleasant, sheath cleaning is a task that must be done for the health and comfort of your gelding. Frequency depends on the horse. Some geldings seem to stay fairly clean, while others need to be cleaned weekly. Signs that a sheath needs cleaning include tail rubbing, difficulty urinating, and visible smegma. Even if the penis and sheath look reasonably clean, the horse should be checked periodically for the presence of a bean—a ball of hard, waxy gray material that develops in the tip of the penis. It can block the urethra and interfere with urination if it becomes too large.

Mares can develop smegma around their udders. A buildup of smegma around the udders can be itchy, irritating, and can even lead to infection. Tail rubbing can be a sign that the mare's udder is itching and needs to be cleaned. Like

What You'll Need

- A bucket of lukewarm, clean water and a small clean sponge (you may need to cut a sponge into smaller sections to get a size that easily fits into the sheath)

- A cleaning product (such as Excalibur sheath cleaner) or gentle liquid hand soap. Try baby oil to soften a large amount of smegma before removing it comfortably

- A pair of latex medical gloves for sanitary and aesthetic purposes, although some people do not use them

- If the horse will tolerate it, a low-pressure hose to rinse the sheath after cleaning it

Cleaning the Sheath

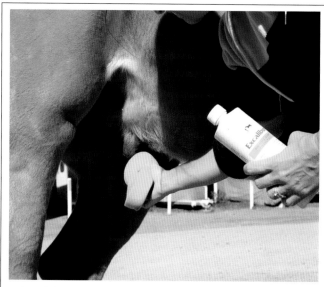

- Stand close to the side of your horse and face the rear. Never put your head down near the sheath; you will rely on your sense of touch to do this job.

- Insert a wet sponge into the sheath and squeeze it out to wet the area. Repeat a few times.

- Put cleaning product on the sponge and insert into the sheath and all areas; when you remove the sponge it will be covered with smegma, dirt, and dead skin.

- Rinse the sponge and repeat the last step until the sponge comes out fairly clean.

geldings, some mares need to be cleaned often, while others rarely, if ever, need attention in that area.

With all horses it is important to keep grime and sweat from building up between their back legs. Toweling regularly between the back legs will prevent this. Also towel around the udder or sheath at this time. If your horse objects, take your time until your horse is used to being touched in these areas. This will make it easier on both of you when it comes time to clean a sheath or udder.

The Bean

• Gently manipulate the slit at the head of the penis to remove the ball of smegma that builds up within; this ball is referred to as the bean.

• Rinse out the sheath with warm water from a hose or a bucket and a clean sponge.

• If this is your or your horse's first time with sheath cleaning you may not get the sheath completely clean or remove the bean. Do what you can and end the session on a positive note, but be sure to rinse out the soap from the sheath.

Cleaning Udders

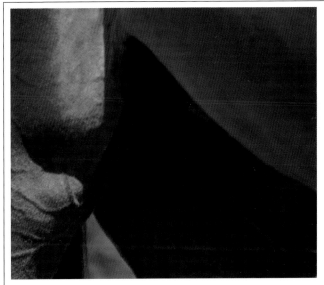

• Cleaning udders is a simpler and less invasive task than cleaning a sheath. Use caution, since mares are very sensitive. Be alert for kick warnings from the horse.

• Stand close to your mare's body to avoid a full-velocity kick. By toweling between your mare's legs regularly, she'll get used to being touched in the udder area.

• Gently lather the udders, using your sponge to carefully wipe all crevices and hidden areas.

• Rinse the sponge in clean, lukewarm water and wash away all soapy residues.

ADVANCED BASICS

WHITE MARKINGS
Tips and techniques for keeping that chrome sparkling clean

Light grays, Paints, and horses with lots of white markings all present a unique challenge to the groom. Mud, grass, and manure stains show up clearly against that pure white canvas. Anyone who rides a gray horse has experienced the pain of giving the horse a meticulous bath the night before a show, only to arrive at the stable the next morning to find a large green smear across the horse's haunch. An additional

problem is that white tails and manes tend to turn yellow over time. Restoring the gleaming white color is a challenge.

Fortunately, there is an arsenal of products available to help. Purple-colored whitening shampoos, such as Quick Silver, work by imparting an imperceptible blue tint to the hair shaft. Under fluorescent light, the coat will seem to have a slightly blue-green hue, but in sunlight, the blue tint makes

Whitening Shampoo

- Whitening shampoos contain special ingredients that remove any dingy stains from the coat while subtly tinting each hair shaft to produce a gleaming white glow.

- After bathing, use a sponge or your gloved hands to work the product into a

light-purple lather, coating any white areas.

- Allow the product to remain on the coat for ten to fifteen minutes.

- Rinse thoroughly and condition as desired.

Dry Shampoo

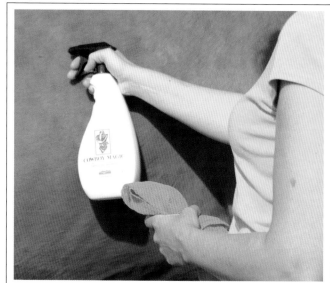

- Dry shampoos and sprays can be used to remove individual stains on the white parts of the coat.

- After bathing, apply a silicone spray (see page 127) to help repel stains. This will cause the dry shampoo to have the greatest effect.

- Apply the powder or spray to the affected area, allow it to set for several minutes, then curry and brush out the stain.

the whites look whiter. Dry shampoos or spot removers (such as Cowboy Magic Green Spot Remover) can be rubbed directly into a stained area without having to resort to a full bath. Silicone coat sprays help prevent stains from setting into the coat. Clipping the lower legs and using white powders also help in a show situation.

Clipping

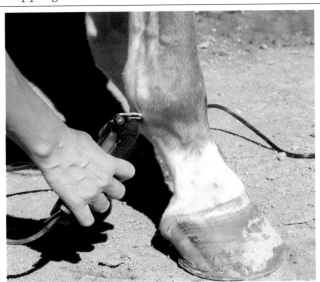

- Clipping the white hair on the lower legs can make markings appear to stand out; sometimes this is referred to as booting up.

- Using a #10 blade, clip the legs at least a week before the show, to allow the hair to grow enough to hide the pink skin beneath. Clip carefully, avoiding clipper lines or bald spots.

- Blend the line into the longer, colored hair above the marking for a more natural appearance.

Powders

- If you are preparing for a show, after bathing dry the legs thoroughly and then apply a coating of baby powder, talcum powder, French chalk, or cornstarch to white markings on the legs.

- If any dirt or manure touches the horse's legs, it will stick to the powder rather than the hair. Upon arriving at the show, brush off the powder to reveal sparkling clean legs.

- As a finishing touch, apply a fresh light dusting of white powder before entering the ring.

ADVANCED BASICS

HORSE VACUUMS

These tools are a luxury that can speed grooming time while reducing airborne dust and hair

Horse vacuums are very popular in some facilities. They can speed up the grooming process. In addition to the dust, dirt, and loose hair, they collect external parasites from the coat and skin of the horse. As with any tool, correct use is the key to getting the best results and is a must for safety to the horse and handler. Horse vacuums come in heavy duty to portable sizes. There are many different attachments available as well. Most vacuums have a reversible action so that they can also be used as a blower.

The grooming area needs to be large enough that the vacuum will not be under foot. Ideally, the vacuum should be on the same side of the horse that you are working on, meaning

Getting Started

- Be sure that the grooming area is large enough for you to work around your horse without the vacuum getting in the way.

- If using an extension cord, do not let extra cord lie near the horse's feet.

- Do not have any extra buckets, rakes, or tack cluttering up the area, which can cause problems for you or your horse.

- Empty the vacuum as necessary; it won't work if it is full!

Neck and Shoulder

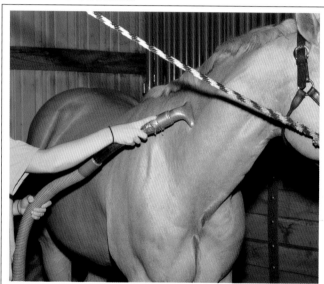

- Start on the neck region of the horse and vacuum in the direction of the hair.

- On the well-muscled areas, move the vacuum element back and forth to loosen and remove the dirt and hair.

- If your horse will accommodate, you can vacuum the entire neck, even close to the ears.

- When finished with an area, move the nozzle in the direction of the hair to lay it down.

that the grooming area needs to be large enough so that the vacuum can be easily moved around. Ideally, there will be an electrical outlet on both sides of the grooming area in which to plug in the vacuum. If not, be very careful to keep the horse from stepping on the electrical cord. Position the vacuum to the side and rear of your horse somewhat out of sight. Many horses are more suspicious of the sight of the vacuum and hose than of the noise. Be sure to empty the vacuum regularly for best performance.

Desensitizing your horse to a vacuum starts by getting him used to the feel of the nozzle on his coat with the vacuum turned off. Starting at the shoulder and working toward the tail, rub the nozzle over the horse. Use a low speed for the first time you start the vacuum, again working from shoulder to tail. Most horses learn to enjoy being vacuumed as much as they enjoy a good currying.

Large Muscle Areas

- The buttocks feature the most well-muscled area of your horse's anatomy, so you can apply pressure there and move the vacuum nozzle back and forth with fervor.

- The top of the horse's croup is a difficult area to get deep-down clean and a perfect area to take advantage of the vacuum.

- Do not vacuum your horse's tail.

- When finished with an area, move the nozzle in the direction of the hair to lay it down.

Legs and Flank

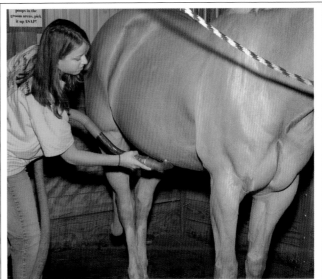

- When vacuuming over lightly muscled areas, such as the legs, go in the direction of the hair.

- Be careful in the flank area not to let the vacuum pull too much on the horse's skin; if you hear the machine straining because it's pulling on the skin, clear the nozzle and start again.

- You may not want to vacuum below the horse's knee or hock, much like when using a hard rubber curry, unless you have a soft attachment to use.

SUMMER COAT CARE

How to prevent a bleached-out coat on dark bay or black horses.

GROOMING HORSES

In the summer months, many horses' coats experience stress from the sun. Sweat combined with sun can cause fading, dulling, and drying of the coat. Dark bay and "fading black" horses are especially vulnerable. To the pleasure rider, some sun bleaching is not generally a cause for concern, unless it is so severe that it seems to be a symptom of a nutritional deficiency (see page 36). But for a competitive rider, sun bleaching can create an unattractive picture in the show ring.

Several strategies can be used to minimize the effects of the sun. First, be sure the horse is receiving adequate nutrition and fresh water. If he is, then turn to alternative strategies. Supplementing with feed additives, such as copper or paprika, helps the coat retain its natural dark color and shine. Keeping the horse out of direct sun is also helpful. Either stall

Sun Bleaching

- A sun-bleached black or dark bay horse may develop an unsightly orange hue or may simply fade to a lighter shade of bay.

- The color change may be accompanied by a dry, coarse look to the coat.

UV-Rated Sheets

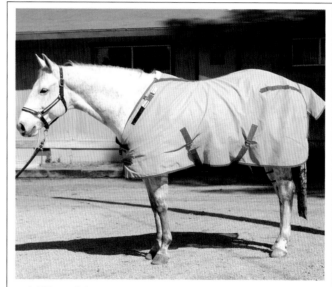

- A UV-rated sheet serves as a physical barrier to block the sun's harmful rays from reaching the coat.

- Use a sheet with a hood whenever the horse is turned out in the sunlight.

- Start using the sheet in May, when the horse's summer coat has grown in and the sun starts becoming stronger.

the horse during daylight hours and turn him out at night, or provide him with a UV-blocking light sheet while he's out during the day. Night turnout has the added benefit of keeping the horse in during the hottest, buggiest times of day, so he will be more comfortable. Sunscreen sprays are also available to prevent UV damage to the coat. For any of these strategies to be effective, they must be initiated in early spring, before the coat has been damaged. Once the hairs are bleached, they cannot be returned to their original luster, except by waiting for the summer coat to shed out in the fall.

Sunscreen Sprays and Supplements

- Sunscreen sprays can be used to prevent the coat from fading, but they must be applied daily for best results. They are not as effective as sheets.

- Add a tablespoon of ground paprika to your black or dark bay horse's daily ration to keep his coat

from fading. Stop using paprika ten days before a show, since the capsaicin in the paprika results in a positive test.

- Commercial supplements are available to enhance the color of a dark or black coat.

Night Turnout

- The simplest and most effective way to prevent sun bleaching is to reverse the horse's daily turnout schedule, keeping him in a stall during the day and turning him out at night.

- An added benefit is that the horse will be protected from the discomforts of hot sun and flies during the day.

WINTER CARE

Winter is a season with its own unique set of horsekeeping challenges, and grooming is no exception

During the winter, horses grow a thick, long coat to protect themselves from cold and precipitation. If they are not being worked, it's best to leave that coat alone as much as possible. It should not be clipped or brushed too much. A thick-coated horse may not even need a blanket except in extreme weather.

On the other hand, if the horse remains in work through the cold season, it is best to clip part of or all of the coat and blanket the horse. When the horse is ridden, he works up a sweat, and a long coat can make him overheat. After the ride, a full winter coat can take hours to fully dry, leaving the horse susceptible to chills. It is healthier for the horse,

Winter Blanket Chart

CLIPPED HORSE	
40°F to 50°F and raining	Turnout sheet
30°F to 40°F	Medium-weight blanket
20°F to 30°F	Medium-weight blanket and liner
10°F to 20°F	Heavyweight blanket
Below 10°F	Heavyweight blanket, liner and hood

UNCLIPPED HORSE	
30°F to 50°F and raining	Turnout sheet
20°F to 30°F and snowing	Medium-weight blanket
10°F to 20°F	Medium-weight blanket
Below 10°F	Heavyweight blanket

Winter Coat

- A horse's natural winter coat consists of a thick, dense layer of insulating hairs and a longer, fuzzier layer of guard hairs that repels water.

- Blanketing can actually make the horse colder, since it flattens down the hair, reducing its natural insulating abilities.

- Currying the winter coat can be a challenge and can cause a buildup of static. Instead, skip the curry and brush thoroughly with stiff and soft brushes.

46

as well as easier for the groom, to clip (see page 70).

Hooves also require special attention in winter. Again, if the horse has the winter off, the natural approach may be best—bare hooves have better traction and resist ice buildup compared to shod hooves. If the horse remains in work and keeps his shoes on, care must be taken to prevent slipping and the buildup of snowballs in the shoes.

(see page 70)

··········· • GREEN ● LIGHT ···········

Feed horses extra hay during cold or wet weather. Digesting the hay produces heat energy that helps keep the horse warm. Horses have a natural urge to chew roughage when the temperature drops, and some will even chew wood if hay is not available. Feed 3 percent more hay for every 3 degrees below 15 degrees F.

Winter Clips

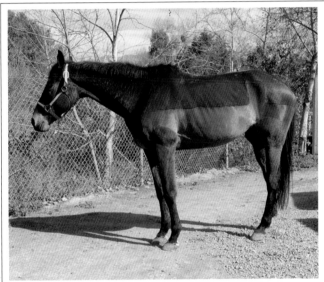

- If a horse is regularly working hard enough to sweat, it is healthier for the horse (not to mention easier for the rider) if he is clipped.

- A heavy, unclipped coat can cause the horse to overheat during work. It also takes a very long time to dry thoroughly, so the horse may get a chill after he cools down.

- A trace clip, shown in the photograph, is a common basic clip for the winter months. See page 78 for more clip options.

Snowballs and Shoe Traction

- The hooves of a shod horse can build up a thick, rounded layer of ice and snow, making it difficult to balance. Specialized snow pads put on by the farrier help prevent this.

- A thin layer of cooking oil sprayed onto the sole also helps prevent the snow from sticking.

- Metal shoes are slippery on ice. Barefoot is best, but if the horse needs shoes, the farrier can add borium, small droplets of metal, to the bottom of the shoe, giving the horse extra traction.

See page 78 for more clip options.

ADVANCED BASICS

RAIN ROT

Rain rot is a bacterial infection caused by the Dermatophilus bacteria

Rain rot develops on the skin of the back, neck, and hindquarters when the horse has been wet. One rainstorm is usually not enough to cause rain rot, but several days in a row of wet weather can lead to an outbreak, especially if the horse never has a chance to get dry or is not groomed regularly.

The best cure for rain rot is prevention. Horses in pasture should be checked routinely to catch skin conditions early. After a rain, take a plastic or rubber curry out and curry the horses' backs and rumps to loosen up their coats. This won't get your horse "show clean," but it makes sure that air gets to the horse's skin to prevent such conditions from starting.

If you do spot the telltale signs of rain rot—hair standing

Rain Rot

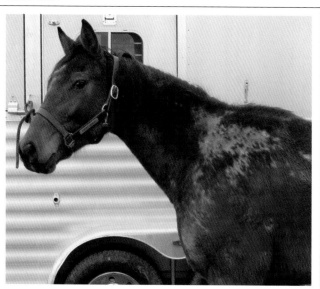

- In the early stages, rain rot simply appears as hair standing on end in the rain-drip pattern on the horse's coat—across the back and rump and down the sides and hips where rainwater would drip off.

- The affected area feels warm to the touch, and the horse may flinch in pain when you touch him.

- If untreated, rain rot quickly develops into scabby, black flaking skin.

Cleaning

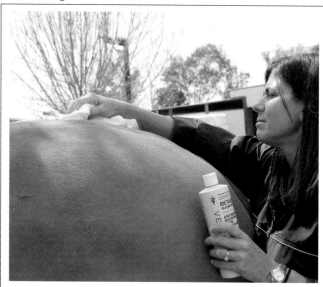

- Bathe the affected areas with an antibacterial shampoo such as Betadine Surgical Scrub. Allow the suds to stand on the horse's skin for several minutes before rinsing off.

- Dry the horse as thoroughly and quickly as possible. Rub gently using clean towels, and cover the horse with a cooler to wick away moisture. Remove the cooler as soon as the horse is dry.

on end, skin warm and painful to the touch, and crusty scabs under the hair—treat it as quickly as possible to prevent it from spreading. If the horse wears a blanket or sheet, remove it and launder it. If the weather is warm enough, bathe the horse with an iodine-based antibacterial shampoo. Do not pick off the scabs, as this is painful to the horse.

If it's too cold for a bath, groom the horse gently but thoroughly with clean brushes, and then soak the brushes in a bucket of bleach water before using them again. Bring the horse into a stall and allow his coat to dry thoroughly. Apply a salve, such as icthammol, MTG, or mineral oil, to the scabby areas and keep the horse dry. Once the salve has loosened the scabs, you may be able to remove them easily. If not, treat them again with antibacterial wash followed by salve. In severe cases, a vet may prescribe a course of penicillin injections.

Treating

- Apply a salve to any scabby areas. MTG works well.

- Keep the horse indoors during rainy weather until the rain rot has cleared up.

- If the rain rot is in the saddle area, do not ride the horse until it heals.

- Launder any blankets, sheets, and saddle pads that have come into contact with the affected horse.

- If the rain rot is quite advanced or widespread and does not respond to treatment, contact your vet for a dose of penicillin.

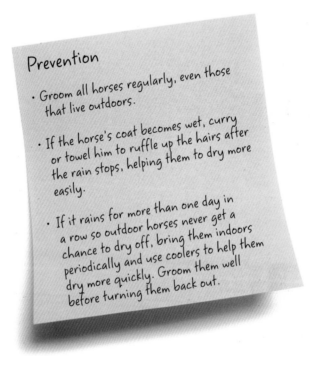

Prevention

- Groom all horses regularly, even those that live outdoors.

- If the horse's coat becomes wet, curry or towel him to ruffle up the hairs after the rain stops, helping them to dry more easily.

- If it rains for more than one day in a row so outdoor horses never get a chance to dry off, bring them indoors periodically and use coolers to help them dry more quickly. Groom them well before turning them back out.

SCRATCHES
Scratches is a fungal infection of the pastern and fetlock

Scratches is also known as greasy heel, mud fever, or pastern dermatitis. Caused by microorganisms present in wet, manure-laden soil, scratches causes painful, scaly scabs, hair loss, and inflammation.

To prevent, keep a careful eye on your horse's pastern and heel area, which should be rinsed off and dried after each use. Don't leave sweat in this area, whether or not your horse uses protective equipment. Keep all boots and wraps clean and dry between uses. If the horse comes in from turnout with muddy legs, rinse and dry them thoroughly. If the horse comes into a dry stall each day, clipping the lower legs helps prevent infection, since the skin is exposed to the air and can dry more quickly. If the horse lives outdoors, it's better not to clip, since the hair protects the area.

Recognizing Scratches

- Each day as you groom your horse, gently run your hands around his pasterns. Bumps under the skin are an early warning sign of scratches.

- More advanced scratches looks like small pus-filled, crusty sores under the fetlock joint.

- Very severe scratches can cause swelling of the lower leg, known as "cellulitis."

Clipping

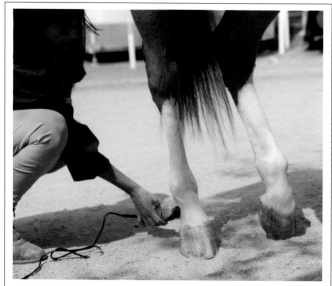

- Clipping the pastern and fetlock area with a coarse (#10) blade allows air to reach the affected areas more easily.

- Clip downward, working very gently around any scabs.

- Follow up by rinsing the legs to remove any scraps of hair that could cause irritation.

- If the scabs are too sensitive to clip over, use blunt-tipped scissors instead to carefully snip away the longest hair.

If an infection does develop, scrub the affected area with an antifungal shampoo, such as Betadine scrub or Nolvasan. If the scabs are loose, pick them off, but if it is too painful to the horse, leave them alone. Rinse and towel-dry the legs thoroughly. Use a blow dryer on a low setting if the horse will tolerate it. If scabs have developed, it's best not to run clippers over them, since this can cause further irritation. Instead, carefully snip away the fetlock hair with scissors. Apply a protective salve to act as a moisture barrier while softening the scabs. Do not wrap the legs. Keep the horse out of the mud until the scratches has healed.

If the scratches does not clear up with a few days of treatment, if it gets worse, or if swelling and heat are present, call your vet. The vet will likely prescribe a course of antibiotics to help resolve the situation.

Treating

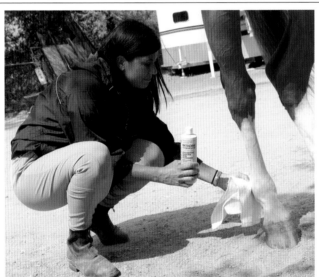

- Scratches must be treated daily until it heals.

- Wash with warm water and antifungal shampoo such as Betadine scrub. Allow the shampoo to stand for several minutes before rinsing thoroughly.

- Carefully and thoroughly dry the legs with clean towels and a hair dryer if possible.

- Apply a salve such as Desitin or icthammol.

- Keep the horse out of muddy or wet areas until the scabs heal.

Prevention

- Clean paddocks regularly to prevent a buildup of manure

- Keep horses out of muddy areas

- For horses that are prone to scratches, clip the pasterns and fetlocks before problems develop, so they will dry more quickly

- Always towel-dry the lower legs after bathing

- Assess the diet. Nutritional deficiencies can suppress the immune system, causing horses to be more susceptible to skin infections such as scratches. (see page 36)

SWEET ITCH
Sweet itch is an extremely irritating condition caused by an allergy to biting Culicoides midges

Sweet itch is also known as Queensland itch, summer itch, or Culicoides hypersensitivity. Affected horses develop symptoms in the summer when insects are most active. It causes severe itching, weepy scabbing, and hair loss. It can occur anywhere on the body, depending on where the insect bites occur, but most commonly affects the mane and tail, as well as the spine, belly, head, and ears. Once a horse develops a sensitivity, it will likely become more severe each year.

Although the allergy itself cannot be prevented, the best way to protect a hypersensitive horse is to prevent insect bites through the use of fly sprays, fly masks and sheets, stabling during times of peak insect activity (morning and eve-

Recognizing Sweet Itch

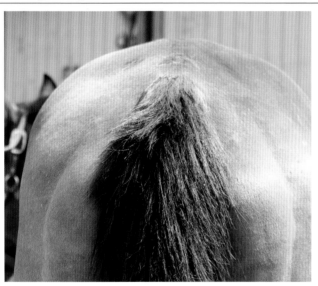

- Sweet itch is quite obvious, since it causes severe discomfort and itching to the horse.

- The horse may rub his skin raw trying to ease the itch, so look for bleeding, swelling, and hair loss around the face, neck, mane, and tailbone.

Topical Treatment

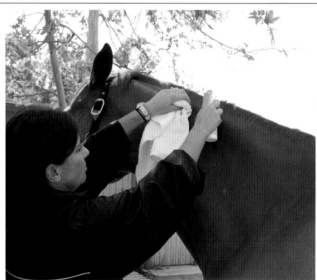

- Bathe the affected area with a mild shampoo to prevent secondary infection.

- Witch hazel, aloe vera, or tea tree oil can alleviate itching.

- Calamine lotion or topical antihistamines also help reduce swelling and itching.

- Wound ointments that contain fly repellents (such as Swat) can be helpful in reducing further exposure.

ning), and keeping the horse away from Culicoides breeding areas (standing water such as ponds or swamps). Note that the midges are very tiny, so any barrier method (sheets, masks, or screens) must have a very fine weave to keep them out. See page 6 for more on insect control.

The symptoms may be treated by antihistamines prescribed by a veterinarian. Topical treatments such as aloe vera and calamine lotions can help soothe the itch. If the horse has rubbed its skin raw, antibiotics may be needed as well to treat secondary infections.

See page 6 for more on insect control.

Antihistamines

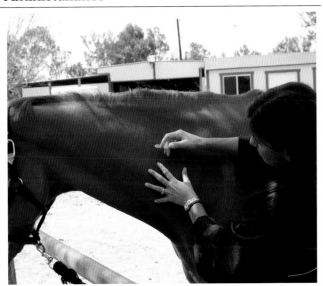

- In severe cases, your vet might prescribe injectable or oral medications.

- Recover is an injectable antihistamine. Corticosteroids may also be used.

- Dexamethasone is an oral anti-inflammatory.

- Trihist is an oral antihistamine that may be prescribed as a preventative.

Prevention

- Fly spray

- Thick ointments such as Swat or petroleum jelly to serve as a barrier

- Fly masks, sheets, and boots

- Keep the horse indoors at dawn and dusk, or all day if necessary

- Use fans in stalls or run-in sheds to blow the insects away

- Eliminate standing water from the area

- In severe cases, the horse may need to be moved to a geographic location where the Culicoides midges don't live

53

SKIN/COAT ISSUES

HIVES

These itchy welts are usually a symptom of an allergic reaction

Technically known as urticaria, hives appear as raised welts on the skin either in a localized area or over the entire body. They generally do not involve hair loss and may or may not cause itching.

If a horse develops hives, the primary goal is to find out the cause of the reaction. Something new in the horse's environment has provoked an allergic response. It could be some-thing that touches the horse's skin or something the horse may have eaten. One very common cause is insect bites.

Once you have determined the cause, take steps to remove the allergen from the horse's environment. Try an all-natural fly spray (although note that some horses are allergic to citro-nella). Launder blankets and saddle pads in a detergent for-mulated for sensitive-skinned people or babies. If insects are

Recognizing Hives

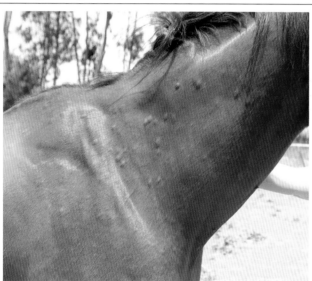

Topical Treatment

- Hives are small, raised welts on the skin, either in a local-ized area or over the entire body.

- Sometimes the location of the hives provides a clue to the cause. Hives in the saddle area might indicate an allergy to the detergent used to wash the saddle pad; hives over the entire body might indicate a food or bedding allergy; hives on the neck, chest, and belly might be caused by insect bites.

- Hives range from the size of a pencil eraser to the size of a half dollar.

- If you suspect that the horse is having a reaction to something on his skin, such as a new bedding or fly spray, bathe him with a gentle shampoo and rinse thoroughly.

- Witch hazel can alleviate itching and reduce swelling.

- Calamine lotion and topical antihistamines also help reduce swelling and itching.

to blame, use a fly sheet and fly sprays to protect the horse, or keep him inside during peak insect feeding times (dawn and dusk).

If the hives are itchy, treat them topically with witch hazel or calamine lotion. In a severe case, your veterinarian can prescribe a topical, oral, or injectable antihistamine and anti-inflammatories. If the hives are very large and occur in the throat area, call your vet right away, since the swelling can cut off the horse's breathing.

Antihistamines

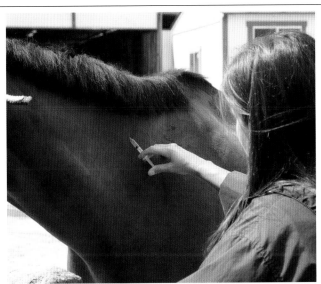

- In severe cases, your vet might prescribe medications.

- Recover is an injectable antihistamine. Corticosteroids may also be used.

- Dexamethasone is an oral anti-inflammatory.

- Trihist is an oral antihistamine that may be prescribed as a preventative to horses that are very prone to hives.

Common Causes of Hives

- Insect bites

- Unusual plant species in hay or pasture

- Feed additives or ingredients

- Various species of wood in bedding, such as cottonwood

- Material in a blanket or saddle pad

- Residual laundry detergent or fabric softener

- Shampoo or other grooming product

- Fly spray ingredients, such as pyrethrins or citronella

- Medications, including antibiotics and non-steroidal anti-inflammatories

55

RINGWORM

Ringworm is a highly contagious fungal skin condition

Ringworm is caused not by a worm, as the name implies, but by the Microsporum or Trichophyton species of fungus. The infection manifests as small, round patches of scaly skin with missing hair. Left untreated, it can progress to larger patches of blistered skin and hair loss. It is easily transmittable to other horses through direct contact or through sharing of brushes, tack, feed buckets, or other equipment. It is also possible for it to be transmitted from horse to human, so wear latex gloves when treating an affected horse.

Conditions that most likely lead to ringworm are damp, dark, dirty environments that can harbor the fungus. Clean stables with sunlight and good air circulation help to prevent it. Horses most at risk are very young, very old, or have a compromised immune system due to disease or poor nutrition.

Recognizing Ringworm

- Ringworm looks like small, round, flaky patches of hairless skin.

- It may appear anywhere on the body but is common in the girth and saddle areas due to transmission via shared girths and saddle pads.

- More advanced cases appear as large hairless patches of scaly, blistered skin.

- Crowded living conditions can contribute to the spread of fungus and other skin ailments.

Cleaning

- First, isolate the horse and sanitize all equipment with a mild bleach solution to prevent spreading the infection.

- Launder saddle pads, blankets, and wraps in hot water and hang to dry in the sun.

- See page 10 for detailed instructions on cleaning your grooming tools.

In case of a ringworm outbreak, immediately isolate the affected horse to prevent spreading the disease. Disinfect brushes, tack, and other equipment with a 1-to-10 solution of bleach and water. Clean the lesions daily with a medicated or iodine-based shampoo provided by a veterinarian for one to two weeks, or until the lesions are all healed. With treatment, ringworm usually resolves without complications. The hair will grow back in the affected areas.

Treating

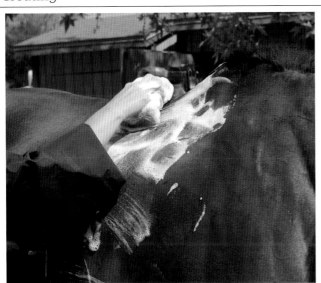

- Bathe the affected areas with an antibacterial shampoo including an ingredient such as iodine or chlorhexedine (or ask your vet for a prescription shampoo).

- Allow the suds to stand on the horse's skin for several minutes before rinsing off.

Prevention

- Avoid sharing brushes and tack. Each horse should have his own supplies

- Groom horses regularly

- Keep stables clean and dry. Allow plenty of ventilation and sunlight into the barn

- Closing up a barn completely to keep it warm in the winter can contribute to many health problems, including ringworm and heaves

- Assess the affected horse's diet. Nutritional deficiencies can suppress the immune system, causing horses to be more susceptible to skin infections such as ringworm

SKIN/COAT ISSUES

LACERATIONS
Treat all cuts, scrapes, bites, kicks, and other minor injuries to prevent infection

Check every horse daily for fresh wounds. These may be bites or kicks from pasture mates or may be caused by scrapes on trees, fences, or other objects. If a horse comes in from the pasture with a severe cut or puncture wound that doesn't seem like a bite or kick, inspect the pasture for a possible source, such as a nail sticking out of a fencepost. Stalled horses are not immune to this type of injury. Good clues to look for when trying to find the "scene of the crime" are horse hair or blood on a protruding or sharp area.

The horse's skin is quite thick. In many cases, a minor wound will involve only superficial hair and skin loss and will not bleed at all. In such a case, simply coat the scrape with a mild

Step 1: Recognizing Lacerations

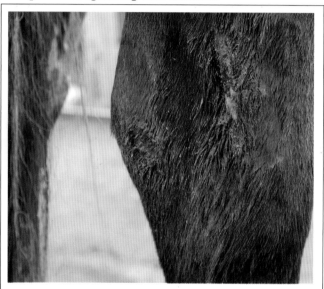

- Each day when grooming your horse, or upon bringing him in from turnout, inspect his skin for injuries.

- If the wound is superficial and the horse is not bleeding, proceed to step 3.

- If the wound is a bit deeper and is or was bleeding, proceed to step 2.

- If the wound is severe or won't stop bleeding, call the vet (see Red Light sidebar).

Step 2: Cleaning

- Using sterile cotton or a clean washcloth, soak the wound with clean water. Carefully remove any dirt, bedding, or other material from the wound.

- Scrub gently with an antibiotic shampoo such as Betadine.

- If the wound has developed a scab, do not try to scrub or pick it off. It is there to protect the wound underneath and will come off easily when it is ready.

- Rinse thoroughly.

- Gently dry the area with a clean towel.

ointment to prevent it from drying out. In most cases, the hair will quickly grow back with no scarring.

If the wound is deeper and bleeding, more attention is required. Wash the area with an antibiotic scrub and rinse it thoroughly. Check to be sure the wound is not deeper than it looks. Coat the wound in an antibiotic ointment. If it is on a lower leg, wrap it with a standing bandage (see page 60) to prevent contamination by dirt or manure.

(see page 60)

Call the vet if a wound is bleeding profusely; a joint is involved (joint infections can be fatal); the horse has a puncture wound, which has a high probability of getting infected; the eye is injured, which can escalate to permanent damage to the eye if not treated properly; the horse seems to be in severe pain; or the wound needs stitches.

Step 3: Treating

- Wearing latex gloves, gently apply a dab of ointment to the wound and spread it into a thin layer.

- If the wound is still bleeding a little, a powdered dressing, such as Furall or Wonder Dust, instead of ointment, helps stop the bleeding.

- If the wound is on a lower leg, apply a gauze patch and a standing bandage to protect it from contaminants (see page 60).

Topical Treatment Chart

Some common wound-treatment products:

Brand	Form	Active ingredient
Bag Balm	Ointment	Lanolin
Betadine Scrub	Shampoo	Iodine
Betadine Solution	Liquid	Iodine
Corona	Ointment	Lanolin
Furall	Powder spray	Furazolidone
Fura-Zone	Ointment	Nitrofurazone
Nolvasan Ointment	Ointment	Chlorhexidine
Nolvasan Scrub	Shampoo	Chlorhexidine
Tea Pro	Spray	Tea tree oil
Wonder Dust	Powder	Potassium alum

SKIN/COAT ISSUES

STANDING WRAPS

These multipurpose wraps reduce or prevent inflammation, protect the legs, and cover wounds

Standing wraps are used to reduce or prevent inflammation, to cover a wound, to support injured legs, and to protect the legs from trauma while a horse is in a stall or trailer. They may be used to prevent swelling after a hard workout, such as jumping, reining, or an intense trail ride. They can help reduce "stocking up" (mild, painless filling of the tissues due to inactivity) in horses that spend a lot of time in a stall. Liniments or poultices may be applied under the wraps.

A standing wrap consists of three parts: a quilted or pillow wrap, which is a thick rectangular wrap that should fit from right below the horse's knee/hock to the bottom of the fetlock; a bandage that wraps firmly around the pillow wrap to

Standing Wraps: Step 1

- Apply the pillow or quilted wrap, wrapping clockwise on a right leg and counter-clockwise on a left leg. (You should always be pulling the bandage toward yourself across the front of the cannon bone, not the back.)

- The wrap should reach from just below the knee joint to the bottom of the fetlock joint.

- Pull the wrap snug across the front of the leg, and with uniform pressure wrap it around the back, being careful not to pull tightly across the tendons.

Standing Wraps: Step 2

- Insert the end 3 or 4 inches of the bandage under the edge of the pillow wrap at the midpoint of the cannon bone. Make one wrap around the starting point, and then begin to wrap downward, overlapping each wrap by half the width of the bandage.

- Like the pillow wrap, the bandage should come toward you across the front of the leg and away from you across the tendons.

- Concentrate on creating even pressure with each pass of the bandaging material.

support it and hold it to the leg, made of flannel or knit material; and a fastening element to keep the bandage in place such as bandage pins or masking tape. Often the material has Velcro already attached to fasten the wrap. Whenever one leg is wrapped, the opposing leg should also be wrapped for support. However, if the wrap covers only a slight skin wound or other injury that won't prevent the horse from bearing weight on that leg, a wrap on the opposite leg is not necessary. They should be checked regularly throughout the day and unwrapped and changed at least every twenty-four hours.

········· **RED ● LIGHT** ·············

If incorrectly applied, a standing wrap will actually cause injury to the tendons in the form of a bandage bow (swelling of the tendon sheath). Don't apply wraps unevenly, too tightly, or over inadequate padding. If you're inexperienced, have an experienced horseperson demonstrate and oversee your initial attempts at wrapping. Don't use when a horse is turned out or being worked, as they restrict the tendons and cause injury.

Standing Wraps: Step 3

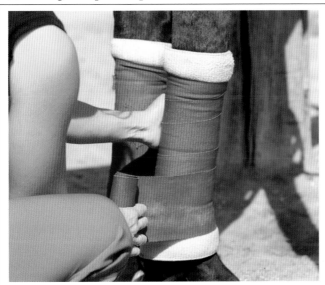

- Wrap down the leg to the bottom of the pillow wrap, leaving at least 1/2-inch of padding exposed.

- With each pass of the bandage, be sure that you use even, consistent tension. Avoid creating any loose spots, tight spots, or wrinkles in the material.

- If you make a mistake, remove the entire wrap and start over rather than trying to fix it as you go.

Standing Wraps: Step 4

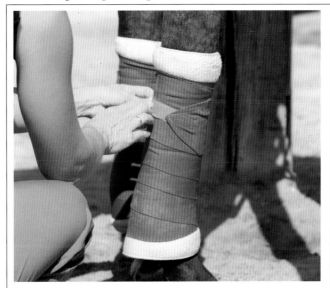

- Wrap back up the leg to the top of the pillow wrap, again leaving 1/2-inch of padding exposed at the top.

- Continue the wrap back down to the middle, and secure the Velcro. If the wrap doesn't have a Velcro closure, use pins or tape.

- The fastening device shouldn't be tight; there shouldn't be an indentation where the tape or bandage pin fastens to the bandage. Also, if tape is used, it should be spiraled on the leg rather than taped in a solid ring, which could impede circulation in the leg.

POLO WRAPS

These classic wraps provide casual, versatile protection for the tendons while riding

Polo wraps are made of stretchy fleece material and are thick enough to be used alone, without padding underneath. They are used to protect the horse's lower legs and tendons from interference during work. They may be worn by horses that are jumping, doing lateral work in dressage, or have conformational or movement faults that make them likely

to interfere (hit their legs with their own hooves).

Polo wraps should not be left on a horse that is turned out or stalled and left unattended, since they could come unwrapped or slip down and cause injury. They are intended only for use during exercise and are not meant to be left on for long periods of time. Polo wraps should also not be used

Polo Wraps: Step 1

- Use a clean, dry wrap, rolled neatly and tightly with the Velcro end on the inside of the roll.

- Start at the inside of the leg, wrapping toward yourself around the front and then away from yourself across the back tendons.

- Make one complete turn around the center of the cannon bone, and then wrap downward, overlapping each layer halfway over the previous one.

- Keep tension on the wrap, and don't let it bunch or sag. The wrap should be snug but not tight.

Polo Wraps: Step 2

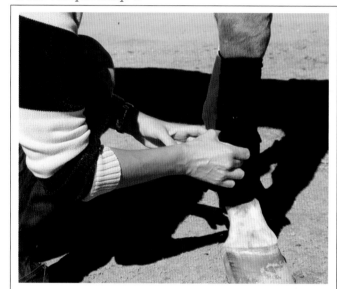

- Continue wrapping in this manner until you reach the fetlock joint.

- Wrap the polo down around the back and bottom of the joint, then reverse direction and begin to wrap back up the leg.

- The wrap should form a tidy inverted V at the front of the fetlock joint where the wrap crosses over itself.

for cross-country riding, hunting, or trail riding—all situations when the horse's legs could become wet. Wet polo wraps are too heavy to support themselves, so they will slide down and become tangled around the horse's feet.

Machine-wash and dry wraps after each use. Long, narrow wraps, such as polos and standing bandages, have a tendency to wind themselves into a tangle in the washing machine. To minimize this, fasten all the Velcro straps, and wash and dry the wraps inside a mesh garment bag. After drying, untangle the wraps and roll each one, ready for the next use.

Polo Wraps: Step 3

- Continue wrapping, remembering to maintain a constant tension, until you reach the top of the cannon, an inch or two below the knee joint.

- Reverse direction again, and wrap downward toward the starting point at the middle of the cannon.

- If you have wrapped well and the polo fits your horse, you will arrive at the midpoint of the cannon just as you reach the end of the wrap.

Polo Wraps: Step 4

- Double-check your work for sagging, wrinkles, or uneven spots. If the wrap is not smooth and snug, you'll have to unroll it and start over.

- Use the Velcro closure to seal the wrap.

- If you need greater security, use duct tape or electrical tape over the Velcro strip. Do not wrap the tape completely around the leg so it forms a loop with itself, as this can bind the tendons.

POULTICE

A non-invasive, non-medicinal way to effectively reduce inflammation in the legs

A poultice is a thick, sticky, white or gray claylike substance that may be applied to a horse's lower legs to draw out inflammation and reduce soreness. Poultices may be used preventatively on horses that have worked especially hard, such as racehorses, barrel horses, endurance horses, or jumpers. They may also be used on injured limbs to reduce swelling.

Wearing disposable gloves, use your fingers to smear the poultice onto the lower legs in a thin layer, thoroughly coating the tendons. Wrap damp brown paper or plastic wrap over the poultice. Make the paper or plastic as smooth as possible on the horse's limb. You do not want to wrap over any wrinkles or ridges. Then cover the paper or plastic with a

Poultice: Step 1

- Wearing latex medical gloves to keep the sticky goo off your hands, scoop up a dollop of poultice.

- Smear it onto the lower leg in the direction of hair growth, coating the entire cannon and fetlock with a quarter-inch-thick layer.

- You can poultice the knee as well, if needed. See above for instructions.

Poultice: Step 2

- Tear off a section of brown paper that is the same height as the area to be covered and long enough to wrap around at least once.

- Wet the paper by dipping it into a bucket of water or hosing it.

- Carefully wrap the paper around the poulticed leg, covering all the white clay. Be very careful not to let the paper wrinkle or bunch; you want a smooth, consistent surface.

pillow wrap and standing bandage, following the directions on pages 60–65.

You may occasionally need to wrap a horse's knee or upper foreleg, either to cover an open wound or to reduce inflammation. Start by applying a standing wrap below the knee to act as a support structure for the upper bandage. Then wrap a second bandage around the upper leg so that it rests on the lower wrap. Do not wrap too tightly around the knee joint, since it needs to bend and is prone to pressure sores.

Leave the poultice in place for twelve to twenty-four hours, and then remove it and the wrap. If the poultice material is dry, you should be able to brush it off with a stiff body brush. If the poultice is still damp, hose it off. Hand-walk the horse to restore circulation, then check the legs for swelling or heat and rewrap if needed.

Poultice: Step 3

- If you want to keep the poultice wet and active for longer, or to create a "sweating" effect, cover the paper with a layer of plastic wrap.

- To keep everything in place and to provide support and gentle pressure to the tendons, finish by applying a standing wrap over the poultice, as described on page 60.

Poultice: Step 4

- Leave the wrap in place for twelve to twenty-four hours.

- Then remove the standing bandage and peel off the plastic and paper.

- If the poultice clay is dry, you can probably brush it off with a stiff-bristled

brush. If it is damp and sticky, use a hose to rinse it off.

- Check the leg for swelling, and reapply the poultice if needed.

BOOTS FOR WORKING

A variety of specialized boots provides protection and support for the performance horse

In addition to polo wraps, there is a wide variety of commercially made protective boots for horses to wear during exercise. These boots protect the tendons from interference and, in the case of sport boots, provide support to the fetlock, thus preventing injury by pulling or straining. They may be made of leather, neoprene, or other materials and

may or may not be lined with fleece or synthetics.

Choose a boot for your horse based on your discipline as well as his specific physical issues. Any horse that travels close behind due to conformation, thus putting himself at risk for injury due to interference, may need to wear ankle boots on his hind legs. A horse that participates in reining or

GROOMING HORSES

Galloping Boots or Brushing Boots

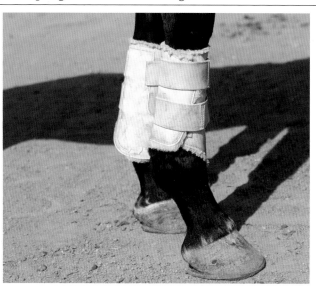

- These boots are used in jumping, eventing, pleasure riding, and trail riding.

- Align the boot so that the larger swell of the protective padding covers the fetlock, while the rest of the pad covers the inner tendons of the cannons. Align the boot a bit higher than it

should be, and then slide it down into position before tightening the straps, so that the leg hair lies flat under the boot.

- The metal buckles go in front, and the Velcro points toward the back.

Ankle Boots

- These boots are used in jumping, dressage, or on any horse that tends to interfere with his hind legs.

- The padding should cover the entire fetlock joint.

- Straps point toward the back.

barrel racing may need the protection of skid boots, which prevent sores on the backs of the fetlocks from sliding across the arena sand. Eventers and jumpers benefit from galloping boots (also known as brushing boots or splint boots), which protect the inner tendons of the legs with a thick cushion.

Some boots may also be used to protect the horse during turnout. In general, it's not advisable to leave the horse turned out in any boots for longer than four hours or so. Heat, moisture, and dirt can accumulate under the boot, leading to abrasions, fungal infections, or other problems.

Sport Boots

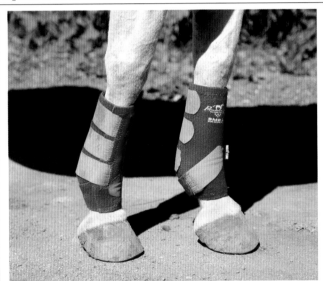

- Sport boots are made of neoprene and differ from most other boots in that they have a strap that runs under the fetlock joint to support the suspensory tendons.

- Apply the boots so that the Velcro closures point toward the back, and wrap them as tightly as possible so they don't slip down. Fasten the suspensory strap under the fetlock joint.

- In cold weather, you may need to retighten the boots after the horse's body heat has warmed and softened the neoprene.

Skid Boots

- These boots are used in Western speed events, including reining, barrel racing, and cutting.

- Apply them like sport boots, ensuring that the hard plastic "shell" covers the back of the fetlock.

HOOF AND SHIPPING BOOTS

A selection of boots protects the hooves during work and the legs during transport

GROOMING HORSES

There are two basic categories of protective boots for the hooves: bell boots and hoof boots. Bell boots fit around the pastern and hang down to protect the coronary bands and the bulbs of the heel from interference. Bell boots also prevent the horse from catching the edge or back of his shoe with the opposite hoof and pulling it off. Use bell boots when

jumping or reining or when riding any horse that tends to overreach.

Quarter boots are similar to bell boots in that they protect the bulbs of the horse's heel. They are firmly attached, however, on the horse's hoof below the coronary band rather than fitting around the pastern. They are typically used on horses

Bell Boots

- Bell boots may be made of rubber, neoprene, or plastic (as in the case of the old-fashioned "petal" boots).

- Put gummy boots (made of stretchy rubber) on by stretching them over the horse's hoof inside out and then flipping them down. Other types may have

adjustable Velcro straps or buckles.

- Bell boots are safe to leave on during turnout or shipping. Check them daily for chafing.

Gaited Horse Boots

- Quarter boots (sometimes referred to as hinged-quarter boots), trotting boots, scalping boots, or bell boots are used on the five-gaited American Saddlebred, fine harness, roadsters, and National Show Horses in the show ring as well as for training.

- Put them on the front feet. This protects the bulbs of the horse's heels from being injured by the horse's hind feet as they stride forward.

- White is the color required in competition.

that perform at speed, such as roadsters, or at the rack, such as the five-gaited Saddlebred. Other boots designed to protect the bulbs of the heel are trotting and scalping boots.

Hoof boots are hard rubber boots that fit over the horse's entire hoof, protecting the sole and frog against hard or rocky ground. They may be used to temporarily replace a lost shoe, or may be used on barefoot horses on exceptionally rough riding surfaces. Hoof boots are a relatively new innovation, and designs are constantly evolving. Some hoof boots feature "gaiters" that fit over the pasterns to help keep the boot in place, while others feature dials that tighten the boot around the hoof. (Note that jumping in hoof boots is generally not advisable, since they can shift or slip.)

Shipping boots are tall, thick, durable boots used only when trailering a horse. They restrict movement and are very bulky, so they should not be used under any other circumstances besides trailering.

Hoof Boots

- Hoof boot designs vary, but in general, they are slipped on over the horse's toe and then pulled up over the heel. The horse may need to step down into the boot to get it all the way on.

- Fasten the boot according to the manufacturer's instructions. It should fit very tight. The boot should not be high enough to rub against the coronary band or heel bulbs.

- Ride or turn a horse out in hoof boots, but remove them daily to check for chafing and pick out the hoof.

Shipping Boots

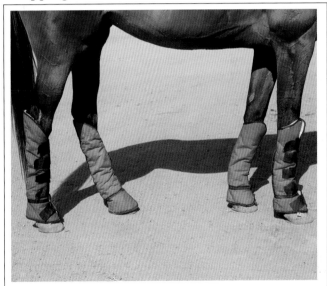

- Shipping boots extend from above the knee or hock to below the fetlock, covering the coronary bands of the hooves.

- The boots should fit snugly so they don't slip down while in the trailer.

- Be sure the Velcro closures are on the outside of the leg and point toward the back.

- On long trailer rides, take rest breaks to water the horses and check boots.

- Be sure your horse is comfortable with these boots. Don't let this ride be his first experience wearing them.

CHOOSING CLIPPERS AND BLADES

There is a broad spectrum of clippers available, varying in quality, size, and intended use

Tiny battery-operated clippers can fit in your pocket for the unexpected touch-up at a show. Large, plug-in body clippers are used only for clipping the hair from the bigger parts of the horse, including the neck, barrel, and hindquarters, and are far too cumbersome to be used on the head and legs. However, to body clip a horse with detail clippers would take hours and would wear out the motor because detail clippers are insufficient for such a job.

Therefore, to be able to do the most complete clip job, you need at least two pairs of clippers for the various tasks: a set of small clippers and a set of body clippers. The smallest touch-up clippers often have permanent blades. If you

Body Clippers

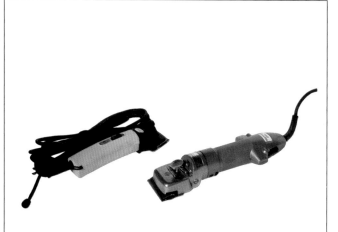

- Body clippers are large clippers that cover large areas of the horse's coat at one time. A complete body clipping kit will include:

- Body clippers, and a set of sharp body clipping blades

- Clipper oil, clipper grease, and blade cleaner

- Screwdriver to adjust and clean the clippers

- Rag or towel to use on the clippers and a towel or brush to use on the horse

- Heavy duty extension cord with grounded plug

Small and Detail Clippers

- Small clippers with detachable blades work well for any clipping or trimming situation except body clipping. If you are going to have only one set of clippers, this is the size to have. They are designed so you can change sets of blades and therefore may be used for many clipping situations.

- Detail clippers, as the name implies, are designed for very specific trimming, such as inside the ears or on the muzzle. The blades on these clippers are very fine and aren't interchangeable.

plan on getting just one set of small clippers, it is worth the investment to get a style with detachable blades. Detachable blades can be sharpened and replaced, adding to the life of the clipper blades. The larger body clippers always have detachable blades.

Clipper blades come in different sizes, which produce different types of cuts. For your small clippers, you'll want a selection of clipper blades. It is nice to have at least two sets of each size blade on hand, in case one set becomes dull or even breaks before you finish the job. Dull blades will cause

discomfort to the horse and do a poor job of clipping. There's no sight sillier or more frustrating than a half-clipped horse! Having the correct equipment for the job is the first step to a good clip.

Clipper Blades

- A successful clipping experience, for both you and your horse, depends on having the correct equipment. In particular the clipper blades must be:

- The correct make for the model of clippers (many small clipper blade sets are compatible with any

of the small clipper styles manufactured by the major brands)

- The correct size for what you are trying to trim

- Sharp and not missing any teeth

- Clean and well oiled

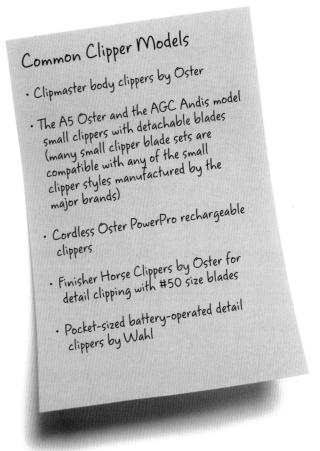

Common Clipper Models

- Clipmaster body clippers by Oster

- The A5 Oster and the AGC Andis model small clippers with detachable blades (many small clipper blade sets are compatible with any of the small clipper styles manufactured by the major brands)

- Cordless Oster PowerPro rechargeable clippers

- Finisher Horse Clippers by Oster for detail clipping with #50 size blades

- Pocket-sized battery-operated detail clippers by Wahl

71

CARE OF CLIPPERS AND BLADES

Extend the life of your equipment through proper lubrication, cleaning, and storage

GROOMING HORSES

The most important thing you can do to keep your clippers in good shape is to read the manual! It will tell you if there is anything you might need to do before using them. For example, there may be a protective coating on the blades that needs to be removed before use. The manual also tells you how to keep the clippers clean, gives safety tips, and pro-

vides the size of the extension cord needed. If an extension cord cannot carry the current needed by the clippers, both the cord and the clippers will overheat.

All clippers and blades will stay the sharpest and continue cutting the longest if special care is taken to clean and oil them throughout the clipping process. To clean the small

Lubricating Small Clippers

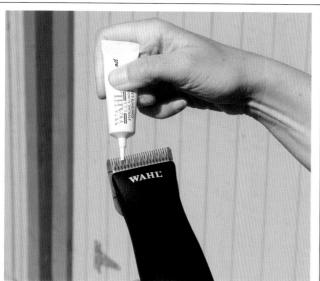

- The bottom blade in a small clipper set is the comb; the upper blade is the cutter.

- To clean, push the cutter half out from the comb and remove all hair and dirt. Repeat in opposite direction.

- Apply oil to the teeth of the blades and on the top of

the cutter; run for fifteen seconds. If you continue clipping, wipe the excess oil off the blades; if you put the clippers away, leave the excess oil on.

- The clipper oil allows the movable metal pieces to rub against each other without overheating.

Cleaning and Oiling Large Clippers

- Clean or brush out the blades at least every five minutes and stop to oil them every twenty minutes.

- To clean, turn off and wipe off hair with a soft rag or brush out with a soft brush. Turn on and dip tips of blades into blade wash or spray with lubricating prod-

uct. Remove from wash and run a few more seconds. Turn off and wipe excess wash or coolant from blades before continuing.

- To oil, place a thin line of oil along the top of the teeth and squeeze a few drops into the small hole on the head of the clippers.

clipper blades, dip and run the blades in a blade-cleaning solution. Dip just the teeth of the blades, not the entire blade, into the liquid. To lubricate, place a few drops of oil along the teeth and a couple of drops on the cutout area in the top of the blades. After cleaning or oiling the blades, run the clippers for a few seconds. Then wipe away the excess product.

Body clippers should have the hair cleaned out of their blades every five minutes (or every few passes) and then sprayed with lubricant or dipped in blade wash. Oil should be applied to the body clippers approximately every twenty minutes. A small tube of clipper oil is usually included with a new set of body clippers. Most body clippers have a small hole on the top blade for adding oil, and add a thin line of oil onto the top of the teeth as well. After you apply the lubricant or oil, run the clippers for a few seconds and then wipe off any dripping product. Dripping the oil or cooling/cleaning product on your horse's skin may cause blistering.

Adjusting Tension of Body Clipping Blades

- On the top of the body clippers is a screw that, when tightened, puts more tension on a set of blades. As blades dull during the body clipping process, tighten this screw to keep the blades "sharp" so you can continue clipping.

- When you begin clipping with a fresh set of blades, be sure this tension screw isn't twisted in too far. Tighten it enough so that the blades give an acceptable clip, but don't start with the screw fully tightened; there won't be leeway to sharpen the blades by tightening the screw. You'll have to change the blades.

Cleaning and Lubrication Products

- Clipper oil

- A cooling product, such as Kool Lube or Blade Ice

- A blade wash product

- A small brush or old toothbrush reserved for getting hair out of the clipper

- A towel or rag to be used on the clippers only

- An airtight container to store clean, oiled clipper blades rust-free

HOW TO CLIP
Basic guidelines, techniques, and tips for a perfect clip job

Clipping a clean horse keeps your blades sharper longer, so groom areas you plan to clip in advance and bathe if necessary. Decide in advance exactly what type of clip you are going to do (see page 78 for some traditional options). If you are body clipping, mark out the clipper lines with masking tape, chalk, or washable marker. Start clipping at the shoulder of the horse and work your way toward the back, always clipping against the grain of the hair. Make long strokes with the clippers so the clip is as a seamless as possible. Also, overlap your strokes. (Some people start at the back and work forward; you will eventually develop your own system.) Keep the blades clean and lubricated, as described on page 72.

The tension of the blades on the body clippers can be adjusted. Tightening the adjustment as you proceed with a

Clipping Area

- Select a clipping area that is well-lit and not in a busy traffic area.

- It is easiest to body clip a horse that is cross-tied.

- Don't clip in a wash rack because of the danger of electrocution.

- If clipping on cement, be careful of dropping the clippers and breaking teeth off the blades or even ruining the clippers completely.

Mark with Masking Tape

- Choose the type of clip you want to do (see page 78) and mark out the pattern on the horse with masking tape.

- Measure from a few different points on the horse's body (such as the mane, withers, point of shoulder, elbow) to ensure that your tape is symmetrical on both sides of the horse.

- If marking with chalk, your method of measuring is the same.

body clip will result in a uniform trim as the blades naturally become dull. Consult the manual for instructions on changing the clipper tension and other blade maintenance.

Work efficiently and gently. Concentrate on getting the job done in as few strokes as possible when clipping sensitive areas. Horses get frustrated if you take multiple tiny little swipes with the clippers. As your clipping techniques improve, efficiency will become habit. If the horse protests at any point, take a break, and review the section on Desensitizing the Horse (page 76).

It is a good habit to clean and oil the blades when putting your clippers away. Do not wipe the oil off of the blades, but allow it to provide a protective coating.

Cutting with the Grain

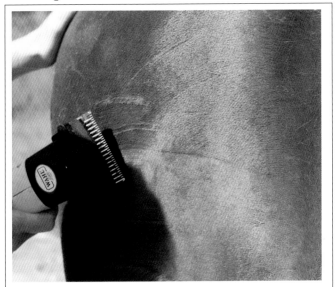

- Make long strokes with the clippers so the clip is as seamless as possible.

- Overlap your strokes by the width of one or two teeth to prevent leaving long lines of hair between strokes.

Important Points

- When clipping near the mane, leave at least a 1/2 inch of winter coat on either side. Don't trim mane hairs as they will take a long time to grow back and lay down correctly.

- When doing a clip that includes the back of the horse, leave a saddle pad–

shaped patch of winter coat to add extra protection.

- To avoid cutting any tail hairs, leave an upside-down V-shaped patch of winter coat at the top of the dock. The wide portion of the V is the width of the tail, and the point aims toward the horse's head.

DESENSITIZING THE HORSE

Train your horse to accept clippers and stand quietly while being clipped

They buzz, they vibrate, they tickle, and they have a long black tail. Yikes! Clippers can be very scary to a horse that is not used to them. It is important to take the time to slowly introduce clippers to alleviate the horse's natural fears.

Introduce the clippers one sense at a time. Start with vision. Let the horse see the clippers while they are turned off. Then

let him smell them and investigate them if he chooses. If he is comfortable at this point, move on to touch: Start rubbing the clippers (still turned off) over his neck, chest, and shoulders, progressing toward the back end if he doesn't become nervous. Also touch the clippers to all the parts of his face, including the top of the head and the ears. If the horse be-

Step 1: Clippers Off

- Let the horse see and smell the clippers while they are turned off.

- Start by touching the horse's shoulder, and slowly move the clippers down his legs, all around his belly, chest, and hindquarters, and up his neck.

- When the horse is comfortable with the clippers near his body, touch them to his face and ears.

- If the horse becomes nervous, back off and start over. The goal is to never frighten the horse.

Step 2: Clippers On

- Hold the clippers well away from the horse but in a place where he can easily see them before turning the switch on.

- Let the horse see and smell the clippers if he wants to.

- Repeat step 1, running the clippers over the horse's

body and legs so he can feel the vibration.

- Once the horse is completely comfortable, you can begin to clip.

comes nervous at any point, slow down or go back a step.

Next, introduce the sound of the clippers by turning them on, well away from the horse's body and in a location where he can see them clearly. The sudden buzzing may startle the horse. Switch them on and off a few times until he relaxes. Let him sniff them again if he likes. Finally, combine sight, feeling, and sound by touching the clippers to the horse while they are on, all over his body, as you did when they were off. If all goes well, you can progress to actually clipping.

Note that this process may not happen all at once. It may take several short training sessions over a period of days for the horse to become comfortable enough to allow you to clip him. Don't progress faster than your horse can handle, or you will only create more fear in the long run.

Step 3: Legs

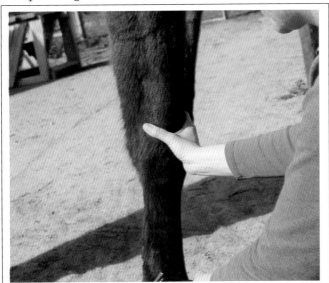

- The legs can be difficult, since the horse may associate you touching his leg with being asked to lift his hoof. You'll have to teach him not to pick up his hoof every time you touch his leg.

- Teach him a cue, such as pressing on the front of his knee or saying the word "stand," that indicates that he should keep his hoof on the ground.

- Use lots of praise. Don't punish the horse for lifting his hoof, since he thinks he is doing what you want.

Step 4: Face

- The face and ears are especially sensitive, and even a horse who will happily let you clip the rest of his body may object when you try to work on his head.

- Proceed slowly and gently. Sometimes the problem is not fear, but ticklishness, so press more firmly with the clippers to avoid tickling the horse.

- You may have to apply a twitch or use one of the other restraint methods mentioned on page 20.

- Never force the horse; it'll frighten him. You'll only make your task difficult.

BODY CLIPS

Horses with different jobs require various traditional styles of clip patterns

There are several different styles of clips, ranging from a minimal bib clip to a full-body clip. Decide what type of clip is best for your horse based on the climate, his level of work, whether you intend to blanket, how much shelter he will have, and what style is acceptable in your show discipline.

A horse in a region with very cold or severe winters needs to keep as much hair as possible. A bib or strip clip may be best for him, removing the hair only where it is most likely to cause sweating. He will only need to be blanketed during very severe weather. On the other hand, a horse doing very heavy work, during which he will work up a sweat every day, should be body clipped; he will then need to be blan-

Bib Clip

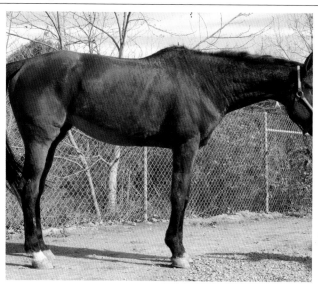

Trace Clip

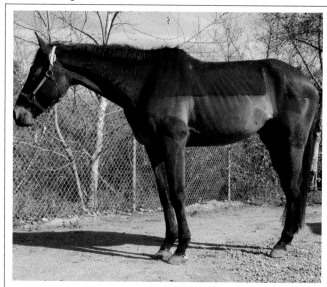

- A bib clip is a very minimal clip for horses in light work. It leaves most of the hair for warmth, removing only the minimum in the most sweat-prone areas. It also exposes some of the large arteries in the neck and chest, which allows for greater heat loss while working.

- Clip the front of the throat and neck, the chest, and the belly to just behind the girth.

- This clip can be easily expanded to an Irish clip, in which a triangle of hair from the throat to the midpoint of the belly is removed.

- A trace clip is a common trim for horses in moderate work but not showing. It removes the hair only from the areas where a horse is likely to sweat.

- Clip the underside of the throat and neck, the chest, belly, and a strip across the stifle and flank.

- A high trace clip removes the hair to about halfway up the sides, neck, and haunches and may include clipping part of the head.

- A low trace clip removes only a narrow strip from the hip to the throat.

keted and kept in a stall during cold or wet weather.

Show hunters, dressage horses, Western show horses, and horses shown in breed shows, if clipped at all, are usually fully body clipped, including the face. Field hunters, eventers, and pleasure or trail horses are more likely to have a partial clip, such as a trace clip. See the show preparation chapters for particulars on clipping for the various disciplines and breeds.

Hunter Clip

- A hunter clip is an ideal clip for horses that are in very hard work or tend to sweat excessively over their whole bodies.

- Clip the whole body, including the head, except for a patch of hair in the saddle area for protection against the cold and saddle rubs.

- Leave the legs unclipped, up to the stifles on the hind legs and a triangular point at the tops of the front legs.

Full-Body Clip

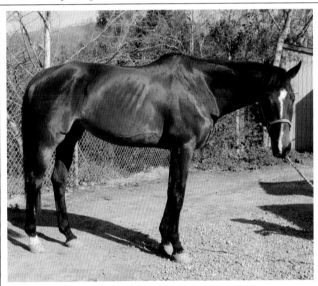

- Horses that are being shown through the winter usually have a full-body clip, since it is more visually appealing than either a shaggy horse or a partial clip.

- Clip the horse's whole body, including the legs and head.

- A body-clipped or hunter-clipped horse must be well blanketed in cold weather, since his natural protection has been removed. See page 34 for more on blanketing.

TRIMMING FOR NEATNESS

How to tidy up your horse for a nice appearance and easier grooming when you're not showing

Pleasure horses, trail horses, and others that are not shown (or will be shown only at local, informal venues) do not require the close clipping of a show horse. In fact, it is better not to closely clip the head and legs if the horse is not going to be shown; the long hairs are there for a reason. Ear hairs protect the horse from insects, as well as from debris that might fall into the inner ear; they also keep the ears warm in cold weather. The whiskers on the muzzle are sensitive to touch and help the horse identify different types of plants when he's grazing. Whiskers around the eyes protect the eye from debris.

Nevertheless, trimming the hair of the head and lower legs

Ears

- Use #10 blades on a set of small clippers.

- Fold the ear closed with your left hand, and run the clippers along the edge from base to tip to remove the long hairs there.

- Allow the ear to open, and trim the inner hairs so they are flush with the edges of the ear.

Muzzle

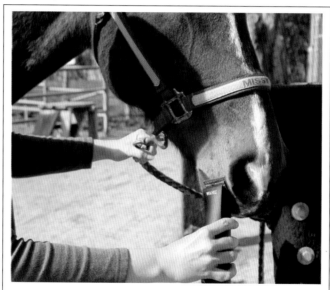

- Use #30 blades on a set of small clippers; #10 blades will work on the horse with a heavy winter coat.

- Pressing the flat side of the blade gently against the horse's skin, trim off the long whiskers on the lips, around the nostrils, and at the end of the muzzle.

- Working downward in the direction of hair growth, carefully clip the whiskers that are higher up on the muzzle. Be careful not to gouge the softer hair of the face.

does give the horse a more refined appearance and helps cut down on grooming time. In some boarding stables, clipped horses are the norm, and owners are expected to keep their horses looking sharp. Clipping the lower legs also allows them to dry more quickly, reducing the chance that the horse will develop scratches or fungal infections (see page 50). Here's how to do a basic trim that will make the horse look tidy while still allowing him some of the benefit of his natural guard hairs.

Jawline

- Use #10 blades on a set of small clippers.

- Working downward in the direction of hair growth, clip the long hair between and along the jawbones from the throatlatch area to the lower lip.

- Blend the clip lines into the rest of the unclipped face hair.

Fetlocks

- Use #10 blades on a set of small clippers.

- Clipping downward in the direction of hair growth, clip the long guard hairs down the back of the cannon bone and fetlock.

- "Scoop" out the hair at the back of the pastern. It may be easier to hold the horse's leg up and allow the hoof to drop toward the ground, opening the fetlock joint.

CLIPPING THE LEGS

Clipping the long hair on the lower legs gives the horse a more refined look

Clipping the legs also helps prevent the hair from collecting ring dust or mud, makes grooming and drying time faster, and makes white markings look whiter. Use medium to coarse blades (#15 or #10) and a smaller set of clippers. Large body clippers will be too cumbersome for this job.

Begin by clipping downward along the backs of the can-nons, from the point of the knee to the fetlock. Press lightly and always work with the grain of the hair to prevent cutting too close. Next clip the sides and fronts of the cannons in the same manner, leaving a V of longer hair below the knee or hock and blending carefully.

Clip the fetlock joint and pasterns, still working downward

Backs of Cannons

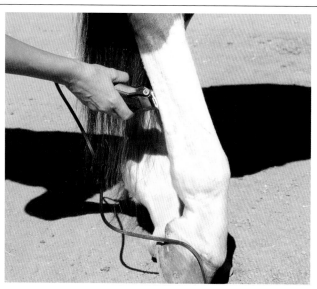

- Use #10 blades on a set of small clippers for the legs.

- Start clipping behind the knee, working downward in the direction of hair growth.

- Clip smoothly down to the top of the fetlock, removing all the long, shaggy hair.

- When the horse has its summer coat, you may find running the #10 blades against the hair up the very back of the cannons gives you the clean look you want.

Sides and Fronts of Cannons

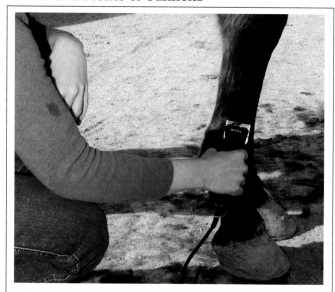

- Continue working around the sides of the legs, gradually tapering the top of the clipped area lower so that at the front, the top of the clipped area is just below the knee joint.

- Make several passes over each area if necessary.

- Blend the clipped area at the top and bottom by gradually increasing and decreasing pressure as you begin and end each stroke.

in the direction of the hair. It may be easier to clip the back of the fetlock if you lift the horse's leg and hold it at the front of the fetlock joint, allowing the hoof to drop down toward the ground. If the horse has large ergots, trim them off with scissors before clipping.

Set the hoof back down gently, and turn the clippers over. Clipping upward against the grain of the hair in short strokes, clip around the coronary band.

Pastern and Fetlock

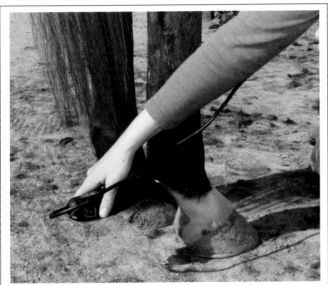

- Clip down around the pastern and fetlock.

- If the horse has long ergots that interfere with clipping, cut them off using a knife or scissors. Like chestnuts, they don't have nerves or cause pain to the horse.

- For access to the back of the pastern, lift the horse's lower leg, cup your hand around the front of the fetlock joint, and let the hoof drop toward the ground.

- If the horse has its summer coat, run #10 blades against the hair up the back of the pasterns.

Coronary Band

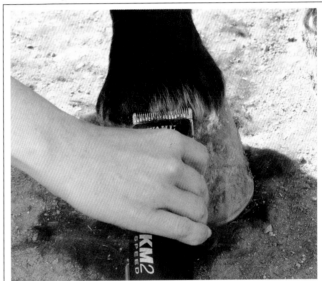

- Now turn the clippers over, and clip upward all the way around the coronary band.

- Trim just the hair that hangs over the top of the hoof wall, not up into the pastern area itself.

CLIPPING EARS AND BRIDLE PATH
Clipping ears is perhaps the most challenging clipping task

Ear clipping is a challenge both because the ears are so delicate and detailed and because horses frequently object to the buzzing and vibrating of the clippers near and within their ears. For this problem, gradual desensitization is the key (see page 76). If the horse is still ticklish, try inserting horse earplugs (available in tack shops and catalogs) to muffle the sound, as well as to prevent hair from falling into the ear canal.

If all else fails, the horse may be twitched, or even lightly sedated by a vet for the procedure. If you are clipping a horse for show, know the rules pertaining to illegal substances. There are very specific rules pertaining to what sedatives may be in your horse's system while competing.

Unless the show standards of your discipline demand it, the fine hairs of the inner ear should not be fully clipped out, es-

Edges

- Gently squeeze the ear shut and clip upward from base to tip along the edges.

- If the outsides of the ears are fuzzy, neaten them up with the #10 blades (no matter what time of year) going against the hair.

- Blend the trim up to the forelock and into the bridle path.

Inner Ear, Minimal Trim

- If it is acceptable in your discipline to keep some hair in the ears to protect against insects or cold, clip the inner ear hair flush with edge of the ear.

- Use #10 blades and clip in the direction of hair growth.

- Be sure your blades are sharp and your clippers cool for any clipping that is needed around the ears. This will make the job go faster and be more comfortable for the horse.

pecially during bug season. These hairs protect the ear from debris and insects. Ideally they should be trimmed just short enough to lie flush with the outer edges of the ear. If you must clip out the ears completely, protect them with a fly mask with ear coverings when the horse is turned out.

The horse's stall is the best place for detailed clipping. He'll feel safer, and you can keep him contained without a battle. If it's too dim in the stall, position your horse so that his tail is against a wall so he can't back away. Have something to stand on; height gives more accessibility to the horse's head.

ZOOM

Saddle-type breeds, such as the American Saddlebred, will have their ears neatly trimmed and cleaned out for competition. However, to emphasize the pointed shape of the ears, 1/2 to 1 inch of hair will be left inside the ear at its very tip. This hair will then be trimmed into the shape of a diamond to accent the shape of the ear.

Inner Ear, Trimmed Clean

- To clip inner ear hair completely, work against the grain of the hair using #40 blades.

- Make each pass with the clippers as gentle but thorough as possible so you do not go over and over the same spot. Always try to end on a good note.

- After clipping, wipe out the ears with a soft cloth dampened with rubbing alcohol. This will remove cut hair and scurf.

Bridle Path

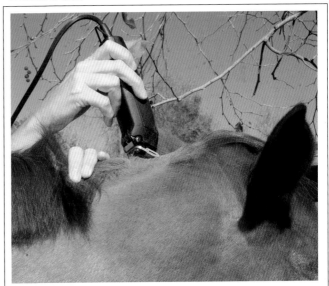

- Be sure to know the appropriate length for your breed. The correct length can be as narrow as the width of the crownpiece of the bridle to 14 inches or more depending on the breed and discipline.

- See the show preparation chapters for specific lengths.

- Also be aware of how much forelock your horse should have. Cleaning up the wispies on the sides of the forelock is important for a finished look.

FACE AND THROATLATCH

Trimming the long hairs of the horse's muzzle and jaw produces a much neater, more refined appearance

An accomplished groom can actually "sculpt" the horse's head with a set of small clippers, bringing out the horse's assets and diminishing the look of less desired points.

The sizes of the blades needed for each area vary depending on the length of the horse's hair coat. Cool weather touch-ups call for #10 blades, while slick summer coats need finer blades, such as #40, with a #10 on hand for blending. For most of this trimming, you will be going against the hair.

Note that many of today's dressage riders do very little detail trimming, leaving muzzle and ear hairs long and natural. In Europe, many of the sport horse exhibitors do no trimming at all, but of course their horses are thoroughly groomed and

Nose

- Remove all the long feeler hairs around the nostrils and muzzle, working in the direction of hair growth with a #40 blade in summer and a #10 blade in winter.

- Clean out the longer hairs on the insides of the horse's nostrils as well.

- Blend into the longer hair above using a #10 blade.

Muzzle/Lips

- Trim off the long feeler hairs around the horse's lips, working in the direction of hair growth with a #40 blade in summer and a #10 blade in winter.

- You do not need to "press" the clippers into the skin at any point; just glide them over the surface.

- Be sure that your horse does not nip or bite the clippers or cord while working around his mouth. Many horses are mouthy and will try to grab the clippers, which would have detrimental, if not fatal, results.

braided. Otherwise, most breeds and disciplines are in agreement about trimming the feelers off the horse's muzzle and inside the nostrils to give him that show ring look.

To make a refined head, such as an Arabian's, more exquisite or to accent a powerful jaw, such as a Quarter Horse's, trim the sides and underside of the horse's lower jawline as described below.

Jaw

- Use #10 blades on the lower jaw. Trim in the direction of the hair growth. For a finer trim, turn the clippers over and use the teeth of the blades.

- Lift the horse's head to trim between the jaw bones, blend into the throatlatch area, and a short way down the front of the neck.

- Trim under and between the horse's cheekbones with a #40 blade. Trim against the hair on the underside of the horse's face and then blend with the hair on either side of the face. Use a #10 blade on the side of the face.

Throatlatch

- To accentuate a powerful jaw, neaten up the horse's throatlatch.

- Use a #10 blade on a set of small clippers.

- Neaten the front of the horse's neck and shape of the jaw by turning your clippers over and running them in the direction of the hair over these areas.

CLIPPING DIFFICULT AREAS

A few areas on the horse's body present special body-clipping challenges

The horse's flank has a whorl of hair growing in all different directions, and it tends to be a sensitive spot for some horses, especially mares. The girth area behind the elbow is difficult to access, since the skin there typically folds and bunches. You may need help during these stages of the clip as the skin in these areas needs to be "stretched" to get a smooth trim.

The horse's throatlatch is also difficult to get to, since it lies between the horse's large cheekbones, and there is excess skin there as well. Trimming this area during a body clip is not exactly the same as when doing a detailed show clip. Use the body clippers for as much of the area as possible to get the best blending with the rest of the coat.

Flank

- Clip slowly and gently against the hair, pressing firmly to avoid tickling.

- The underbelly can be a sensitive area as well, so get an assistant if your horse is especially anxious.

- Have the assistant pick up one of the horse's front legs to prevent it from trying to strike or kick at the clippers.

- Do not put your head underneath the horse's belly as you clip.

Elbow

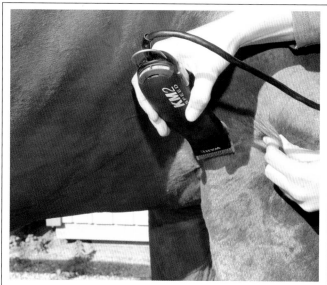

- Have an assistant lift the front leg on the side of the horse that you are working.

- Gently pull the horse's forearm forward to expose and stretch the skin at the girth area and directly behind the elbow.

- Clip against the direction of the hair.

The top of the tail is not difficult to access, but it can be a challenge to decide just where to stop clipping and how to blend the clipped area into the tail hair. The photos below show you how to work in these difficult areas for the best possible results.

Throat

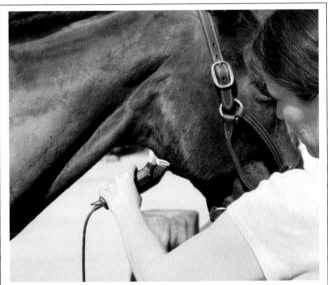

- Lift the horse's head up and forward to reveal and stretch the area of his throatlatch.

- Use the body clippers for as much of the trimming as you are comfortable with. The horse's head is trimmed with the #10 blades on your small clippers.

- Use the small clippers in the direction of (not against) the hair to blend between the two blade sizes.

Top of Tail

- Leave an upside-down V shape on the horse's croup directly above the dock of the tail. The V will start on either side of the width of the tail and taper to up to a point. There is no universal size for this V; it will vary depending on the size of your horse.

- Because of the way the horse's hair grows, one side of the V will usually be easier to clip than the other.

FIXING COMMON MISTAKES

The first few times you clip a horse, you are bound to make some mistakes

Clipping is a difficult skill to master. Several errors can cause unattractive irregularities in the clipped coat—pressing too hard, not pressing hard enough, using incorrect blade angle, using wrong size or dull blades, not blending carefully, or a host of other problems. Sometimes it's truly not your fault—perhaps the horse moved unexpectedly, causing the clippers to gouge into the coat and leave a bald spot.

In any case, it's helpful to recognize what causes these "mistakes" and to have some ideas for how to smooth out the rough spots. Rest assured that with time and practice, clipping will get easier. In the meantime, at least your horse doesn't know how silly he looks.

Streak Marks or Lines

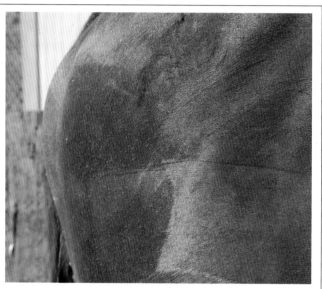

- If you get streaks, stop and take care of your equipment.

- Streak marks are caused by dull blades or blades that are missing teeth. The only way to fix them is to get a sharper set of blades with all of their teeth.

- Going over the rough area with the better blades will smooth it out as much as possible.

Bald Spots

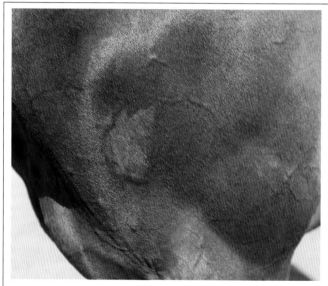

- Bald spots are caused by using clipper blades that are too fine or by clipping against the direction of hair growth instead of with it.

- The only way to truly fix spots that have been clipped too closely is to wait for the hair to grow back.

- You may be able to buy a coloring product to disguise the area, but some breed rules strictly forbid color alterations.

As always, the first step to a satisfactory clipping experience for both you and your horse is to have all of the clipping equipment at hand and in good working order (review page 72). A complete body clip is very time consuming, especially if you or your horse is new to the experience. When you first learn to clip, it's best to practice on a quiet, experienced horse, so you don't have to struggle with behavior issues.

Nicks on Legs

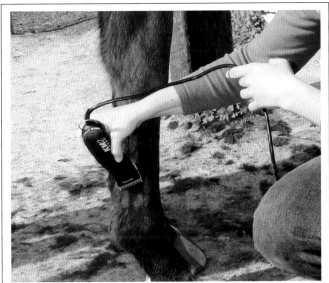

- Nicks are caused by clipping too close, clipping dirty legs, clipping over old scars, or clipping over new cuts that have scabbed over (and sometimes clipping off the scabs).

- Thoroughly groom or wash legs before clipping. (Note that legs need to be dry before clipping can begin.)

- Run your hands down the horse's legs, looking for old scars or new scabs.

- If the horse has older scars or healing cuts, you will not be able to trim the legs as close as you might wish.

Ragged Ears

- Ragged ears are caused by dull blades or missing teeth or by a horse not comfortable with getting its ears trimmed and continuously moving its head.

- Introduce him to the clipping process before you need that quality trim.

- Clip in a safe and secure place and stand on something sturdy.

- If the horse is uncooperative, use a twitch or other means of mechanical restraint; although this might seem inhumane, when used correctly, such restraint will prevent a battle.

BRAIDING KIT

The critical tools and equipment needed for easier, better braiding

The braiding kit is a subcategory of the basic grooming kit. It includes everything you'll need to pull, braid, or band a mane. Many tack shops and horse supply catalogs offer pre-stocked braiding kits, and these are a good choice for the beginning braider. Your kit should fit into a belted pouch to keep everything handy while you work.

At a minimum, you'll need a pulling comb, scissors, a "pull-through," a seam ripper, and yarn or small rubber bands. An inexpensive source for a pull-through is a latch hook used for making latch-hook rugs. It can be purchased at any store where crafts are sold. Other helpful tools include thinning shears, a specialized mane-thinning tool such as Solocomb, a Braid Aid (a four-pronged comb that divides the hair into three equal sections to be braided), a large plastic needle,

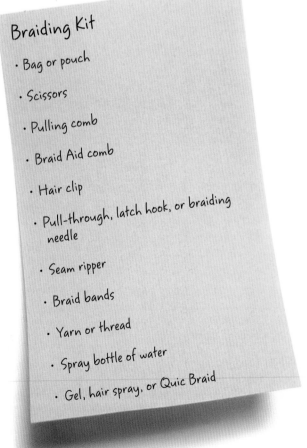

Braiding Kit

- Bag or pouch
- Scissors
- Pulling comb
- Braid Aid comb
- Hair clip
- Pull-through, latch hook, or braiding needle
- Seam ripper
- Braid bands
- Yarn or thread
- Spray bottle of water
- Gel, hair spray, or Quic Braid

Tools

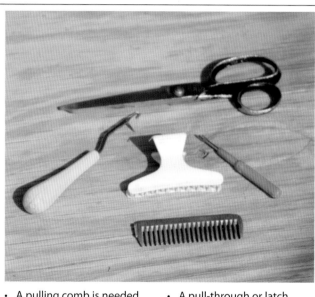

- A pulling comb is needed to thin and shorten the mane before braiding (see page 94) as well as to separate and comb the mane as you work.

- A Braid Aid helps create uniform-sized strands for braiding.

- A pull-through or latch hook is used to pull up the braids into knobs or buttons.

- A seam ripper is used to remove the braids after the show.

white tape (for taped braids), hair gel or hair spray, and a spray-on braiding product such as Quic Braid.

A sturdy stool or hay bale is also necessary if you aren't tall enough to reach the top of the mane easily. If you're straining to reach above your head, you will get fatigued, and you also won't be working at the correct angle to make the braids come out neatly.

Elastics, Thread, or Yarn

- Whether you choose elastic bands, thread, or yarn to secure your braids depends on personal preference and the type of braiding.

- Banded manes are secured with elastic. Elastics are also used for hunter braids, but they are not as secure as yarn and also not "tradi-

tional" and not considered as correct to use as yarn.

- Yarn is used for hunter braids. Buy braiding yarn or any inexpensive cotton yarn in a color that matches your horse's mane.

- Thread or rubber bands are used for button braids.

Optional Products

- Additional products can help make braiding easier and help hold in the finished product.

- Quic Braid is a spray-on product that makes the hair easier to handle and less slippery.

- Hair gel can be applied to each strand before braiding to help keep each section organized and can also be used as a finishing touch to smooth down flyaway hairs.

- Hair spray can be applied to the finished mane to help prevent braids from loosening.

MANE BASICS

MANE PULLING

The traditional method for shortening, thinning, and tidying the mane

Banding and braiding demand a short, thin, uniform-length mane. This cannot be accomplished by simply cutting the mane, since this results in a blunt-edged but still thick mane, which looks silly when unbraided and is almost impossible to work into braids. Instead, thin and shorten the mane by pulling the hairs out a few at a time using a pulling comb.

While this sounds cruel, most horses don't suffer, but a few sensitive souls do object strenuously. There are several ways to make mane pulling as painless as possible. First, pull only very few hairs at a time. Pulling out a big chunk at once is bound to hurt. Second, schedule your mane-pulling sessions for after a ride. The horse will be quieter and less reactive, and

Comb the Mane Flat

- Begin with a clean, dry mane. Do not apply any conditioner or detangler, as these products will make the hair slippery and difficult to work with.

- Comb the mane down flat, removing any tangles.

- Make sure the mane all falls on the same side of the neck.

Tease Up a Section

- Starting at the top of the neck, nearest the ears, grasp the longest hairs from a small section of mane. It's best to pull the hairs on the underside of the mane to help it lie flat.

- Using your pulling comb, tease the mane upward to isolate the long hairs in your fingers.

the pores will be open so the hairs will come out easier. Also try steaming the pores open by holding a very hot, damp towel over the spot just before you begin working. Finally, an analgesic spray, such as Chloraseptic, helps numb the area.

Most importantly, don't expect to get the whole mane done in one session. The horse will be happier if you spread out the process over several days. Once the mane is the appropriate length, maintain it over time by pulling a little bit here and there, so you won't have to repeat the whole process again in a few weeks.

Wrap and Pull

- Wrap the hairs once or twice around the pulling comb.

- Hold the crest of the neck with your left hand and the comb in your right hand.

- Pull hard, with a jerk in a downward direction. Don't pull toward you or upward.

- If the hairs do not come out easily or the horse reacts painfully, you are trying to pull too much at once. Try fewer hairs next time.

A Pulled Mane

- Comb the mane flat again and repeat, moving gradually down the neck until you reach the withers. Keep the mane a consistent length and thickness.

- If the mane is not as short as you want it to be, start again at the top.

- The finished mane should be neat and tidy, resting against the neck with a uniform length and thickness.

MANE BASICS

CLIPPING THE BRIDLE PATH
The first step toward a well-groomed mane

At the top of the mane, just behind the ears, the hair grows in two different directions. Some of it still hangs to the side, along the neck, while some starts to grow forward into the forelock. This is also the spot where the crownpiece of a halter or bridle rests. To avoid bunching up the mane under the crownpiece, clip off a short strip of the mane just behind the ears. This is the bridle path.

Bridle paths also serve a cosmetic function, creating the illusion of a cleaner throatlatch or a longer or more shapely neck, depending on length. In general, horses shown with a long, natural mane will have a longer bridle path (8 inches or more), while horses shown with pulled and braided manes will have a shorter bridle path, perhaps just the width of the crownpiece of the halter or bridle.

GROOMING HORSES

Measure

- First, decide how long you want the bridle path to be, depending on your breed and discipline.

- For a short bridle path, use two fingers to measure the distance. For a 3- to 4-inch path, gently fold the horse's ear down flat against the neck and make the path as long as the ear.

- Use a comb or hair clip to hold back the hair that you do not want to remove.

Trim with Scissors

- Use #10 blades on your small clippers for this step.

- Be sure that the mane is well-groomed and free of dirt and debris before trimming.

- This trim does not need to be uniform and precise because you will go over all of it again with smaller clipper blades.

- Brush away the cut hair to help in keeping as much as possible off you and your horse's face.

First, determine the desired length of the bridle path. Start by making it a bit short, rather than a bit long. You can always remove more hair later, but if you clip off too much, it will take months to grow back. After trimming the bridle path with scissors, use clippers with a fine blade (#30 or #40), being careful not to clip any of the coat alongside the bridle path.

Clip

- Use #30 or #40 blades to clip the trimmed path as closely as possible.

- Be careful not to cut into the forelock or the rest of the mane.

- Once the bridle path is established, you can skip the first two steps and touch it up with the clippers whenever it starts to grow out.

Bridle Path Length

Each discipline and breed has specific standards and traditions regarding the length of the bridle path:

• Arabian	8 to 12 inches
• Saddlebred (Five-Gaited)	6 to 8 inches
• Saddlebred (Three-Gaited ASB)	Roached mane
• TWH	6 to 8 inches
• Morgan	6 to 8 inches
• Western	4 to 6 inches
• Hunter or jumper	Width of the crownpiece of the bridle
• Dressage	Width of the crownpiece of the bridle

TRAINING BRAIDS

A simple method for getting the mane to lie flat and neat on one side of the neck

For show purposes, the horse's mane should fall on one side. In the hunter/jumper world, for example, the horse's mane is braided on the right side, while at American Quarter Horse Association shows the horse may be braided on either side. In any case, unruly manes that fall on both sides of the neck are not desirable.

Unfortunately, most horses' manes naturally flop to both sides at different points along the neck. To "teach" the mane hairs to favor one side, use training braids. These are simple braids that hang straight down, as opposed to show braids that are folded and sewn together. They are not difficult or time consuming to do.

Unruly Mane

- An unruly mane is in need of training braids.

- Training braids are good for manes that fall to both sides of the neck, fall on the "wrong" side of the neck, or stick up.

- Training braids also help prevent tangles in a long mane.

Braiding

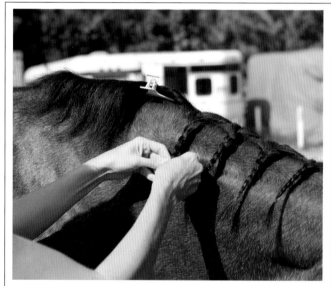

- Dampen the mane with water and brush or comb it all to the same side of the neck so it lies as flat as possible.

- Beginning at the top, divide out a section of mane approximately 2 inches wide, and apply a dab of hair gel.

- Separate the section into three strands, and braid them together. Don't pull too tight at the beginning of the braid, as this can pull out the hairs as well as cause itching and rubbing.

Some horses' manes stick up straight after being pulled. Training braids help the mane lie down after being pulled.

Start by wetting the mane and applying a leave-in conditioner or braiding product such as Quic Braid. Comb the mane over to the desired side of the neck, and braid it into training braids, as shown in the photos below. You can use a mane tamer over the braids if desired (see Zoom sidebar). Leave the braids in for one to three days, depending upon the tenacity of the mane. Then, remove the braids, wet the mane, and comb it straight. Repeat as needed.

Finishing a Braid

- Finish the braid by simply securing the end with a few wraps of a braiding elastic. You do not need to fold and sew the braids, as with show braids.

- Continue down the mane, repeating the process, to create nine to twelve wide braids.

Completed Training Braids

- The photograph above shows the finished braided mane.

- Training braids can be left in for several days to a week. When desired, remove the braids and comb through the hair with water to straighten it.

- If the mane still sticks up or flops over to the wrong side, redo the braids and leave them in for another week.

ROACHING THE MANE

Clipping or shaving the mane completely off to meet show standards

Some horses have their manes completely clipped off for competition, which is called roaching. In the American Saddlebred division, the Three-Gaited and saddle seat Equitation horses are shown with roached manes. The polo pony has its mane roached, as do some stock-type Western horses. Roaching the mane will make the horse's neck look leaner and more elegant or athletic. For some events it is done to minimize interference of the mane with the reins or other equipment the horse may be wearing.

Roaching the mane basically means shaving it completely off. However, there are slight differences between breeds in the trimming details. With the Saddlebred, the entire mane

Roaching the Mane

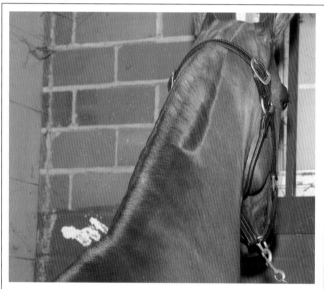

- Groom the mane thoroughly before trimming, and cut off the mane with scissors or #10 blades on your small clippers.

- Then, press the clippers along the crest of the neck, cutting the mane hairs as close as possible.

- Hold the clippers parallel to the crest, and, going with the direction of the hair, blend and straighten out the line of the clip on either side of the crest.

- During cooler months, this may be all that is needed for a finished look.

Finer Roaching

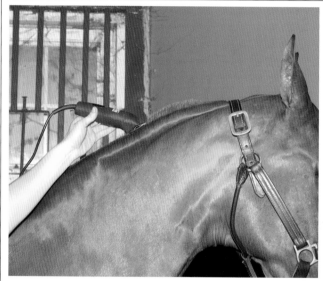

- During hot weather, when your horse's show coat is at its finest, finish off the crest with #30 or #40 blades to get the finished look needed.

- First, follow the steps mentioned in Photo 1 with #10 blades.

- For the final step, change to the sharper set of blades and press the clippers along the crest of the neck, cutting the mane hairs along the top of the crest as close as possible.

should be taken off, including the forelock. With the Quarter Horse and other stock-type breeds, the mane is trimmed off, but the forelock and a tuft of mane over the withers must be left. In the Western stock-type breeds, roaching the mane is optional but more commonly seen in the working-type events.

Roached Mane—American Saddlebred

- The American Saddlebred showing in the Three-Gaited or saddle seat Equitation divisions will need to have a roached mane for the show ring.

- The complete mane and forelock are trimmed off.

Roached Mane—Stock-Type Breeds

- American Quarter Horses and other stock-type breeds may be shown with a roached mane.

- Roaching the mane is not as common with the pleasure and halter show horses; however, in the speed and working events (other than reining), it is a matter of personal preference.

- When roaching the mane of the stock-type breed, leave a tuft of hair over the withers and do not cut off the forelock.

MANE BASICS

CARE OF A LONG MANE
Long manes have their own unique set of concerns for the groom

In some breeds and disciplines, a long mane is essential. Arabians, Morgans, Five-Gaited Saddlebreds, Friesians, and Andalusians, for example, are all shown with a long, full mane. Reining and cutting horses often have long manes that emphasize the horses' athletic movement when they fly in the breeze during the spins and quick changes in direction.

Like long tails, the hair of the long mane is precious and takes months to grow back if it is broken or pulled out. Because mane hair is usually finer and more delicate than tail hair, it's much more prone to tangling. In the worst-case scenario, the mane can become hopelessly tangled into long, matted "witch's knots."

To preserve the integrity of the mane and avoid breakage and tangling, keep the mane clean and well-conditioned

Witch's Knots

Finger-Combing

- A long mane left uncared for can become horribly tangled by the wind and the elements.

- These dreadlock-like snarls are known as witch's knots.

- You may be able to straighten out the mane with liberal use of detangler

and finger-combing. In a worst-case scenario, the knots will have to be cut out.

- Prevent this situation by taking the steps listed with Photo 2.

- After bathing, apply a conditioning and detangling product while the mane is still damp to seal in moisture, repel dirt, and prevent tangles.

- It's best not to brush or comb the mane every day, since some hairs will inevitably break off.

- Instead, carefully work through the mane with your fingers, gently removing any tangles.

with a leave-in conditioning product. Each time you bathe the horse, be sure to rinse the shampoo thoroughly from the base of the mane. Soap residue can cause itching, prompting the horse to rub out his mane. Training braids and mane tamers (see page 99) help keep the mane from tangling. Be careful not to braid too tightly, since tight braids can also cause itching.

Training Braids

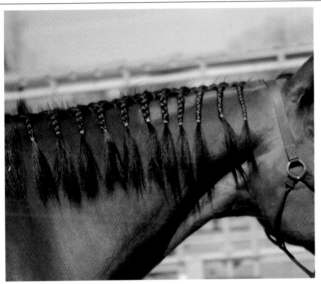

- Long training braids help prevent tangles long-term, such as when the horse is on pasture and you can't finger-comb the mane every day.

- See page 98 for instructions on training braids.

- Braids can be left in for up to a week. Check them regularly for rubbing or hair breakage.

Lovely Long Mane

- Arabians, Morgans, Saddlebreds, Friesians, and several other breeds all take pride in their long manes.

- All your hard work is rewarded by a gorgeous, flowing mane in the show ring.

MANE BASICS

HUNTER BRAIDS

This sign of tradition and respect for the sport creates a finished look in the show ring

Braiding is both an art and a science. Professional braiders are paid handsomely for the service they provide, often braiding several horses before dawn on the morning of a show while the riders and trainers sleep soundly. Learning to braid your own horse can save you money (or can even make you money if you become skilled enough to braid professionally) and

is an important part of becoming a well-rounded horseman.

Well-made braids take practice, however. You'll need to braid quite a few manes before you feel confident and comfortable with the process. Practice any time you have an extra hour at the barn, and always braid for schooling shows to hone your technique in a lower-pressure environment.

Hunter Braids: Step 1

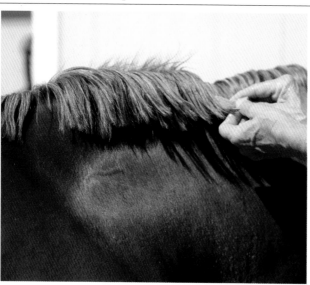

- Wet the mane and brush it flat, all on one side of the neck.

- Keep the drips to a minimum. Water running down the horse's neck will cause him to shake his head.

- Stand on a sturdy mounting block or small ladder so you are able to look down on your horse's neck. (If you have a small ladder, wood is preferable, as, in the case of a "collision," the wood will break rather than severely injuring your horse's legs.)

Hunter Braids: Step 2

- Starting at the top of the mane, divide out a 1-inch section and use a clip or comb to hold back the rest of the mane.

- Spray Quic Braid onto the section, or apply a dab of hair gel and work it into the mane.

- Some braiders do not use any additional products but have the best results simply using water and keeping the mane very wet.

Hunter braids are the "default" braids of the show world. They are appropriate for nearly any English show discipline—hunters, jumpers, equitation, dressage, sport horses in hand, and English classes at breed shows. They consist of many tiny braids, folded under and tied into either flat plaits or "knobs," along the crest of the neck. The goal is twenty to thirty braids, depending on the length of the horse or pony's neck and the thickness of the mane. The more braids there are, the longer the neck will appear to be.

ZOOM

Traditionally, if you are showing in an English discipline, all braids should be on the off (right) side of the horse. If you are showing in Western events, the mane should be braided or banded on near (left) side. See page 98 for instructions on training the mane to lie on one side.

Hunter Braids: Step 3

- Separate the 1-inch section into three equal parts either by hand or using a Braid Aid comb.

- You may have slightly smaller or slightly larger sections of mane depending on the thickness of your horse's hair and what part of the neck you are working on. Some horses have very wide crests, for instance, so your sections will become narrower but contain the same amount of hair.

- Near the withers, the mane may become finer and wispier. Use a slightly wider section of hair to keep the braids looking equal.

Hunter Braids: Step 4

- Begin to braid the three sections tightly against the horse's crest. Since you are standing above your horse looking down on the neck your hands should be at about waist height.

- As you braid the section of hair, direct it downward, not out from the horse's neck.

- Each of the three individual sections of the braid should be pulled tightly out to the left or to the right, rather than down or up.

BRAIDING/BANDS

Braid in yarn and tie the braids off to complete the process

A prerequisite for a neatly braided mane is a neatly pulled and thinned mane (see page 94). It's difficult, if not impossible, to braid a mane that has been cut with scissors or that is too long or thick. For hunter braids, pull the mane to a uniform length, not longer than 4 1/2 inches. Don't wash your horse's mane before braiding it! A squeaky clean mane is next to impossible to braid.

There are several methods for securing the braids, including sewing them in with thread, braiding in yarn, and using small elastic bands. Generally speaking, professional braiders use yarn, since it is the most secure and provides the most polished look. Braiding with elastic bands is quite a bit easier than using yarn or thread, but the braids will have a less professional appearance and will be much less secure. Below, we

Hunter Braids: Step 5

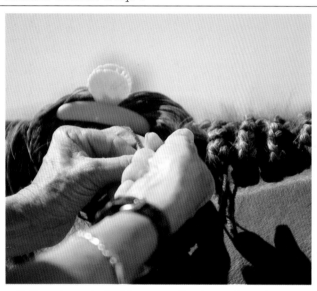

- Halfway down the braid, add in a 16-inch piece of yarn in a color that matches the horse's mane.

- Align the center of the yarn behind the braid, and work in each side of the yarn with one of the three sections of hair.

- Continue to keep the tension and tightness uniform from the top to the bottom of the braid, with or without the yarn.

Hunter Braids: Step 6

- Complete the braid, and use the yarn to tie a slip knot around the bottom of the braid to secure it.

- Starting at the poll and working your way back to the withers, complete all of your braids before pulling any of them up.

- If you keep the braids uniform and tight, you should be able to see uniform and distinct parts between your braids as you look down on the horse's neck.

- Step down and back to see that your braids are as uniform in width as possible.

GROOMING HORSES

show how to braid using yarn. To finish a braid with elastics instead, wrap one band tightly around the bottom of the straight braid, and then fold the braid under itself twice. Wrap a second band twice around the middle of the folded braid to hold it in place.

To remove the braids, lift each one and cut through the yarn cross on the underside of the braid using a seam ripper, being careful not to cut any of the hair. Pull the braid down straight. Use the seam ripper again to cut the slip knot at the end of the braid, and carefully separate the strands of hair using your fingers. When all the braids are out, wet down the mane and brush it flat.

Hunter Braids: Step 7

- Insert the pull-through down through the top of the braid, practically on the other side of the crest, and hook it onto the yarn. Pull only the yarn up through the center of the braid.

- Pull up all of the braids before you tie any of them off to make it easier to see the uniformity of the braids.

- Be sure the braids are approximately the same length when pulled through. You want the bottom line to be even.

- Pull up all of the braids before tying them off.

Hunter Braids: Step 8

- Divide the two ends of the yarn; wrap the ends around the underside of the braid, crossing them in back, and tie down tightly in front using a double square knot.

- When tying the yarn, push up a knob of the braided hair. This knob, or bump, should be level with the crest of the horse's neck but not sticking up so it is visible from the other side.

- Make a final knot on the back of the braid to secure.

- Finish by snipping off the ends of the yarn. If your braids are uniform, your knobs should be uniform.

BUTTON BRAIDS

A good choice to accent the crest of a dressage horse with a longer, more muscular neck

Button braids are the style more commonly used by European riders of all disciplines and are also common on American dressage horses and jumpers. They are not typically seen in the hunter ring or at breed shows. They are larger and puffier than hunter braids, and it takes fewer braids to complete the mane. They tend to look better proportioned on large horses with big, thick necks. Never braid a forelock without braiding the mane, but in dressage it is permissible to braid the mane without braiding the forelock.

A tiny version of button braids can also be made using smaller sections of hair pulled up into tight little balls. These smaller buttons are acceptable on a hunter and look es-

Button Braids: Step 1

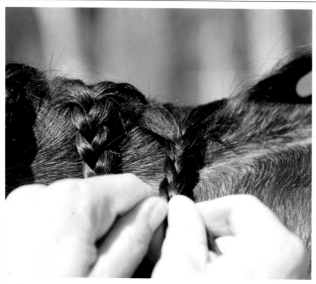

- First, prepare your needle and thread by cutting an 18-inch strand and threading it through a plastic braiding needle. Tie the ends of the thread together in a large knot.

- Begin by braiding a section of mane as in steps 1 through 6 of hunter braids

(page 104) with a section of mane that is about 2 to 3 inches wide. (The result is nine to thirteen large braids rather than twenty to thirty small braids.)

- Instead of braiding in yarn, secure the end of the braid with a small rubber band that matches the mane.

Button Braids: Step 2

- Take one of your prepared threaded needles and pierce the end of the braid, just above the rubber band, from front to back.

- Fold the braid under and push the needle up through the center of the base of the braid, where it meets the horse's neck.

- Sew the needle downward through the two layers of braid, about a third of the way down from the crest. Bring the needle up through the two layers, another third of the way down the braid, then down through the tip of the braid.

pecially cute on ponies. For hunters, it is preferable for the "bumps" to not be visible from the other side.

Use heavy braiding thread in a color that matches the horse's mane, plastic braiding needles, and rubber bands. The mane should be pulled to a length of 4 to 5 inches before beginning to braid.

Button Braids: Step 3

- Thread the needle back up through the center of the braid at the crest, and pull the thread tight, which will pull the braid up into a ball.

- Take a pass with the thread around each side of the braid to gather in any loose hairs, pass it back under one of the earlier stitches, and secure with a knot.

Button Braids: Step 4

- Repeat the steps until you have nine to thirteen round braids along the crest.

- Braiding will go faster if you have enough needles to prepare one for each braid in advance.

- Another tip for quicker and more even braiding is to start by braiding the entire mane into straight braids before going back to sew up the buttons.

BRAIDING/BANDS

FRENCH BRAID

What to do with a very long mane in classes that require braiding

Dressage is becoming more and more popular among enthusiasts of "nontraditional" dressage breeds, such as Arabians, Half-Arabians, Saddlebreds, and Morgans. If they are shown only in dressage shows, these horses can have their manes pulled and braided like any other dressage horse. If, however, the horse also competes in breed-specific shows, or if the owner simply wishes to maintain the traditional breed standards of a long, full mane, the French braid is a good solution to the braiding problem.

The French braid, also known as a running braid, is an acceptable option for the hunter ring, although it is not common. Ideally, it is better to pull the horse's mane and braid it into true hunter braids. If the mane is not too thick, it may also be possible to braid a long mane into button braids.

French Braid: Step 1

- Dampen the mane with Quic Braid, plain water, or a small amount of human hair gel on the upper part of the mane to make it easier to braid and to reduce wisps in the finished braid.

- Separate three strands of hair at the top of the mane, just behind the bridle path. Each strand should be about 1/2 to 3/4 inch wide.

- Begin braiding the three strands together, left strand over the center strand and then right strand over the center strand.

French Braid: Step 2

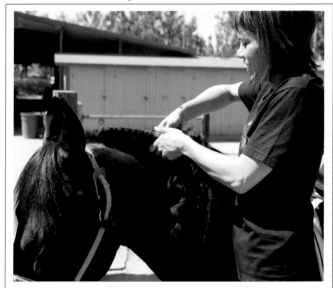

- The second time you bring the left strand over, add in another 1/2- to 3/4-inch strand of hair from the mane.

- Continue in this manner down the length of the neck, keeping the braid tight and close to the crest.

- Continue to dampen the mane with Quic Braid, water, or gel as you proceed.

Baroque breeds, such as Friesians and Andalusians, traditionally have long manes as well. For dressage competition, they may be shown with the mane loose or may be braided with a French or Continental braid (see next page).

(see next page)

∙∙∙∙∙∙∙∙∙∙∙∙∙∙∙∙ YELLOW ● LIGHT ∙∙∙∙∙∙∙∙∙∙∙∙∙∙∙∙

The French braid can also be used at home on long-maned horses in the summer to keep the hair up off the neck, allowing the horse to be cooler. Be careful not to braid the mane too tightly, since the neck must stretch to allow the horse to graze. If the braid is too tight, hairs will pull out.

The braid will get thicker toward the center of the neck.

French Braid: Step 3

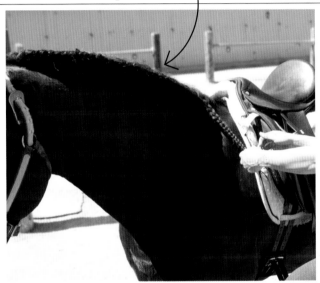

- Pull the strands forward toward the ears to keep the braid snug and neat.

- Nevertheless, there will be an inch or two of mane between the braid and the crest, which is needed to keep the braid from pulling apart when the horse stretches.

- The braid will naturally get thicker toward the center of the neck, where the mane is thickest. Still, use strands of only 1/2 to 3/4 inch.

Completed French Braid

- At the end of the mane, finish by braiding the final three strands into a normal braid. Add in a piece of yarn, as for hunter braids, step 5 on page 106.

- Finish the braid by tying up a knob, as with hunter braids.

- Alternatively, fold the end of the braid up under the French braid, thread the yarn up through the French braid, and tie it off.

- Or, just let the end of the braid hang loose, tied off securely with the yarn or a rubber band.

BRAIDING/BANDS

CONTINENTAL BRAID

A beautiful, striking, and unusual look for the elegant, long-maned horse

The Continental braid is very rarely seen these days and is almost exclusively used on Baroque breeds (Andalusians, Lusitanos, Lippizaners, and Friesians) or Arabians in dressage competitions or breed shows and inspections. Some draft breeds, such as the Suffolk Punch or Haflinger, may be shown with a Continental braid as well. It can be used on any long-maned horse for a unique and striking show-ring look.

It is not really a braid at all but is a method of dividing and banding the mane into sections to create a pattern that looks like macramé. The sections are secured using small elastic bands and are then wrapped with braiding tape. Only black or white tape should be used, depending on the color of the

Continental Braid: Step 1

- Begin by banding the mane, as described on page 116.

- Use elastics that are the same color as the horse's mane, or use white to create a striking contrast with a dark mane.

Continental Braid: Step 2

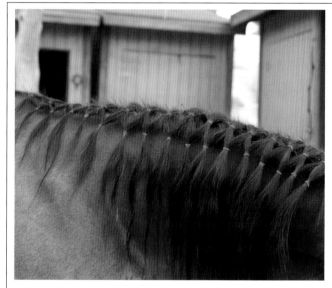

- Starting at the poll, take two of the banded "pony-tails" and divide each of them in half.

- Combine half of each of the two ponytails into one new segment, and band them together with elastic, as shown.

- Repeat, moving down the mane toward the withers, to create the first row of diamonds.

mane. Black tape is best for black or dark gray manes, while white tape can be used on any color mane—black, white, gray, chestnut, or flaxen.

The Continental braid is also known as a macramé braid, fish-net braid, basketweave, or diamond braid.

Continental Braid: Step 3

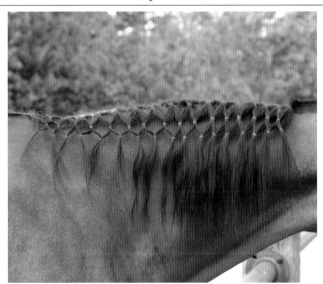

- Repeat step 2 to create a second row of diamonds.

- Depending on the length of the horse's mane, you can add a third, fourth, or even fifth row.

- Continue the net pattern almost to the end of the mane, or leave several inches of mane loose at the bottom.

Completed Continental Braid

- The completed Continental braid is stunning on a horse with a shapely neck.

- If desired, accent each banded joint with braid tape in a contrasting color.

BRAIDING/BANDS

SADDLEBRED OR TWH BRAIDS

A single braid at the top of the mane provides understated elegance in the saddle seat arena

The American Saddlebred and the Tennessee Walking Horse are two breeds exhibited in the saddle seat style of riding, in which specific divisions or classes call for "braiding." In this case, braiding is done with ribbon, which is braided into the horse's mane and sometimes into the forelock as well. The best ribbon to use for these braids can be found at a tack store or florist. It is made of rayon or other synthetic material in a satin finish, 1 inch wide, and is available in 50- or 100-yard rolls. This ribbon is stiffer than traditional satin ribbon and holds up to the demands of the horse show environment.

When finished, both the mane and the forelock braid will have 2 inches remaining at the top and bottom of each

Saddlebred Braid: Step 1

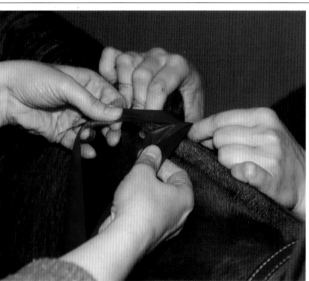

- Stand on a sturdy stool for easy access to the mane, or if you are fortunate to have a horse that stands still, have him lower his head.

- Separate less than 1/2 inch of mane hair out for the braid; the less you use, the easier it is to hide.

- Divide hair into two sections and wet it.

- Cut three strands of ribbon and layer together with the shiny side facing up.

- The length of the strands depends on the length of your horse's mane, but it is usually about 24 inches.

Saddlebred Braid: Step 2

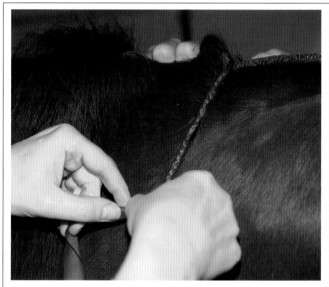

- Have an assistant stand on the opposite side of the horse and hold the top 3 or 4 inches of the braiding ribbon tightly to that side of the horse's crest, with the ribbon secured between her fingers and thumb.

- Add a section of hair behind the ribbon making up the outside strands of the braid (wrap the ribbon around the hair if desired).

- Start braiding tightly, keeping the shiny side of the ribbon to the outside and the hair to the back.

strand of ribbon. These will be finished off in a dovetail cut. A good braid starts tight at the crest of the neck or forelock, is uniform in size from top to bottom, and is no wider than 1/2 inch and usually tighter. No hair from the mane or forelock will show, and the satin side of each ribbon strand will be to the outside. A "lucky" braid is often saved after a successful ride in an important class or a significant win.

Saddlebred Braid: Step 3

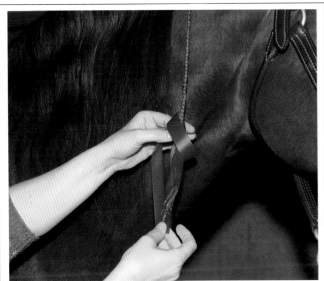

- Braid the ribbon until it is approximately as long as the longest part of the horse's mane.

- If the horse has an extravagantly long mane, end a little short so that your braid isn't hanging too far below the bottom of the neck.

- When you reach the desired length, tie off the braid at the bottom.

- To tighten at the top, tie off the ribbon at that end as well.

- Cut the ends of the ribbon, both top and bottom, into "dovetails."

Completed Saddlebred Braid

- If adding a forelock braid, have the braid be as long your horse's face, so it would go from poll to nose. The forelock braid lies under the browband and then is tucked under the cheek pieces on the mane side of the bridle. It is usually wrapped around the throatlatch.

- In today's show ring, the forelock braid is optional.

- Braids should not be left in overnight because they will be limp, dirty, and not of show quality the next day.

BRAIDING/BANDS

BANDED MANE

A superior banding job highlights the good points of a horse's neck and downplays any faults

Stock-type horses showing in halter, pleasure, horsemanship, showmanship, trail, and Western riding classes will usually have their manes banded. Banding a mane serves many of the same purposes as braiding the mane of the hunter. It calls attention to the horse's neck, enhancing its shape and creating the image of length. In addition, bands will help the

mane to stay still as the horse goes through the requirements of the class, even outside on windy days.

The mane to be banded first needs to be shortened. A thin, athletic neck can pull off a shorter mane, whereas the mane on a thick, punchy neck should be left a little longer. The shortened mane will be between 3 1/2 and 4 1/2 inches

Banding: Step 1

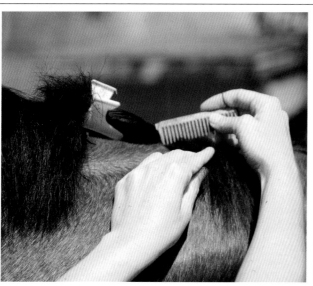

- Wet the mane and brush it flat, all on one side of the neck.

- Keep the drips to a minimum. Water running down the horse's neck will cause him to shake his head.

- Have a sturdy mounting block or small ladder to stand on so that you are able to look down on your horse's neck. (If you have a small ladder, wood is preferable as in the case of a "collision" the wood will break rather than severely injuring your horse's legs.)

Banding: Step 2

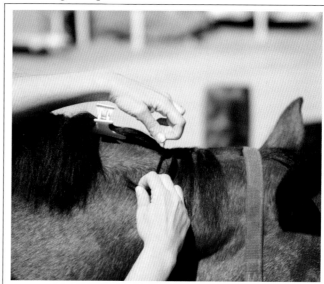

- Starting at the top of the mane, divide out a 1/2- to 3/4-inch section; use a clip or comb to hold back the rest of the mane.

- You may have slightly smaller or larger sections of mane, depending on the thickness of your horse's hair. Some horses have

very wide crests, so your sections will become narrower but contain the same amount of hair.

- Near the withers, the mane may become finer and wispier. Use a slightly wider section of hair to keep the braids looking equal.

in length. A finished banding job will have approximately fifty 1/2-inch sections of banded hair, uniform and lying very tightly to the horse's neck. Banding is done with small rubber bands designed for this purpose and available at tack stores. The bands used should coordinate with the color of your horse's mane and forelock. Horses with multicolored manes require bands for each color.

Banding: Step 3

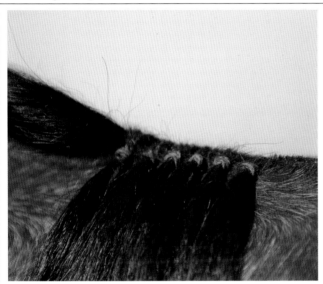

- Comb the mane to smooth out the hair. Then, add the rubber band as close to the horse's crest as possible while still having it on the side of the neck.

- Wrap the band three or four times around the hair so that the band is tight and won't slip.

- Be sure the band lies against the horse's neck, not "poofing" away from it. If the band isn't tight against the neck, pull some of the hairs on the underside of the banded segment to coerce it into lying down.

Completed Banded Mane

- Now continue down the neck, separating and banding the mane into equal sections.

- You want the finished look to be uniform and tight.

- You also want to have distinctive crisp parts between bands for the most professional look.

- A good way to assess your bands is to have your horse lower his head and to look at the line that the rubber bands make. It should be perfectly straight.

117

COMMON BRAIDING MISTAKES
Poorly done braids or bands will do more damage than good to a show turnout

Mistakes in the techniques mentioned in this chapter are usually solved with practice, practice, and more practice. It is important to understand the look that your horse should have when sporting a well-done set of braids or bands. Going through the effort is not enough; you need to become accomplished in turning out your horse in your chosen discipline.

Give yourself the best chance of success by having the correct supplies to do the job. For example, trying to band or braid a horse without having a sturdy stool to stand on handicaps you before you even begin, providing the wrong viewpoint or leverage to do a quality job. Do not try something for the first time the day of a show! You will not have the time or

Braids Too Loose

- Stand on a sturdy stool or ladder so that you are able to be above your horse looking down on his neck.

- Be sure that the mane is wet down well. Unwashed manes will braid better than clean ones, and do not use a detangling product before braiding!

- If you are having a very difficult time, you may have to simply practice your braiding skills on a friend's hair or somewhere other than your horse.

Braids Sticking Up

- Stand on a sturdy stool or ladder so that you are able to be above your horse looking down on his neck.

- Braid each section so it lies against the horse's neck—do not pull the braid out toward your body.

patience to do an acceptable job. Educate yourself by watching other riders or braiders at shows and reading magazines that cover your discipline. Pay attention to the turnout of the horses and riders that you admire. As you become proficient in achieving a professional look, you may find yourself "personalizing" your technique. That is to be commended, as long as you keep your standards high.

Uneven Braids

- Braid your horse's entire neck before pulling or tying up any of the braids.

- Concentrate on uniformity in size, paying attention to the parts of your horse's mane that are thicker or thinner, and compensate accordingly when separating out your sections.

- Braid tightly from the very top of the braid to the bottom.

- Pull up all of your braids before you tie them up. Focus on the bottom line of your braids. The bottom line needs to be level. It doesn't mean the braids are the exact same length!

Stray Hairs Sticking Up

- Keep the mane well wet down when braiding.

- Use hair gel on the completed braids to flatten down stray hairs.

- When pulling your braids up and the yarn through at the top of each braid, be sure not to pull any of the mane hair through.

BATHING AND CONDITIONING
A simple way to produce a clean, soft, silky, tangle-free tail

Each time you bathe your horse, you'll also want to shampoo and condition his tail. Shampooing too often can dry the hair and make the skin itchy. Don't bathe more than once a week unless a show schedule demands it.

After bathing the rest of the horse's body, fill a bucket with shampoo and hot water. Dunk the tail into the bucket, and use a sponge or body brush to scrub the shampoo into the dock. Rinse thoroughly with a hose.

For a light gray or white tail that has yellowed or is stained with grass or manure, put on a pair of gloves and massage a whitening shampoo into the long hairs below the tailbone. Allow the shampoo to set in the tail for ten to twenty min-

Shampoo Tail

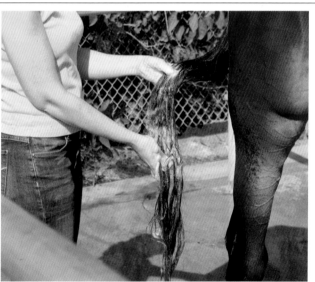

- Fill a five-gallon bucket with hot water and horse shampoo.

- Soak the tail either with a hose or a sponge and warm water. When using a hose on the tail, always aim it downward to avoid spraying into delicate areas.

- Lift the bucket of sudsy water and dip the horse's tail into it, using a sponge or brush to work the suds into the tailbone.

Rinse Tail

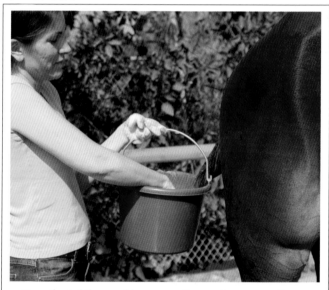

- Rinse the tail thoroughly, using a hose or a clean sponge and a bucket or two of clean, warm water.

- Squeeze the water out of the skirt of the tail (do not wring) and repeat the rinsing.

- Be sure to remove all residue from the tailbone. If any is left, it will cause itching, and the horse may rub out his tail hair.

- If desired, use a vinegar rinse (see Make It Easy sidebar).

utes before rinsing. (You can use these shampoos on the tail-bone as well, but do not leave them in for so long, as they can irritate the skin.)

To avoid breaking the tail hairs, which can take years to grow back to full length, never comb or brush the tail. Instead, while the tail dries after a bath, spray or massage in a leave-in conditioner or detangler, and use your fingers to separate each individual strand from top to bottom. The result will be a full, soft, beautiful tail.

MAKE IT EASY

An inexpensive, simple rinse for manes and tails is vinegar. Add a 1/2-cup of white vinegar to a bucket of water and dip in the tail. Use your hand or sponge to wet the top of tail, as well as the mane. Rinse again with clean water. The vinegar removes any product left in hair that could cause itching.

Condition Tail

- After gently squeezing out as much water as possible, apply a conditioner to the tail to seal in moisture, add shine, resist tangling, and reduce static.

- Read the instructions on your conditioner. Some are meant to be left in, and some are meant to be rinsed out.

Blow Dry and Finger-Comb

- Apply a detangling product, such as Show Sheen or Cowboy Magic, if desired.

- Move the horse out of the wash rack, and use a blow dryer on a low temperature setting to help dry the tail more quickly.

- Finger-comb the tail as it dries by separating each individual hair by hand from top to bottom, resulting in a full, beautiful, knot-free tail.

BRAIDING UP THE TAIL
Braiding protects the tail hairs to help them grow length and thickness

A tail left loose can easily be damaged in many ways. The horse can rub it out on a fence or stall wall. The hairs can become caught in stall hardware or splinters of wood and be ripped out as the horse moves. They can simply break off as the horse swats at flies or be chewed off by playful pasture-mates. A very long tail can easily be stepped on or dragged through the mud. Exposure to the sun and wind can dry the

hairs, making them more prone to breakage and loss.

To get the extra length or thickness desired for the tail of some show horses, braid it up between competitions. There are different ways of braiding up a tail depending on the exact outcome desired, but there are some universal points that apply to all situations. The most important point is to not begin the braiding too tightly. The braid should start just

Starting the Tail Braid

- Have the tail dry and the tail hair well picked through.

- Begin braiding the length of the tail about one fist below the end of the tailbone.

- Braid in all of the tail hair, including the feathers (the shorter tail hairs that grow from the top of the tail

through the mid-point of the dock).

- Braiding the feathers into the tail braid will keep them from being pulled out when caught on anything in the horse's stall or paddock.

Finishing the Braid

- Alternatively, leave the feathers out of the tail braid to keep them from breaking off when the horse swishes its tail. Hold the tail just below the end of the tailbone and lift it up and slightly away from the horse.

- Some of the feathers automatically hang down.

Others will need to be separated out from the hand holding the tail.

- Continue braiding to the end of the tail.

- Simply tie off the braid with an elastic, or finish it as described in the next photo.

below the end of the tailbone. If it starts too tightly it will be uncomfortable, and the horse will work to get it out. The tail needs to be completely dry before being braided up as well.

If a braided-up tail gets wet, it needs to be taken down and the long hair dried out. Left up wet, a dense braid will mildew and rot in the center, totally destroying the tail.

MAKE IT EASY

A good rule of thumb is to start your tail braid approximately one fist length below the end of the tailbone. Any higher, and it may prove too tight and uncomfortable. Any lower, and the beginning of the braid will be too loose so it can easily catch on things, breaking and pulling out significant amounts of hair.

Tying Up the Braid

- Add a braiding material (flannel, bunting) into the braid, leaving extra length to tie it up.

- After you braid the entire tail, finish with a knot.

- Thread the end back through the top about a fist below the end of the tailbone.

- Pull the braid through until the doubled portion is about 8 to 12 inches long.

- "Sew" the remaining length of braid through the doubled portion or simply wrap the remaining length around the folded braid.

Finished Tail

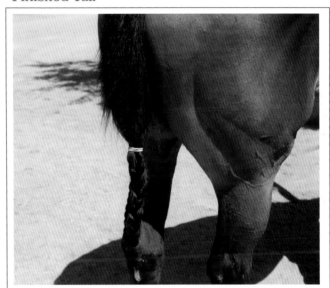

- Cover the finished tail with one of the options on the next page to keep the braid intact and clean for the longest time possible.

- Put up correctly, this tail should stay up for weeks.

- During the off season, a tail will need to be taken down only if it gets wet or starts to come out.

- Some grooms work a leave-in conditioning product into the long hairs before braiding them up, especially if it will be weeks or months before the tail comes down again.

TAIL BAGS AND COVERS
Extra protection for the ultimate show-quality tail

Another way to protect the tail is to cover it with a commercial or homemade protective wrap. Braid the tail, as described on page 122. If it is long and touches the ground, tie it up. Once braiding and tying up are complete, cover the braided section to keep it clean and help the tail stay braided.

Tail covers, also known as tail wraps or tail bags, can be homemade or commercial. What you use depends on the type of horse you have or the discipline you are in. Many people in the various breeds and disciplines use a specific tail covering because it was how they were taught. If you understand what to expect of a tail cover and see no reason why another style wouldn't work for you, it is certainly worth a try. Today there are waterproof and breathable tail wraps or bags available.

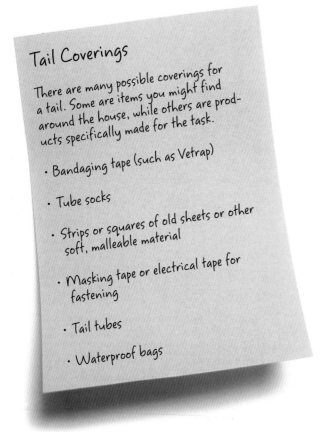

Tail Coverings

There are many possible coverings for a tail. Some are items you might find around the house, while others are products specifically made for the task.

- Bandaging tape (such as Vetrap)

- Tube socks

- Strips or squares of old sheets or other soft, malleable material

- Masking tape or electrical tape for fastening

- Tail tubes

- Waterproof bags

Tail Bag

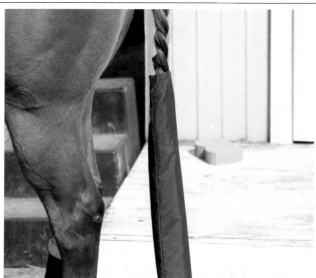

- Commercial tail bags slip on over the braided tail and fasten with a loop through the top of the braid.

- During fly season, be sure to use a bag that has a tassel at the end for swatting flies.

- Nylon is more durable than Lycra, but Lycra is gentler on delicate hair.

- Look for a waterproof/breathable tail bag.

When a horse's tail is braided and wrapped, he can't use it as effectively to protect himself from flies. So during fly season, be sure to help him out by using the fly protection methods discussed on pages 6-7. In addition, some commercial tail bags have a tassel at the end to whisk away flies.

ZOOM

Having a braided-up tail doesn't disqualify your show horse from pasture turnout; you will just have added responsibilities. Fly spray the horse before turnout because a braided tail does not swish away flies efficiently. If the braided tail gets wet, it must come down and be dried. If left up wet, your carefully braided length will rot.

Vetrap or Other Bandaging Tape

- Follow the instructions for braiding and tying up a long tail (see page 122).

- Wrap the Vetrap or other bandaging tape around the mass of braided tail.

- You will need to wrap around the tail braid many times, as this type of bandaging material strengthens as it sticks to itself.

- Since horses have no feeling in the braided hair, it can be wrapped quite tightly. Be sure that it is tight at the top of the braid, or it will eventually slip off.

Braided-In Tail Tubes

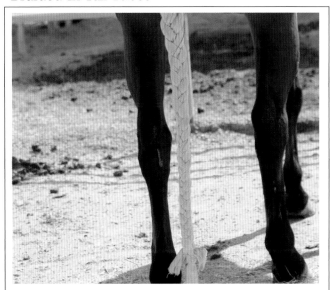

- Braid-in tail tubes consist of three tubes of Lycra. Slip each one over a strand of hair before braiding the tail.

- A homemade tail tube can be fashioned out of strips of material, such as an old sheet, as shown in the photograph above.

- As you braid, wrap each of the three strands with a strip of material. Tie off at the bottom.

TAIL WRAP

A tail wrap covers the top part of the tail for protection while shipping or for smoothing out the dock before a show

Horses' tailbones can be bruised, or the hairs can be rubbed out, by the butt bar or door of the trailer during shipping. To prevent these problems, horses' tails may be wrapped before a long trailer ride. A tail wrap can be a bandage that is wrapped around the dock, or it can be a product made specifically to fit around the top of the tail and anchored by

Velcro or other fastening device.

In addition, wrapping the top of the tail for an hour before the horse enters the ring at a horse show helps smooth down the puffy or frizzy short hairs along the dock, providing a more streamlined and elegant look. This strategy is used on dressage horses, show hunters, and Western horses. It works

Wrapping with a Bandage: Step 1

- Start at a point about 8 inches down from the top of the dock.

- Wrap the bandage snugly around the tail one or two times in the same spot.

- Pull out an inch or two of tail hairs from under the wrap. Take one or two turns around these hairs, so that they will hold the bandage in place and keep it from sliding down.

Wrapping with a Bandage: Step 2

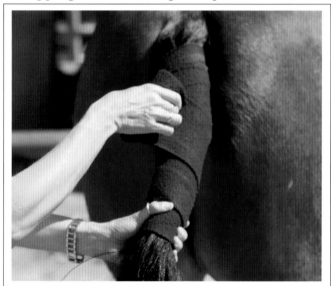

- Begin to wrap upward toward the base of the tail. Keep an even tension on the bandage.

- Overlap each turn of the bandage over the previous one by half its width.

- When you reach the top of the dock, reverse direction and wrap downward toward the bottom of the tail.

especially well on a horse with a pulled tail (see page 130). Spray the tail lightly with plain water or silicone coat dressing before wrapping. A wrap can also be used to protect a French braided tail (see page 110) so the horse doesn't rub out the braid.

Remember, this is a temporary bandage or wrap. Its purpose is to protect the tail during hauling or to put finishing touches on a tail ready for the show ring. It is not intended to be left on the tail for extended periods.

• • • • • • • • • • • • RED ● LIGHT • • • • • • • • • • • • •

As with any wrap, a poor tail wrap job will lead to injury to the horse. Be sure that each pass you make with the bandage is of equal pressure. Don't wrap over a wrinkle or a fold. When using tape to secure the wrap, don't pull tape tight or make it one continuous band. All of these situations can lead to compromised circulation in the dock of the tail.

Finished Tail Wrap

- Stop wrapping just before the end of the dock.

- If you still have bandage material left, wrap back up the tailbone until you reach the end of the bandage.

- Secure the wrap with the Velcro closure. For extra security, apply electrical tape or duct tape over the Velcro, but not tightly.

Wrapping with a Commercial Product

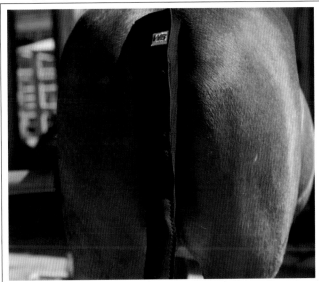

- The tailbone can also be protected with a commercial product, such as Professional's Choice neoprene wrap.

- Apply the tail wrap around the top of the tailbone, smoothing down the hairs underneath it so they lie flat.

- Fasten the Velcro closure so that the wrap is snug enough not to slip, but not so tight as to cause discomfort to the horse.

MUD KNOT

A mud knot is used to protect and keep a long tail clean during muddy conditions

Originally used in the hunt field and for carriage horses, well-braided mud knots are still quite acceptable in the hunter or hunt-seat equitation show ring during rainy weather, even at the top levels of the sport. As an added benefit, they accentuate the hindquarters of a horse with particularly nice conformation in that area. They look especially flattering on ponies.

They are also used to disguise a tail that is wispy or short.

There are many variations on the mud knot. The method shown below is one way to accomplish the goal of a tidy, tied-up tail. Practice making a mud knot before you use it during a show, both to perfect your technique and to allow the horse to become accustomed to the unfamiliar feeling.

Mud Knot: Step 1

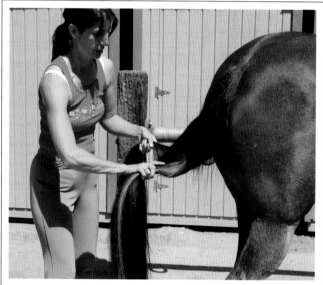

- Braid the upper part of the tail if desired for showing, following the instructions for a French braid on page 110.

- Braiding is not needed for a non-show mud knot.

- At the bottom of the tailbone, rather than finishing off the braid as on page 110, simply incorporate the hair from the French braid into one of the two sections in Step 2.

Mud Knot: Step 2

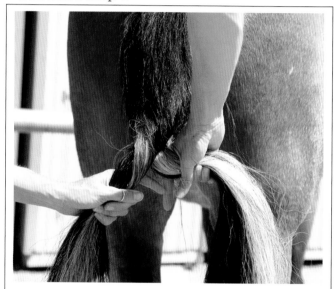

- Divide the skirt of the tail into two equal sections.

- If you are doing a braided knot, braid each section in a normal braid, all the way to the bottom, and secure each side at the bottom by braiding in a strand of yarn, like you do when hunter-braiding a mane, and then tying it. Leave several inches of yarn hanging loose. The yarn color should match the tail.

An unbraided mud knot may be used to keep the tail out of the mud when the horse is turned out or being ridden in a non-show environment. Do not leave the mud knot in during fly season, since the horse will have no way to protect himself from insects. The method for making an unbraided mud knot is the same as that shown below, except without first braiding the tail. Simply separate the skirt of the tail into two sections, tie the sections together in a knot at the end of the tailbone, and wrap them around the tailbone in the same manner as the braided tail.

Mud Knot: Step 3

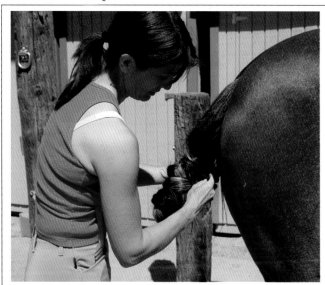

- Cross the two sections of tail at the bottom of the tailbone, bring them up behind the tailbone, and cross them again.

- Bring the sections around in front and cross them again.

- Pull the sections very tight with each pass, keeping them close together and snug to the bottom of the tailbone.

- Continue in this manner until the entire tail is wrapped neatly and tightly around the tailbone, leaving only a few inches loose.

Finished Mud Knot

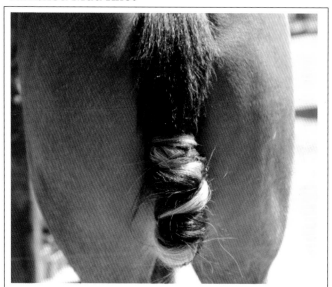

- Finish the mud knot by tying those last few inches together like shoelaces.

- Wrap the ends of the tail around to the underside of the dock and tie them securely in a double knot.

- If your mud knot is braided, use yarn in the braid to tie off the ends.

PULLING THE TAIL

Removing the hair along the sides of the dock creates a crisp, tidy appearance

In some English disciplines, including dressage, eventing, jumpers, and hunt-seat equitation, the dock of the tail is tidied up by pulling out the hairs along the sides. Do not pull the tail of a show hunter or any tail that you intend to braid.

When pulling the tail, pull only a few hairs at a time, and pull straight downward, not to the side. Use short, sharp jerks rather than a slow tug. This will minimize discomfort to the horse. Use a mane-pulling comb, your fingers, or a pair of pliers to grasp each hair.

Pull enough hair that the underside of the dock is visible when the horse's tail is held in a natural carriage while in motion, but do not remove a strip more than an inch or so wide.

Tail Pulling: Step 1

- Assess the tail and decide how long and wide to make the pulled sections.

- Depending on the length of the horse's tailbone, the pulled section may be 4 to 6 inches long. It should end at the point where the tail naturally begins to drop down when the horse is carrying it in motion.

- The pulled section should be narrow enough that when the tail is at rest against the hindquarters, you can't see the bald part.

Tail Pulling: Step 2

- Begin by pulling a 1/4-inch strip from each side of the tail.

- Wrap a few hairs at a time around a pulling comb (see page 95) or your fingers.

- Stand back and assess your work. If needed, pull another 1/4-inch strip from each side, slightly shorter than the first strip.

(To check this, lift the tail and let it rest on your forearm. This is approximately the level at which the horse will carry his tail when trotting or cantering.)

To avoid pulling too much hair, pull only a narrow section at a time along each side of the tail, and then stop to appraise your work. The pulled area should be no longer than 8 inches and should taper gradually back into the natural, full tail. Never pull any hairs from the top of the dock.

Tail Pulling: Step 3

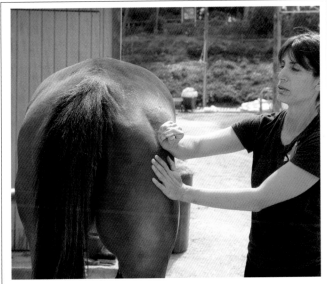

- Continue in this manner, gradually tapering each strip until you reach the desired width.

- When in doubt, it's better to pull too little than too much. Tail hair takes quite awhile to grow back.

- If the horse objects at any point, you may be pulling too many hairs at once. Pull only a few at a time, using a quick, hard, outward jerk.

Finished Pulled Tail

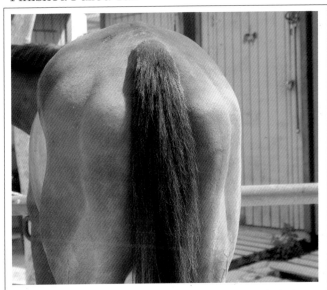

- If there are very short hairs remaining that are too short to grasp with your fingers, use a pair of pliers to pull them out.

- Finish by wiping down the sides of the dock with a damp cloth to remove any stray hairs and specks of blood.

- If the pores bleed a little, this is to be expected. The bleeding will soon stop.

- Just before a class, you can smooth down the dock with a tail wrap (see page 126).

BANGED TAIL

Cut the tail straight across at the bottom for a clean, polished look

A "banged" tail is simply a tail that has been cut straight across the bottom, rather than hanging in a natural, uneven point. Banging the tail is common in many show disciplines, including dressage, eventing, jumpers, and some Western classes. It tidies up the appearance of the horse and can make a straggly, thin tail seem fuller.

Banging may be done in combination with pulling (see page 130) or may be done on an unpulled tail. Banging or pulling is not mandatory in any event but may be done if it helps accentuate an attractive set of haunches or improve the look of a scruffy or straggly tail.

In most cases, you will want to cut the tail straight across at a point that will be level with the fetlocks when the horse is in motion. (To determine this, slide your forearm under the

Banging a Tail: Step 1

- Begin with a clean, dry, conditioned, and tangle-free tail.

- Have an assistant stand to the side of the horse's hindquarters.

- Lift the horse's tail, insert the assistant's forearm under the tailbone as shown,

and allow the tail to drop back down over the arm.

- This will approximate the position of the horse's tail when he elevates it as he trots or canters.

Banging a Tail: Step 2

- Grasp the top of the tail skirt gently in your fist, and run your hand downward until you reach the point where you want to make the cut.

- If the horse's tail is long enough, it should be banged at the bottom of the fetlock for most disci-

plines or a bit shorter for Western performance (see Zoom sidebar).

- If the tail is straggly or short, bang it so that it is as long as possible but still looks full at the ends.

horse's tailbone, which will hold the tail at approximately the level that the horse will carry it when he's active.) If the horse's tail is too short to allow this, cut it so it is as long as possible but still looks straight and full at the point of the cut.

In the past, it was fashionable to cut the tail almost to the point of the hocks, but this is no longer a common style.

ZOOM

In different disciplines, tails are banged at different lengths. In general, tails are banged at the fetlock in English disciplines. In Western performance, banging the tail a bit shorter—halfway up the cannon bone—helps prevent the horse from stepping on his tail when he backs or spins.

SHOW TAILS

Banging a Tail: Step 3

- Use sharp scissors or clippers to cut straight across the bottom of the tail.

- Release the skirt of the tail from your grasp and shake it out gently.

- While the assistant keeps his arm under the tailbone, check for uneven hairs and trim them off.

Finished Banged Tail

- A banged tail skirt generally looks best with a pulled dock (see page 130).

- Banging the tail can tidily shorten an extremely long tail and helps a wispy tail look a bit fuller.

FRENCH BRAID

Braid the top of the tail for added elegance in important hunter and equitation classes

French braiding of the tail is a style seen almost exclusively in the hunter and hunt-seat equitation ring. Hunter ponies look very cute with their tails braided. Eventers occasionally braid the tail for the stadium jumping phase as well, and show jumpers may have their tails braided for high-profile competitions.

By slimming down the profile of the top part of the tail, a French braid accentuates a well-conformed set of hindquarters and presents a polished image to the judge. It is correct to braid the tail only if the mane is also braided. If the horse's tail has been pulled (see page 130), you will not be able to braid it.

French Braid: Step 1

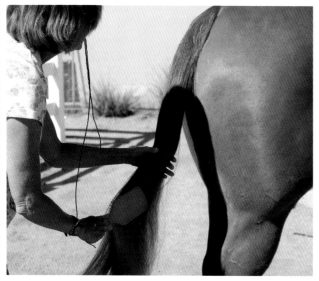

- Begin with a clean, dry, unpulled, tangle-free tail.
- Dampen the top of the tail by spritzing it heavily with plain water or Quic Braid. Do not use any conditioner or detangler, as it will make the hair too slippery.

French Braid: Step 2

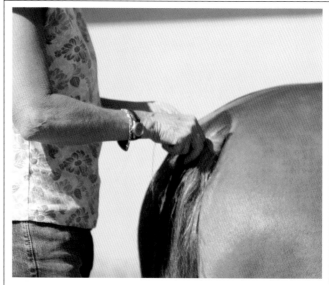

- Gather a small section of hair, about 1/4 inch wide, from the very top of each side of the tailbone, and cross the left side over the right side.
- Gather another small section, of an equal size, from the right side, and cross it over the left-side piece. This forms the beginning of your braid.

134

Begin with a clean, dry, conditioned tail. Do not use any detangler or silicone spray, since it will make the hairs too slippery to handle. Carefully pick through the tail by hand to remove any knots or tangles. Before you begin, dampen the top of the tail with water or Quic Braid. You'll also need a 2-foot-long piece of yarn that matches the color of the tail, a pair of scissors, a pull-through, hair gel or hair spray, and a stool to stand on if the horse is quite tall.

······· GREEN ● LIGHT ·············

If a show hunter has a damaged, short, or skimpy tail, a false tail may be used in the show ring. See the instructions on page 140 for tying in a tail switch on a stock horse. The method for hunters is essentially the same.

SHOW TAILS

French Braid: Step 3

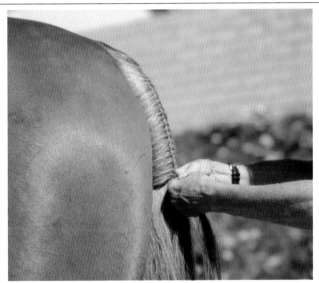

- Continue braiding down the tail in this manner, adding equal-sized sections of hair to the braid as you progress.

- Pull each strand very tight, and hold onto the strands carefully so they don't loosen.

French Braid: Step 4

- When you reach the end of the tailbone, continue to braid normally, not adding in any more hairs, to create a long, thin braid.

- A few inches from the end of the skirt, add in a piece of yarn as you would when braiding the mane.

- Tie off the end of the braid by making a slip knot in the yarn.

- Finish the braid with one of the three options shown on pages 136–137.

FINISHING THE FRENCH BRAID

There are three options for finishing a French braid: A tucked-under loop, a wraparound, or a pinwheel

The tucked-under loop is the most straightforward method. After tying off the end of the braid, simply push the end back up under the French braided part, using a pull-through to help pull it up snug. Use the pull-through to bring the two ends of the yarn out the sides of the braid, and tie them together in a tidy knot. Snip off the ends of the yarn.

The second option is to wrap the pigtail part of the braid around the base of the dock and secure it in place with yarn or thread.

A third option for finishing the braid is to form a pinwheel by rolling up the end of the braid and securing it with yarn or thread. The pinwheel is a more difficult technique, but it

Loop

- After tying off the braid in Step 4 on page 135, insert a long braiding needle down through the French braid, about 6 inches up from the bottom of the tailbone.

- Insert the tip of the braid into the eye of the needle, and pull it up into the

French braid. Leave a short loop hanging out.

- Pull out the two ends of the yarn, one on each side of the French braid, tie them together in a knot, and trim them short.

Wraparound

- After tying off the braid in Step 4 on page 135, wrap the long, thin braid around the bottom of the French braid.

- Stitch the end of the braid into the French braid with the yarn.

- Tie the yarn off with a square knot and trim it short.

creates a stylish picture in the show ring. With a little practice, you will be able to master it.

With any method, finish the braiding job by spraying it with hair spray or lightly coating it with hair gel to keep it in place. A tail wrap (see page 126) can be used as well.

ZOOM

Quarter marks are a checkerboard-pattern combed into the hair of the hindquarters. Spray the hair with water, and use a 2-inch section of a comb to brush the hair perpendicular to its growth pattern, creating the image of a checkerboard. You can purchase plastic stencils that help create the pattern. Finish with hair spray.

Pinwheel: Step 1

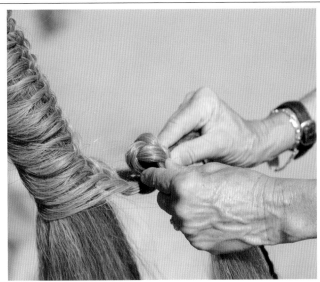

- After tying off the braid in Step 4 on page 135, thread the yarn through a large needle.

- Roll the braid up from the bottom, keeping it tight and even.

- Use the yarn to sew the roll to itself as you progress.

Pinwheel: Step 2

- When you reach the bottom of the French braid, secure the pinwheel to the dock with a stitch or two through the braid.

- Tie off the ends of the yarn in a square knot, and trim them short.

TAIL EXTENSIONS

When your stock or hunter horse's natural tail doesn't quite cut it, add an extension

In a competitive show ring, every detail counts. A long, full tail is definitely the goal. If your horse has a tail that is thin or short, the addition of a tail switch or extension is permissible for most Western classes as well as hunters. Sometimes this is referred to as the addition of a false or fake tail, but that is a misnomer, as the hair used is real horse hair, not synthetic.

A high-quality tail extension for a Quarter Horse or other stock-type breed, or for a show hunter, should be 100 percent natural horsehair. It needs to be as close in color as possible to that of your horse's actual tail; the idea is to add the hair without looking like it is added.

Tack stores that service the Western show industry usually

Tail Extension: Step 1

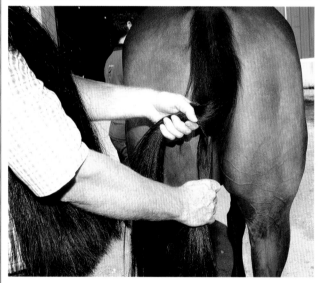

- For best results, the horse's own tail should have a soft, natural edge—do not bang the tail straight across. Both the natural and artificial tails should be clean and free of tangles.

- There is more than one way to tie in the extension. This method is very secure and results in a lifelike appearance.

- First, divide horse's natural tail in half—an upper half and an underneath half. Flip the upper, or top, half up and clip it out of the way.

Tail Extension: Step 2

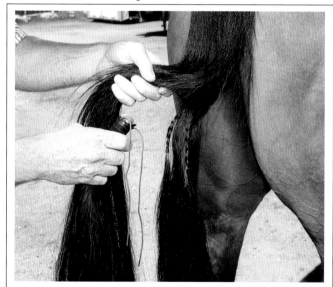

- Separate two small strands of hair, one on each side of the tailbone, each about 1/4-inch wide and 2 to 3 inches up from the bottom of the tailbone.

- Braid each of the two quarter-inch sections into a short, tight braid as shown above. Use an elastic band to finish each one.

carry common colors, such as black and sorrel. White, flaxen, and other light-colored tails are more difficult to come by and therefore more expensive. Stores that specialize in tails will have more color choices or may suggest that you send in a sample of tail hair from your horse to get a perfect match.

In addition to providing the fuller look desired, a tail extension also adds some weight to your horse's tail. This additional weight may keep the tail quieter when the horse is moving.

YELLOW LIGHT

A tail switch or extension is an investment that needs special care. Remember, these hairs cannot grow back! A quality extension should come with instructions. Universal rules include careful washing and drying just as you would your horse's actual tail, with conditioning as needed. Be sure the tail is completely dry, and store it in a tail bag to keep it clean and tangle-free.

Tail Extension: Step 3

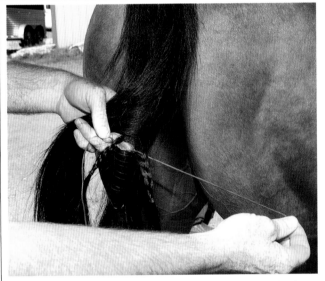

- Next use the two strings at the top of the tail extension. Thread one through the top of each braid, pull them up tightly, and tie them together in a neat, secure bow.

- For extra security, apply a piece of electrical tape around the knot.

- Pull a few strands of tail hair over the top of the extension to cover it. Then wrap a turn or two of tape around it.

Finished Tail with Extension

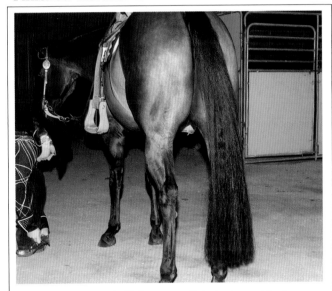

- Unclip the upper half of the natural tail and let it fall down over the braid to hide the attachment.

- Shake the tail gently to blend the natural tail with the extension.

- If desired, use thinning shears, a razorblade, or scissors held vertically to very carefully shorten and blend the end of the tail extension to create a natural look at the desired length.

TAIL SWITCH

Use a tail switch to improve the look of your American Saddlebred and Tennessee Walking Horse's natural tail.

The saddle seat show horse is shown with a long, flowing tail, the longer, the better. Some breeds, such as the American Saddlebred and Tennessee Walking Horse, can show wearing a tail switch, also called a wig, to add length and fullness to their tails. In other breeds that show saddle seat, such as the Arabian and Morgan, a tail switch isn't allowed.

There are individuals who specialize in making saddle seat tail switches. The more unique the color of the tail needed, the more expensive the switch will be. The saddle seat tail switch will usually be longer than the stock type, both because the natural tail carriage of these horses is much higher (even more so in the case of a set-tail horse) and because it

Making a Part for the Switch

- Carefully wash, dry, and pick out the horse's natural tail. The switch should be clean, dry, and picked out as well.

- Select the place on the tailbone where the switch will be attached. Add it where the tail has feathers to cover it so it blends in.

- At the point where you decide to add the switch, part the tail with the part being a circumference around the tailbone.

- Have an assistant hold the hair above the part up while simultaneously holding the hair below the part neatly together and down.

Wrapping the Tape

- Wrap the tailbone with electrical or friction tape. The top of the tape will be directly below the part you made, covering the flowing tail hair but not overlapping the hair held up by the assistant.

- Wrap the tape snug around the tail several times.

- Next, make a few wraps of the tape with the tape "twisted" into a thinner corded form. This will give you a ledge to rest the shoestring of the switch on when you tie it to the tail.

- Cover the ridge of tape with another pass of the tape flat to cover the ridge.

can touch or drag on the ground. Even if you are allowed to attach a switch to your horse's tail, keep its natural tail as long as possible. Many Saddlebreds and Walking Horses are shown without switches because their tails already have the desired length and fullness.

The switch for the saddle seat tail is attached directly to the horse's tailbone. Therefore it needs to be removed as soon as the horse is finished showing so as not to interfere with circulation in the tail.

Tying on the Switch

- The switch is tied directly to the tailbone with shoestring. The strings are usually cut off of the switch as it's removed from the tail. As a result, the switch needs to be rethreaded with new string before each use.

- Lay the top of the switch just above and resting on the ledge you made with the tape wrapped around the tail. A wet shoestring makes for a tighter knot.

- Tie the shoestring around the tail. Knot it on the underside of the bone. Then bring the string to the front of the bone and make another knot. Trim off excess.

Finished Tail with Switch

- Drop the tail feathers that are above the added switch.

- Using your fingers, comb through the horse's natural tail and the switch to blend it together.

- Your goal is for the tail to look natural and the switch to give realistic fullness and length to the horse's actual tail.

- The tail switch should come out as soon as possible after the horse's class. Double-check to be sure you remove the tape as well. Don't leave a switch in all day, as it can impede the tail circulation.

THE RIDER
Proper dress and equipment for hunter, equitation, and jumper riders

The rider's attire for hunter/jumper shows is typically classic and reserved, particularly in the hunter ring. The goal for a hunter rider is not to distract the judge's eye from her horse, so bright colors or helmet "bling" are not welcome, although this trend is changing. Equitation riders, while dressed essentially the same as hunter riders, may choose brighter colors for their shirts and jackets. Boots should always be black, and breeches should always be a light, solid color. ASTM/SEI-approved helmets should always be worn when jumping, whether at home or at a show. For hunter and equitation riders under twelve, there are a few variations to the clothing theme (see photo).

Jumper riders have more freedom to choose their own outfits. Approved helmets, tall black boots, and light-colored

The Show Hunter or Equitation Rider

- The rider wears a conservatively colored hunt coat and a white or light-colored riding shirt with a stock tie or choker (sometimes called a ratcatcher).

- Light-colored breeches are worn with tall black field boots.

- Hair should be neatly arranged under a hair net and tucked beneath an approved helmet in a conservative color.

- Spurs, crops, and bats are optional.

Child Hunter or Equitation Rider

- For riders age twelve and younger, turnout should be similar to a junior or adult in the appropriate division, with a few exceptions.

- Jodhpurs and brown jodhpur boots with leather garters are appropriate, rather than breeches and boots.

- A young girl's hair may be braided into two pigtails tied with colorful ribbons, rather than tucked under her helmet. A matching ribbon can be used in the pony's tail braid if desired.

breeches are still the norm, but hunt coats are generally not worn except at the upper levels of showing. A solid-colored, clean, tucked-in polo shirt is the typical jumper attire at lower-rated and local shows. Remember to wear a belt to complete the look. In the jumper world, coat color can have meaning. Grand Prix riders who are on the USET, or have been on it in the past, can wear scarlet coats (known as pinks). In the hunter and equitation divisions, any rider may wear pinks, but it is not common and may be viewed as pretentious.

Field hunters have a unique set of rules and traditions regarding attire and appointments (such as flasks, sandwich cases, whips, and horns). General standards are noted below, but check with your local hunt club for its particular dress code before you attend your first hunt.

Jumper Rider

- The attire requirements of a jumper rider are much more permissive than in the equitation or hunter divisions. Riders do not need to wear a hunt coat except in classes where formal attire is specified. A solid-colored shirt with a collar, tucked in, is appropriate.

- Light-colored breeches may be worn with tall black field boots or with paddock boots and half-chaps.

- Riders should always strive to appear neat, clean, and workmanlike.

Field Hunter Rider

- Wear tall black dress boots, light-color (not white) breeches, and black riding helmets with chin harnesses.

- Formal attire requires a black or navy wool hunt coat, white shirt with white stock tie, canary yellow vest, and black or white gloves. (Red coats are worn only by hunt staff and honored members.)

- Ratcatcher attire, worn by junior members, consists of a light-colored hunt coat, a tattersall vest, a ratcatcher collar, and brown gloves.

SHOW HUNTER
The look of the show hunter is classic, conservative, and refined

In the hunter divisions, horses are judged on their manners, style over fences, and way of moving. Judges are looking for a pleasant, quiet, well-trained horse with a flat-kneed, ground-covering stride. Hunters may be shown over fences or under saddle (a group class with no jumps in which the horse is shown at a walk, trot, and canter).

Hunters are traditionally in very good weight, with no ribs showing and perhaps even a bit of extra fat (but not too much!). The overall look should be conservative and classy, with no bright colors or poorly fitting tack to distract from the refined elegance of the horse. "Bling," or decorative, colorful embellishments on the horse's tack or rider's apparel, is not welcome in the hunter ring.

Turnout is of vital importance in this division, since the

Show Hunter

- The horse must be impeccably groomed for the hunter divisions. Whites must be bright white, and the coat should gleam.

- The horse's body should either be unclipped or completely body clipped (see page 78).

- Closely clip the fetlocks, coronary bands, and lower legs for a clean look.

- Hooves should be neatly trimmed and shod. Wipe them clean just before the horse enters the ring, and apply a coat of hoof polish.

Head and Mane

- Pull the mane to approximately 3 inches in length, and braid into approximately thirty hunter-style braids (see page 104) along the right side of the crest.

- Closely clip the entire head and ears with #30 blades. Ears should be fully clipped out. The bridle path should be very short, just longer than the width of the bridle's crownpiece.

- Wipe the horse's nose and muzzle with a damp cloth before entering the ring.

horse's style and conformation are being assessed. Hunter horses require more detailed clipping than most other disciplines. Braids should be small, neat, and evenly spaced. (Tradition dictates that mares should have an even number of braids and geldings or stallions should have an odd number, but many competitors do not follow this code.) A poor clip or braiding job can detract from the judge's overall impression.

ZOOM

The most common bit in the hunter ring is a D-ring snaffle. A Pelham or Kimberwicke curb bit is also acceptable. Severe bits should not be used, and the judge may penalize "non-conventional" bits. Strive for ease and grace—don't give the judge the impression that the horse needs a mouthful of hardware to be controlled.

Tail

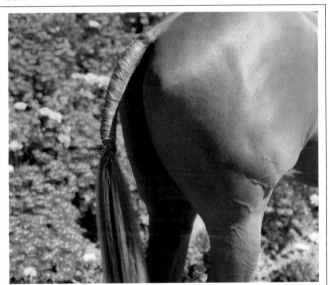

- The tail should not be banged or pulled, but rather left natural, although well conditioned and brushed, of course.

- For very formal classes such as hunter classics, braid the tail in a French braid (see page 134).

- If the horse's tail is unattractively skimpy, a false tail may be used. Take care that the tail looks like a natural tail and is securely fastened.

Tack

- The bridle is classic and understated, of plain or raised brown leather with a simple cavesson noseband. Dropped and flash nosebands are not allowed.

- For over-fences classes, the horse may wear a standing martingale. Remove it for under-saddle classes.

- Use a jumping-type close-contact saddle made of brown leather, with a matching girth. The saddle pad should be a well-fitting shaped white fleece pad.

- Hunters are never shown with boots or wraps of any kind.

EQUITATION HORSE

Turnout and tack for the equitation horse should be conservative and functional

In the equitation divisions, the rider is judged, rather than the horse. The judge looks for excellent position on the flat, form over fences, effectiveness of the aids, and ability to communicate with the horse over a complex series of jumps. To test the rider's abilities, equitation courses tend to be more complicated and difficult to ride than hunter courses, and equita-

tion horses may be somewhat hotter than their hunter counterparts. For these reasons, stronger bits and martingales may be used. Don't forget to remove martingales, whether standing or running, before the flat class.

Equitation horses should be in peak physical condition, neither too thin nor too fat, and should be trained to a high

Equitation Horse

- The horse must be impeccably groomed as in the hunter division. Whites must be bright white, and the coat should gleam.

- The horse's body should either be unclipped, or completely body clipped (see page 78).

- Closely clip the fetlocks, coronary bands, and lower legs for a clean look.

- Hooves should be neatly trimmed and shod. Wipe them clean just before the horse enters the ring, and apply a coat of hoof polish.

Head and Mane

- Pull the mane to approximately three inches in length, and braid into approximately thirty hunter-style braids (see page 104) along the right side of the crest.

- Closely clip the entire head and ears with #30 blades. Ears should be fully clipped

out. The bridle path should be very short, just longer than the width of the bridle's crownpiece.

- Wipe the horse's nose and muzzle with a damp cloth before entering the ring.

degree. Most top-level equitation horses have training equivalent to second- or third-level dressage, including counter canter, half pass, and other complex movements.

For the most part, equitation horses should be turned out like hunters, including hunter-style braids (see page 104). The exceptions are that equitation horses can wear leg protection and running martingales (in over-fences classes only), if needed. Boots or wraps should be of a conservative, neutral color, such as black, white, brown, or natural leather.

ZOOM

Like hunters, plain snaffle bits or Pelhams are the norm for equitation horses, and the judge may penalize non-conventional bits or nosebands. However, stronger bits, such as those with curbs and ports, are more common in the equitation than the hunter ring, and figure-8 nosebands are occasionally seen.

Tail

- The tail may be banged and pulled or may be left natural.

- For very formal classes, you can choose to French braid the tail (see page 134). (Do not pull the tail if you plan to braid it.) Ponies usually have their tails braided.

- If the horse's tail is unattractively skimpy, a false tail may be used. Take care that the tail looks like a natural tail and is securely fastened.

Tack

- The bridle is made of plain or raised brown leather with a simple cavesson noseband. The judge may penalize another noseband.

- For over-fences classes, the horse may wear a standing or running martingale. Remove it for under-saddle classes.

- Use a jumping-type close-contact saddle made of brown leather, with a matching girth. The saddle pad should be a well-fitting shaped white fleece pad.

- The horse may wear boots for protection, including splint boots, bell boots, and hind ankle boots.

PONY HUNTER
Although the ponies and their riders look cuddly and cute, competition in these divisions is fierce

Pony hunters should be turned out similarly to show hunter horses (see page 144), except that there is a bit more allowance for the "cute" factor. Tails are usually braided in a French braid, and a ribbon may be added to match the ribbons in the young rider's hair. Note, however, that red ribbon in the tail is used as a warning that the horse may kick if other horses come too close. For safety reasons, a child's pony should not be a kicker, so the judge may look unfavorably upon a hunter with a red ribbon in his tail. Choose another color for your decorative bows.

Ponies should be in good weight, neither too fat nor too thin, and should have excellent conformation, with clean

Pony Hunter

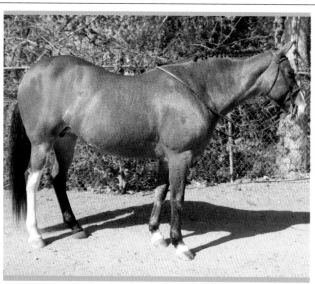

- The pony must be impeccably groomed for the hunter division. Whites must be bright white, and the coat should gleam.

- The pony's body should either be unclipped or completely body clipped (see page 78).

- Closely clip the fetlocks, coronary bands, and lower legs for a clean look.

- Hooves should be neatly trimmed and shod. Wipe them clean just before the pony enters the ring, and apply a coat of hoof polish.

Head and Mane

- Pull the mane to approximately 3 inches in length, and braid into hunter-style braids (see page 104) along the right side of the crest.

- Closely clip the entire head and ears with #30 blades. Ears should be fully clipped out. The bridle path should be very short, just longer than the width of the bridle's crownpiece.

- Wipe the pony's nose and muzzle with a damp cloth before entering the ring.

legs, a refined, typey head, small ears, and a balanced physical appearance. Pony owners sometimes struggle with their ponies' weight, since it is so easy for these little ones to eat too much and become overweight. Most ponies need very little grain, if any at all, and subsist quite well on a diet of good-quality hay, perhaps supplemented with a vitamin/ mineral supplement if needed.

ZOOM

There are no special bitting rules for pony hunters beyond those for larger hunter horses (see page 145). However, the safety of the child rider should always be paramount, so if the pony needs a stronger bit, such as a Pelham or Kimberwicke, it is wise to use one, rather than choosing a snaffle for appearance's sake.

Tail

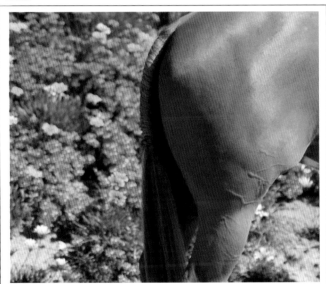

- The tail should not be banged or pulled, but rather left natural, although well conditioned and brushed.

- Braid the tail in a French braid (see page 134), using ribbon that coordinates with the rider's hair ribbons if desired.

- If the pony's tail is unattractively skimpy, a false tail may be used. Take care that the tail looks like a natural tail and is securely fastened.

Tack

- The bridle is classic and understated, of plain or raised brown leather with a simple cavesson noseband. Dropped and flash nosebands are not allowed.

- For over-fences classes, the pony may wear a standing martingale. Remove it for under-saddle classes.

- Use a jumping-type close-contact saddle made of brown leather, with a matching girth. The saddle pad should be a well-fitting shaped white fleece pad.

- Hunters are never shown with boots or wraps of any kind.

SHOW JUMPER

The show jumper is the ultimate equine athlete and should look the part

In the jumper divisions, judging is objective. This means that placings are awarded based on speed and accuracy, rather than on the judge's impression of how well the course is ridden. For this reason, jumpers require a slightly less stringent grooming standard than hunters, but they should still look well-groomed, shiny, and in top condition.

Braiding the mane is not required. Nevertheless, many jumpers are shown with hunter-style braids or with dressage-style button braids (see pages 104 and 108). If the horse is not braided, the mane is still pulled to a uniform length and thickness, although it tends to be left a bit longer and thicker than a hunter's mane. Jumper tails may

Show Jumper

- The jumper is a true athlete and should be presented as such. Although turnout is not taken into consideration in the placings, excellent grooming shows respect for the sport, the judge, and the horse.

- The horse's body may be unclipped or fully body clipped (see page 78).

- Lower legs should usually be clipped, depending on the breed (draft crosses may be left unclipped, for example).

Head and Mane

- The show jumper should be clipped neatly, with the ears trimmed but not fully clipped out. The muzzle and jawline should be clipped.

- The unbraided mane should be pulled short but is usually longer and thicker than the hunter's mane, at about 5 inches long.

- If braided, the mane should be pulled to a length of 3 to 5 inches. Hunter-style or button-style braids are appropriate (see pages 104 and 108)

- If the mane is braided, the forelock should be braided as well.

be left natural or pulled and banged like a dressage horse's tail (see page 157).

Jumpers are allowed to wear leg protection, including brushing boots, polo wraps, sport boots, and bell boots. There are few limitations on tack, and jumping hackamores, running martingales, and specialized bits are common sights in the jumper ring. Girths may feature a wide center section called a belly protector, which guards the horse against cuts or bruises inflicted by the jump rails or by his own front hooves as he tucks them under his body.

Tail

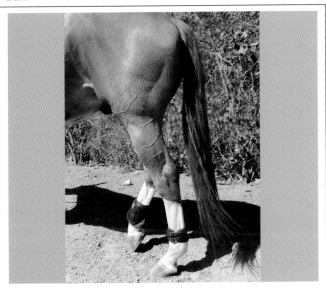

- The tail may be left natural, may be banged and pulled like a dressage horse's tail, or may be French braided like a hunter's tail (although this is rare).

- Do not braid the tail if the mane is not also braided.

Tack

- The saddle should be an English jumping saddle, usually brown leather, although black or other colors are also acceptable. Any girth may be used. The saddle pad may be white fleece and shaped, like a hunter's pad, but white or colored square pads are also seen.

- The bridle should be of a color to match the saddle. A noseband or bit may be used. Running or standing martingales are allowed.

- The jumper usually wears boots for leg protection, including open-front boots and ankle boots, as shown.

FIELD HUNTER

A field hunter's turnout is rooted in a blend of serious tradition and practicality

The tradition of fox hunting traces back to early American and British formal practices. Most of the tack and turnout rules are fundamentally based in safety and practicality specific to the hunt field. For example, field hunters usually don't wear boots or wraps. This is because after hours spent galloping through mud and water, the boots would inevitably pick up dirt and cause abrasions on the horse's legs. Many hunts also frown on the use of running martingales, since the rings can be caught on buckles or brush and make it difficult to pony the horse if the rider has to dismount.

The hunt season proper begins in late fall, so horses will have grown their winter coats by Opening Day. Hunting is

Field Hunter

- The field hunter usually sports a full or partial clip so he does not overheat. Body clips, hunter clips, and trace clips are all acceptable (see page 78).

- Many riders choose not to clip the legs, since thicker hair serves as protection in the field.

- The horse should be neatly groomed and well conditioned for the day's activities.

Head and Mane

- For formal occasions, such as Opening Day, the horse's mane should be braided in button braids or hunter braids, which should be fewer in number than on a show hunter (nine to fourteen, rather than twenty to thirty).

- If not braided, the mane should be neatly pulled to a uniform length.

- If the horse is body-clipped, the head should also be clipped. Do not fully clip out the ears, but do tidy them up (see page 84).

hard, sweaty work, so horses should have a hunter clip or full clip (see page 78).

The rule of thumb for hunting tack is that if you don't need it, don't use it. Martingales, breastplates, complicated bits, and the like are all acceptable if they are needed, but otherwise simpler is better. The exception is when using formal tack and attire, in which case certain traditional appointments are needed, including a flask, sandwich case, wire cutter case, and a leather hunt whip.

ZOOM

As with jumpers and the cross-country phase of eventing, the field hunter will be jumping at speed, so safety and control are the most important factors when choosing a bit for your horse. Curbs, double bridles, and even gag bits are acceptable choices for a hunter.

Tail

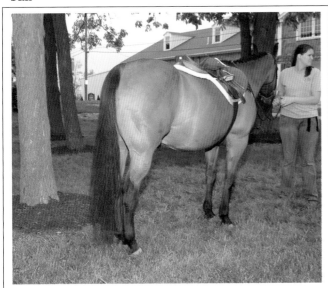

- Braid the tail only if also braiding the mane, as for Opening Meet.

- The tail may also be pulled and banged or simply left natural.

- A mud knot is sometimes a practical choice in wet weather (see page 128).

Tack

- A flat bridle is the traditional bridle for hunting, but any conservative leather bridle is acceptable.

- Use a martingale and breastplate only if needed. Check with your hunt regarding whether it prefers running or standing martingales.

- Use a jumping saddle with fitted white pad, not a square pad.

- Field hunters usually don't wear boots, since they tend to cause more harm than good when left on for such a long time.

THE RIDER

Appropriate attire and equipment for dressage riders and eventers in each of the three phases

The rider's turnout for the dressage phase at lower level events is essentially the same as for dressage riders at United States Equestrian Federation (USEF) levels (Beginner Novice through Preliminary eventing or Training through Fourth Level dressage). It consists of a black short coat, white breeches, black tall boots, and a helmet. At the FEI level (Intermediate through CCI**** eventing or Prix St. Georges through Grand Prix dressage), rider turnout becomes much more formal, including top hats and tails. The derby or top hat is traditionally worn only by riders at the FEI level, but it is allowed and is becoming more popular among lower-level riders at dressage shows. (See page 158 for an explanation of the upper levels.)

USEF Dressage

- Dress conservatively in a black or navy blue short coat. Wear a white or very light solid-colored shirt with a choker or stock tie and white or black gloves (white is preferred).

- Wear a black riding helmet or hunt cap.

- Full-seat riding pants should be white or light-colored. Wear black dress boots or field boots.

- Spurs may be worn. A black dressage whip no longer than 43.3 inches may be carried.

FEI Dressage

- Wear either a dark-colored four-button short coat with a helmet, as in USEF dressage, or wear a tailcoat (also known as a shadbelly) with a top hat, shown here. The tailcoat should be worn with a white shirt with a stock tie and white gloves.

- Riding pants should be white full-seat breeches worn with black dress boots.

- Spurs are mandatory. A black dressage whip no longer than 43.3 inches may be carried.

The rider's attire for stadium jumping is similar to that of show hunters and equitation riders: a dark hunt coat and light-colored breeches, black tall boots, and a helmet.

The cross-country phase of eventing is the one time when a rider can be creative with his fashion. Eventers often sport flashy colors on the cross-country course, both to have fun and to allow spectators to easily identify who they are as they gallop by. Riders wear a stopwatch so they may assess their speed as they progress through the course. In all phases, the rider's clothing should be neat, clean, and well-fitting.

Eventing, Stadium

- Wear a conservative, dark-colored or tweed hunt coat over a shirt with a stock tie or choker. Gloves in a conservative color are okay.

- Wear a solid black or dark blue ASTM/SEI-approved protective helmet with a chinstrap. A safety vest is allowed.

- Light-colored breeches are worn with black or brown field boots. Half-chaps are not allowed, except for smooth black leather with matching boots.

- Spurs and a whip no longer than 30 inches are allowed.

Eventing, Cross-Country

- Wear a shirt of any color or style. Jackets are not required.

- A protective vest and an ASTM/SEI-approved helmet with a chinstrap, which can be any color, are mandatory.

- Riding pants may be any color. Boots should be black or brown and can be field, dress, or jodhpur boots. Half-chaps are not allowed, except for smooth black leather with matching boots.

- Spurs and a whip no longer than 30 inches are allowed.

LOWER-LEVEL DRESSAGE

The dressage horse is a picture of classic elegance in black and white

The dressage horse should be in good flesh, with a shiny, well-groomed coat. Ears do not need to be fully clipped out, since insects could cause head-tossing that may be interpreted by the judge as resistance.

Braid the mane in hunter or button braids. The braids may be accented with white tape, but this style is less common.

The forelock may be left unbraided if desired. In the case of breeds shown with a long mane (Friesians, Andalusians, and Arabians, for example) do not pull the mane, but braid into a French or Continental braid (see pages 110 and 112).

Wipe the nose and muzzle clean before entering the ring. However, in a dressage horse some degree of white foam

Dressage Horse

- The coat may be left natural or may be fully clipped.

- For most horses, the legs should at least be tidied up, with the feathers and lower legs clipped neatly.

- The exception is for draft breeds, ponies, and Baroque breeds, for which leg feathering is a breed trait. In these cases, the leg hair may be left natural but should be clean and well groomed.

Head and Mane

- Trim the ears, but do not fully clip them out. Clip the muzzle, jawline, and throatlatch. Clip the bridle path to a maximum length of 2 to 3 inches.

- Pull the mane to a length of 3 to 5 inches, and braid in dressage braids or hunter braids (see pages 104 and 106). (A long mane may be braided with a French or Continental braid; see pages 110 and 112.)

around the lips is actually desirable, since it is assumed to show the horse's relaxation and acceptance of the bit. A lump of sugar encourages salivation.

The traditional colors for tack and attire are black and white. Saddles and bridles are typically black, with square white saddle pads. Fleece half-pads are popular, and if used they should fit the saddle well without being distracting. The bridle's cavesson and browband may be padded with white leather. Browbands with "bling" (rhinestones) or brass clinchers are also fine. Leg protection for the horse is not allowed.

ZOOM

In the lower levels, the ideal dressage bit is a simple loose-ring, double-jointed snaffle bit. Any snaffle bit made of smooth metal or plastic is allowed. Twisted, wire, roller, ported snaffle, and curb bits are not allowed. At Third Level and Fourth Level, the rider may choose to use a full bridle. See Zoom sidebar on page 159.

Tail

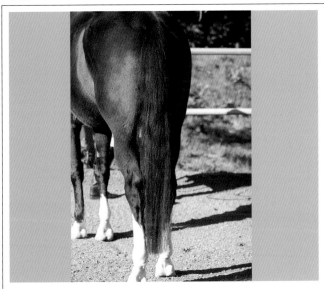

- The horse's tail should not be braided, to avoid causing a stiff carriage.

- Pull the tail (see page 130) and neatly trim it along the dock.

- An alternative to pulling is to closely clip the sides of the tail. Care must be taken

not to create an unnatural appearance.

- The tail should be banged (see page 132) to hang at or just above the level of the fetlock when the horse is in motion.

Tack

- The saddle should ideally be a dressage-style saddle, but in the lower levels any English saddle is acceptable. Most dressage saddles are black, but brown saddles are also allowed. The saddle pad should be white and rectangular in shape.

- The bridle should be black (or of a color to match the saddle) and traditionally features a cavesson or crank noseband with a flash attachment.

- Dressage horses must never wear martingales, wraps, or boots of any kind during competition.

FEI DRESSAGE HORSE

Turnout for the horse is similar to lower-level dressage, except that it should be more formal

Above a certain level, dressage and eventing are governed by the Fédération Equestre Internationale (FEI) rather than the USEF. In dressage, these levels include Prix St. Georges, Intermediare I and II, and Grand Prix. In eventing, the FEI levels are designated by the abbreviation CCI, and are divided into four starred levels (CCI* through CCI****). These first three stars roughly correlate to the USEF designations of Preliminary, Intermediate, and Advanced, while the CCI**** events are even more demanding than Advanced level. There are only three annual CCI**** events—Badminton and Burghley in England and Rolex Kentucky in the United States—as well as the quadrennial Olympics and World Equestrian Games.

FEI Dressage Horse

- Generally speaking, turnout is similar to that of a lower-level dressage horse, but with more attention to detail.

- In cooler weather, horses are usually fully body-clipped.

- Clip the lower legs, except for draft breeds, ponies, and Baroque breeds, for which leg feathering is a breed trait. (See specific breed chapters.)

Head and Mane

- Trim the ears, but do not fully clip them out. Trim the muzzle hairs neatly and tidy up the jawline (although the European style is not to trim at all). Clip the bridle path to a maximum length of 2 to 3 inches.

-

- Pull the mane to a length of 3 to 5 inches, and braid in dressage braids (see page 104). (A French or Continental braid is acceptable for a long mane.)

- The forelock may be left unbraided, particularly on a stallion.

To achieve this level of athleticism, it is a given that the horse will be in peak physical condition with plenty of muscle. The coat should gleam, and white markings should stand out brilliantly. White markings on the lower legs can even create the illusion of more extravagant movement.

Grooming must be impeccable. The mane must be braided neatly, the saddle must be a dressage saddle (rather than an all-purpose or even a jumping saddle, as is allowed in the lower levels), and all tack should be black. The square saddle pad should be gleaming white.

Tail

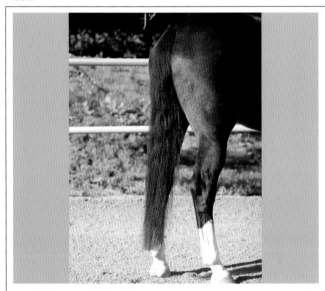

- The horse's tail should not be braided to avoid causing a stiff carriage.

- Pull the tail (see page 130) and neatly trim it along the dock.

- An alternative to pulling is to closely clip the sides of the tail. Care must be taken

not to create an unnatural appearance.

- The tail should be banged (see page 132) to hang at or just above the level of the fetlock when the horse is in motion.

Tack

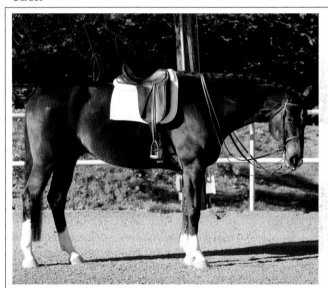

- At the FEI levels, a true dressage saddle is required; it should be black.

- The saddle pad should be white and rectangular in shape.

- The bridle should be black and should have a plain cavesson or crank nose-

band with no flash. At PSG level and above, a full bridle is mandatory.

- Dressage horses must never wear martingales, wraps, or boots of any kind during competition.

EVENTING: STADIUM JUMPING

Top quality turnout reflects the rider's degree of commitment to her sport

The stadium jumping phase of eventing is roughly comparable to the jumper division in the hunter/jumper world. Judging is objective and is based on the pair's ability to complete the course within the time allowed, with no knockdowns, refusals, or other faults. Therefore, turnout is not specifically being judged. Nevertheless, riders should always strive to present a respectable picture to the judge and to their fellow competitors.

While the rules state that type of saddlery is optional, the only logical choice for safety, comfort, and security is a jumping or all-purpose English saddle. At the lower levels, most riders use the same saddle for stadium and cross-country,

GROOMING HORSES

Stadium Jumper

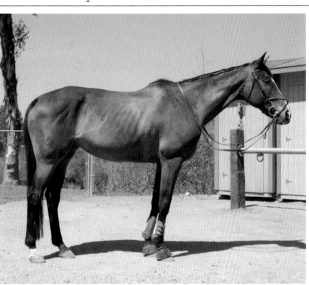

- The horse can be un-clipped, body clipped, or trace clipped (see page 78).

- Lower legs should be clipped to remove the longer hair.

- Some competitors apply quarter marks to the horse's haunches (see page 137). This is a somewhat old-fashioned style but can be used to "dress up" the horse's appearance and draw attention to a nice hip.

Head and Mane

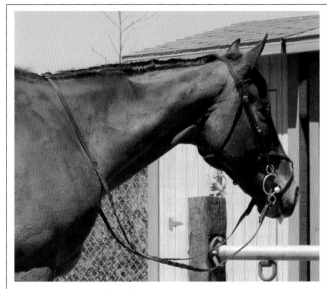

- The horse's head should be clipped as for dressage, with the muzzle and jawline tidied up and the ear hair clipped even with the edges of the ears.

- The horse's mane should be braided neatly with hunter-style braids.

- At a one-day horse trial, the same braids can be left in for both dressage and stadium.

- At schooling shows and horse trials, some competitors may choose not to braid, but the mane should be pulled to a neat, uniform length.

and use a dressage saddle for dressage. At the higher levels, separate saddles for stadium and cross-country may be needed.

Running martingales with stoppers or Irish martingales are allowed. (Unlike other martingales, an Irish martingale is not used to control the horse's head position. It is simply a length of leather with rings on each end, which connects the two reins together so they can't flip over the horse's head.) The horse may wear leg protection including boots or wraps and bell boots.

Tail

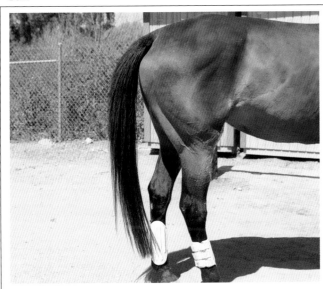

- The tail may be pulled and banged (see page 132) or left natural.

- A tail wrap applied for an hour before the class can slim down the appearance of the dock for a tidier look (see page 126).

- A French braid may be used in the tail, but only if the horse's mane is also braided.

- Do not pull the tail if you plan to braid it.

Tack

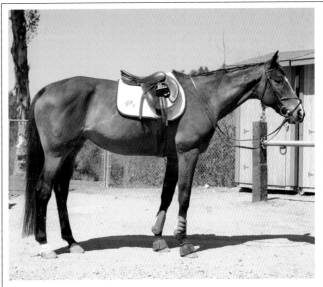

- Ride in a jumping saddle with a square or fitted pad.

- The horse may wear boots, such as bell boots or galloping boots, if needed for protection.

- Breastplates and martingales are acceptable if needed.

EVENTING: CROSS-COUNTRY

The turnout and tack of a cross-country horse are based on safety and functionality

In the cross-country phase of eventing, horse and rider gallop over uneven ground and jump large, solid, natural obstacles such as stone walls and logs. In the horse's turnout, safety and protection are paramount, and appearance is of secondary concern.

The mane need not be braided, but at a one-day event in which cross-country closely follows stadium or dressage, it is acceptable to leave the braids in if there's no time to remove them. Martingales are allowed but must be either running martingales with stoppers or Irish martingales.

Boots or wraps and bell boots are strongly advised for the protection of the horse's legs. Use colored duct tape to se-

Cross-Country

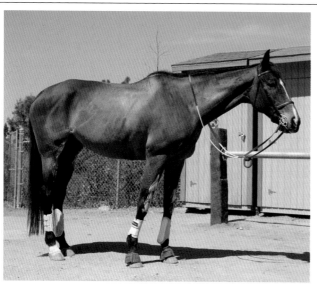

- Many event horses are shown with a trace clip during the late fall and early spring season.

- Grease on the legs helps prevent hang-ups and scrapes as the horse jumps solid fences. (The grease is either Crisco or a product made specifically for this purpose.) It is usually used only at the Preliminary level and higher.

Head and Mane

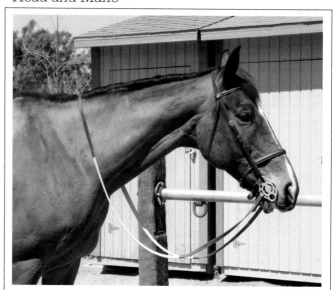

- Clipping is the same for dressage and stadium.

- Horses are normally not braided for cross-country, and, in fact, it is probably safer not to—the rider may need to grab a handful over a fence!

- If the cross-country is run on the same day as dressage or stadium, the braids may be left in.

- The mane should be pulled to a uniform length of 3 to 4 inches.

cure the boots or wraps so they do not come loose after a few minutes on course.

The rulebook is generous in its allowance of tack, colors, and leg protection for the horse. Many riders decorate their horses with brightly colored saddle pads and leg boots and even colored reins or bridles. These may match the rider's own apparel, including the helmet cover, shirt, and compulsory protective vest. In the English worlds of hunter/jumpers, dressage, and stadium jumping, the cross-country phase is the rider's best opportunity for creativity in wardrobe.

ZOOM

The USEF rulebook allows nearly any type of bit for cross-country, even specifically allowing gag bits and hackamores. Control is of the highest importance for the safety of horse and rider. Choose whatever bit is most effective. The only specific restriction is that the reins must connect directly to the bit or bridle; draw reins are not allowed.

Tail

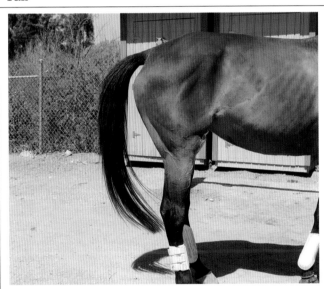

- The tail need not be braided.

- It may be pulled and banged (see page 132), or left natural.

Tack

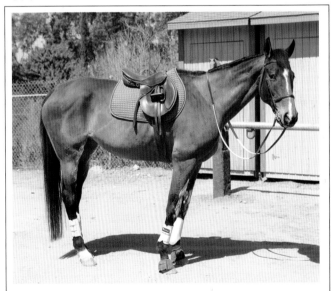

- Ride in a jumping saddle. For higher levels, there are saddles specifically designed for cross-country, with a more forward flap and lower cantle.

- Boots are needed for protection. They may be secured with colored electrical tape or duct tape.

- Breastplates and running martingales are acceptable, but standing martingales are not allowed.

- An overgirth may be used to help prevent the saddle from shifting.

CLEANING/CARE OF ENGLISH TACK
Tack care is an important aspect of show preparation

While not specifically considered a part of grooming, leather care is a key part of the overall picture presented in the show ring. Furthermore, tack that has not been well cared for is potentially unsafe. Old, dried-out leather reins or billet straps are more prone to breaking. Regularly cleaning and conditioning your equipment are an opportunity to check it for loose stitches, cracking leather, or other unsafe conditions.

Leather should be clean, supple, and well broken in. A light-colored "orangey" saddle with a stiff, shiny appearance is probably brand new and not yet broken in and should not be used for showing. It needs to be oiled with light oil specifically made for saddle leather, and the flaps should be rolled by hand to soften them.

Any leather item that comes in contact with the horse's

Cleaning the Saddle

- Remove the stirrups and leathers.

- Soak the sponge in warm water and squeeze it out. Apply leather cleaner to the sponge, never directly to the saddle, and squeeze it to produce a lather.

- Gently scrub the saddle

one small section at a time, paying special attention to crevices and the indentations around hardware.

- Wipe off each section before moving on to the next. If the suds dry on the saddle, they'll leave a mark.

- Clean leather girths often.

Cleaning the Bridle

- For daily cleaning, leave the bridle assembled but undo the buckles and slide off the keepers.

- For deep cleaning, take the bridle completely apart and lay out each piece on a clean towel.

- Clean and condition one piece at a time before reassembling.

- Lather and scrub the bridle as you do the saddle, carefully wiping off the suds with a damp, clean sponge before they dry.

skin—including the bridle, girth, and martingale—should be cleaned each time it is used. Otherwise, tack should be cleaned and conditioned at least once a week and certainly the night before a show. Saddle pads, girth covers, and other cloth equipment should be laundered using an allergen-free detergent after each use.

Conditioning Leather

- Brand new leather must be oiled with leather oil. Dip a clean cloth in the oil and generously slather it over the leather. Wipe off the excess with a dry cloth and allow the leather to set overnight before use.

- Periodically re-oil to keep it supple and moist. Warm oil may absorb better than cool oil.

- Between oilings, use a leather conditioner to maintain the tone of the leather. Wipe it on and rub it in with a dedicated sponge after cleaning the leather.

Bits and Hardware

- After every ride, immediately dip the bit in water and wipe it clean before it dries.

- For a thorough cleaning, remove the bit from the bridle and soak in hot water.

- Scrub the bit and rings with a toothbrush and tooth-paste. Rinse and wipe dry.

- Rub all metalwork and hardware on the bridle and saddle with a metal-cleaning product, such as Nevr-Dull, being careful not to get it on the leather. (Do not use these products on the mouthpiece of the bit!)

ADVANCED BASICS

THE RIDER

Cowboy hats, jeans, and boots are always in style

The attire of riders in the Western stock seat competitions is greatly influenced by regional styles and annual fashions and trends, but there are a few constants.

In most classes, a cowboy hat is required. In some cases, especially for younger competitors, it is optional to replace the cowboy hat with a safety helmet. Read the rulebook for your specific event. Jeans should be scrupulously clean and should fit well, neither too baggy nor too tight. Starching and ironing your jeans are a nice touch. Wranglers are by far the most popular brand seen in the show pen. Always wear a leather belt with a large Western buckle (preferably one won in a show!).

Chaps are optional in most riding classes. Shotgun chaps, which cover the whole leg from hip to heel, are the most common style for pleasure, rail, and pattern classes. They zip

Western Pleasure, Open Show/4H/Local

- The rider wears traditional Western-style attire, including a long-sleeved shirt, shotgun chaps, a cowboy hat, and cowboy boots.

- Jeans or dress pants (for women) are worn under the chaps.

- Vests or jackets may be brightly colored or accented with rhinestones.

- Gloves and spurs are optional.

Western Pleasure, Breed Circuit

- The rider wears traditional Western-style attire, including a long-sleeved shirt, shotgun chaps, a cowboy hat, and cowboy boots. Women wear "slinky" polyester shirts. Men wear silk neck scarves.

- Vests or jackets may be brightly colored and accented with rhinestones and fringe.

- Female riders wear polyester dress pants that match their shirts or chaps, while men wear jeans.

- Gloves and spurs are optional.

up the back and may have embellishments such as fringes and conchos. Chinks, which end at the knee, may be seen in speed and cattle events. They buckle around the thigh and usually have fringes.

The rider's shirt should be a long-sleeved, button-down collared Western-style shirt. Women in Western pleasure classes often wear tight "slinky" shirts in bright colors with rhinestones and fringes. Younger riders can wear brighter colors, with the youngest riders having the greatest color choices.

ZOOM

The selection, size, and shape of a Western rider's hat are of utmost importance. Different Western events, a rider's face, and even the showing of different breeds all call for differences in the shape of the brim and height of the crown. Light-colored hats are worn with light-colored outfits, while dark outfits go with a dark hat. Always place your Western hat brim up when you set it down.

Reining

- The rider of a reining horse must wear Western-style attire, including jeans, boots, a long-sleeved Western-style shirt, and cowboy hat or safety helmet.

- Leather shotgun chaps or chinks are optional.

- Spurs are optional, but most competitors do wear them.

Cattle and Speed Events

- In most events the rider must wear Western-style attire, including jeans, boots, a long-sleeved Western-style shirt, and cowboy hat or safety helmet (if the rules allow it).

- Leather shotgun chaps or chinks are optional (or may be required for certain events, such as cutting).

- Gloves and spurs are optional, depending on the specific event.

WESTERN STOCK

OPEN SHOW

Grooming is the same for stock seat equitation, Western pleasure/riding/horsemanship, trail, and other rail or pattern classes

The vast majority of stock seat riders show at the level of the open show, 4H show, or other local show. These shows are great for entry-level riders and usually offer some opportunities for the more advanced rider as well.

Rail classes are classes in which all competitors ride together and are asked to walk, jog, lope, and reverse direction around the perimeter of the ring. Depending on the class, the judge may assess the horse or the rider. Such classes include Western pleasure and equitation classes. Pattern classes are those in which each competitor enters the ring alone, one at a time, and completes a designated pattern of movements. These classes include Western riding, Western horsemanship,

Western Pleasure Horse

- Clip and boot up the legs, making sure all white markings gleam.

- Apply hoof polish or hoof black before entering the ring.

- Wipe the muzzle, eyes, and ears clean before entering the arena, and apply baby oil or a polishing product if desired.

Head and Mane

- Clip the head and ears with a detailed show trim.

- Pull the mane to 3 1/2 to 4 inches in length, making sure it is very even. Thin it from the bottom to encourage the top hairs to lie flat against the neck.

- Band the mane with bands matching the color of the mane (see page 116).

- The forelock may be braided and tucked under the browband or simply left free.

and trail classes. Grooming for the various events is basically the same, since the same horse and rider combination may cross-enter into various divisions.

The saddle and bridle leather may be a darker color and does not necessarily need tooling and silver embellishments. Local shows are more casual than larger breed shows, so tack does not have to be as high quality as that expected at, for example, the AQHA World Championships. Nevertheless, tack should fit well and be cleaned and conditioned.

ZOOM

Historically, ranchers trimmed manes in various styles to indicate the horse's level of training. A horse with an untrimmed mane was untrained. A horse with two tufts of mane at the withers was a young horse just starting training, usually still going in a bosal. A horse with one tuft at the withers was a fully trained horse going "straight up in the bridle," that is, trained to go in a curb bit.

Tail

- The tail should be long, loose, and flowing. Do not pull or bang it.

- Maintain the tail by keeping it braided up and/or in a tail bag so it is as long and full as possible.

- Bathe, condition, and pick out the tail thoroughly.

- A skimpy or short tail may be enhanced by using a tail extension (see page 138).

Tack

- Use a Western saddle and bridle with a snaffle or curb bit, depending on your horse's level of training and the requirements of the class.

- The saddle blanket should match the rider's attire; Amateur and Youth exhibitors can select brighter colors and designs.

- Boots and wraps are not worn in the show ring.

WESTERN STOCK

WESTERN PLEASURE, BREED SHOW

The look of the Western pleasure horse at the top levels of the breed circuits is slick, sleek, and streamlined

The Western pleasure division at stock-type breed shows, including Quarter Horses (AQHA), Paints (APHA), and Appaloosas (ApHC), showcases horses that have been meticulously prepared for the show ring in terms of breeding, training, and grooming. The ideal Western pleasure mount shows three elegant, smooth gaits (walk, jog, and canter) on a loose rein.

Judges look for a relaxed walk and a flat-kneed, slow-legged jog and canter. The horse should appear calm, consistent, and responsive to the rider at all gaits and should maintain a level topline, carrying his head so that the poll is even with the withers. The rider's cues should be so subtle as to be nearly imperceptible to the casual observer.

Western Show Horse

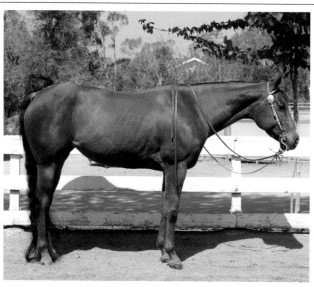

- Clip and boot up the legs, making sure all white markings gleam.

- Lightly sand the hooves for a smooth surface, and apply hoof polish or hoof black before entering the ring.

- Wipe the muzzle, eyes, and ears clean before entering the arena, and lightly apply baby oil or a polishing product if desired.

Head and Mane

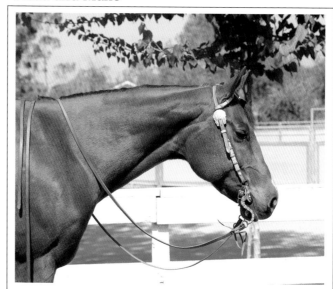

- Clip the head and ears with a detailed show trim.

- Pull the mane to 3 1/2 to 4 inches long, making sure it is very even. Thin it from the bottom to encourage the top hairs to lie flat against the neck.

- Determine the length of the bridle path by gently laying the horse's ear back, and add an inch to that length.

- Band the mane. The forelock may be braided and tucked under the browband or simply left free.

When it comes to the horse's appearance, heads are delicate, necks are slender, legs are long, coats gleam like gold, manes are neatly banded, and tails are smooth. Riders invest a lot of time and money in their turnout. Saddles, bridles, and breastplates are made of the finest light-oil leather, with elaborate silver embellishments and tooling. Riders' clothing is custom made and conforms to the latest fashion trends.

Grooming for other rail and pattern classes—Western riding, Western horsemanship, trail, and so on—is essentially the same as for Western pleasure.

ZOOM

Junior horses (those age five and under) may compete in AQHA, APHA, and ApHC shows in a bosal, snaffle, or curb bridle. Senior horses (those age six and older) are expected to be fully trained and therefore are shown in a curb bit in performance classes.

Tail

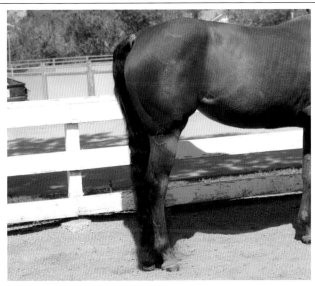

- The tail should be long, loose, and flowing. Do not pull or bang it.

- Maintain the tail by keeping it braided up and/or in a tail bag so it is as long and full as possible.

- Bathe, condition, and pick out the tail thoroughly.

- A skimpy or short tail may be enhanced by using a tail extension (see page 138).

Tack

- Most riders use a tooled light-oil Western saddle with silver accents and a leather or neoprene girth.

- Use a light-oil one- or two-eared Western show bridle with no noseband, with silver conchos matching the saddle.

- The square saddle pad should be a solid color that matches the rider's attire.

- Boots and wraps are not used in rail classes.

WESTERN STOCK

REINING

An event that highlights the athletic ability and versatility of the working ranch horse

Reining horses compete one at a time, each performing a designated pattern. The reining pattern includes all of the moves that a ranch horse working cattle might perform, only in a more extreme form. Today's reining horses have perfected the individual maneuvers to breathtaking precision.

All reining patterns require the horse to execute small, slow circles, large, fast circles, flying lead changes, rollbacks over the hocks, 360-degree spins done in place, and the signature sliding stop. The reining horse should work with a loose rein and respond immediately to the practically invisible cues of the rider. Reining patterns have been approved and published by the National Reining Horse Association (NRHA),

Reining Horse

- The reiner should be immaculate, with a glowing, shiny coat to accentuate the horse's muscular structure.

- Clip and boot up the legs, making sure all white markings gleam.

- Apply hoof polish or hoof black before entering the ring.

- The reining horse may wear "sliders," which are specialized flat shoes with trailers that allow the horse to slide in the sliding stop.

Head and Mane

- Clip the head and ears with a detailed show trim.

- Wipe the muzzle, eyes, and ears clean before entering the arena, and apply baby oil or a polishing product if desired.

- The reiner shows with a long, full, flowing mane and forelock.

- The current style is not to clip the bridle path at all. If clipped, however, the bridle path should be 6 to 8 inches long.

similar to the organization of dressage tests by the USDF.

Approved reining patterns will all include the required maneuvers. Contestants compete, or "run the pattern," one at a time. There is a specific system for judging reining classes, in which each horse starts out with a numerical score of seventy points. During the test, reiners will have points added and deducted according to their performance of the different elements of the test. Reiners are judged on smoothness, finesse, attitude, quickness, and authority.

Tail

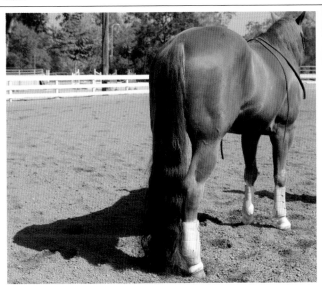

- The reiner should have a long, full, natural tail.

- Maintain the tail by braiding it and/or using tail bags (see page 124) to keep it as long and full as possible.

- Wash, condition, and pick out the tail by hand before a show.

- Tail extensions are not advisable, since the horse may step on the extension while backing or spinning.

Tack

- Ride in a Western saddle, preferably one made for reining.

- Ride in Western bridle with a curb bit.

- Leg wraps or boots are advisable. Most competitors use Professional's Choice sport boots or skid boots.

- Martingales, tie-downs, nosebands, chinstraps narrower than 1/2 inch, and mechanical hackamores are not allowed. Illegal bits include slip, gag, or donut bits and flat polo mouthpieces.

WESTERN STOCK

SPEED AND CATTLE EVENTS

Grooming is similar for cutting, roping, team penning, reined/ working cow horse, gaming, and barrel racing

The cattle events are those most closely associated with the Western stock horse's historic origins as a working ranch horse. Cattle events (also known as rodeo events) in particular showcase the special talents of the cow horse. In cutting, a horse separates (or cuts) a cow from the herd and then prevents it from returning to the herd. Once the rider indicates to the horse which cow is to be worked, the rider cannot guide the horse. Horses, who have two minutes to perform, are judged on their agility and success, with the degree of difficulty of the cow also taken into account. Other popular cattle events include team penning, dally team roping, tie-down roping, working cow horse, and reined cow horse.

Cattle Events

- The cow horse shows with a full, natural mane and tail or may have the mane pulled to 3 1/2 to 4 inches, but not banded.

- As for any discipline, the horse should be healthy, fit, and in good weight.

- Appearance is secondary to performance.

Tack

- Use a Western saddle, preferably one made for your sport. For roping, the saddle needs a rear cinch. The saddle needs to fit well and be rugged, but not fancy.

- Use a Western bridle with a curb or snaffle bit and no noseband, or a bosal.

- Breast collars are permitted, but in some events, such as cutting, choke ropes, tie downs, tight nose bands, quirts, and bats are not. Horses often wear boots for leg protection.

Speed events are timed events in which competitors compete against the clock. Barrel racing is the most popular speed event. Barrel racing is a timed event in which riders maneuver around three barrels in a cloverleaf pattern at a gallop. It originated strictly as a sport (that is, without any practical ranching antecedents). Although events are open to both men and women, barrel racing is more popular among women. Pole bending and roping (also a cattle event) are other speed events.

Grooming and tack for cattle and speed events focus on functionality and practicality. Horses typically show with natural, unbanded and unbraided manes and tails. In most classes, tie-downs are allowed, since the horse's style is not being judged. (Cutting is one notable exception to this.) Saddles and bridles should fit well and be of a type suitable to the sport.

Barrel Racing

- There are no rules regarding the appearance of a barrel horse, but they usually have a full, long mane and natural tail.

- The bridle path, if present, should be 4 to 6 inches long.

- Barrel racers may even paint designs on their horses' rumps and use glitter on hooves or in manes and tails.

Tack

- Barrel racers tend to use brightly colored tack, saddle pads, boots, and rider clothing.

- Use a Western saddle made for barrel racing, and a bridle with a curb or snaffle bit or a hackamore with a bosal.

- Breast collars, tie-downs, and leg boots are all allowed.

THE RIDER

Equipment and attire for the Western rider are similar to those of the stock-type breeds

The Western rider showing an American Saddlebred, Arabian, Morgan, or any of the other "saddle type" breeds under Western tack has the same basic clothing requirements as the Western stock horse exhibitor, as described on page 166.

Riders will wear a Western hat, long-sleeved shirt with any type of collar, trousers or pants, chaps or chinks, a belt, and cowboy boots. A vest, jacket, coat, and/or sweater may also be worn. All clothing should be clean and fit well; clothes should not be baggy or too tight. Some riders choose to wear a one-piece "equitation suit," which has long sleeves and a collar.

There are some minor differences between breeds, particu-

Western Pleasure Amateur/Youth

- The rider wears traditional Western-style attire, including a long-sleeved shirt, shotgun chaps with fringe, a cowboy hat, and cowboy boots.

- Jeans or dress pants (for women) are worn under the chaps.

- Vests or jackets may be brightly colored or accented with rhinestones. An amateur or youth may choose brighter colors.

- Gloves and spurs are op-tional

Western Pleasure Professional

- The rider wears traditional Western-style attire, including a long-sleeved shirt, shotgun chaps with fringe, a cowboy hat, and cowboy boots. Women wear "slinky" polyester shirts. Men wear silk neck scarves.

- Vests or jackets may be brightly colored and accented with rhinestones and fringe.

- Female riders wear polyester dress pants that match their shirts or chaps, while men wear jeans.

- Gloves and spurs are optional.

176

larly in the accessories a rider is required or allowed to wear around his or her neck. In most cases a tie, kerchief, bolo tie, or pin is allowed. For example, the USEF rulebook specifies that the rider of an American Saddlebred may wear "a necktie, kerchief or bolo tie, bow tie, peddle-tie, rosette-tie, or pin used as a tie." Protective headgear, such as a helmet, is always acceptable, especially for junior riders, and is not required to be of Western style.

YELLOW LIGHT

The way the reins are held is of great importance in any Western class. In using split reins, with a curb bit, one finger between the reins is permitted if the ends of the split reins fall on the near side. If you use a romal or when the ends of split reins are held in the unused hand, no finger is allowed between the reins. Reading your breed's rulebook for all details is a must.

Reining and Other Performance Classes

- In most events the rider must wear Western-style attire, including jeans, boots, a long-sleeved Western-style shirt, and cowboy hat or safety helmet (if the rules allow it).

- Leather shotgun chaps or chinks are optional (or may be required for certain events, such as cutting).

- Gloves and spurs are optional, depending on the specific event.

Coordinating the Look

- The rider's attire should coordinate with the color of the tack and the horse.

- This rider wears a light-colored hat to match her light-colored chaps and light oil saddle and bridle.

- The silver accents on the tack are reflected in the silver colors on the rider's shirt.

- The result is an overall impression of style and elegance that shows the horse and rider to their best advantage.

WESTERN PLEASURE
The rules for the Arabian/Morgan divisions are detailed and can be complicated, so read them carefully

The preparation of the Arabian and Morgan Western horse follows both the guidelines set forth by their respective breed associations and the rules that govern the Western divisions. Sometimes you will need to review more than one area of a rulebook to find the answers to all of your questions. As with all equestrian competitions, the more advanced or competitive one is, the more details and rules there are to know and follow. At local competitions, an individual of either of these versatile breeds may be competitive in hunter/saddle seat pleasure and also in the Western pleasure division. At the regional or national level, the competitive Arabians and Morgans are specialists, concentrating in the Western division.

Western Arabian (or Morgan)

- Horses are shown with natural mane and tail, both long and full for pleasure classes. Tail extensions and other modifications are not allowed.

- Hooves should be clean, with dark hooves blackened and polished. White hooves should be washed and left natural or painted with a clear coat.

- White leg markings should be sparkling clean. Arabians may not have white powder applied.

Head and Mane

- Both breeds show with a long forelock and mane.

- The ears, muzzle, and a 6- to 8-inch bridle path are clipped, and ears may have diamond tips (see page 85).

- Lightly wipe the face with highlighting gel or baby oil. (Although in Arabian classes a judge may penalize an entry for excessive grease on the muzzle or face.)

The Arabian and Morgan are both shown in all Western classes turned out according to their breed standards. They will have full manes and tails, a suitable show clip to clean up their faces and legs, and be thoroughly groomed. Both of these breeds look very nice under Western tack.

The Western tack used by the Arabians and Morgans is similar to that found on the stock horses. The darker stained tack is more readily found in the saddle-type Western classes and silver is always in.

Tail

- Tails should be full, long, natural, and well picked out.

- Tail extensions are not allowed, and altered or crooked tails will be penalized.

- The tail may need to be shorter (not dragging on the ground) for Western horses in divisions calling for pattern work, to prevent the horse from stepping on the tail.

Tack

- Tack needs to fit the horse. Many times a Western saddle built for a stock-type animal will not fit the saddle-type Western horse, so look for a saddle specifically made for your breed or type.

- The headstall can be of any Western style.

- Consult your breed's rulebook for detailed guidelines on what is legal in regard to Western bits.

- Boots and wraps are not allowed in pleasure and other rail classes.

WESTERN PLEASURE (CONTINUED)

It's increasingly popular to show the American Saddlebred under Western tack

The American Saddlebred shown under Western tack is a slightly different type of horse than other pleasure Saddlebreds. The horse's conformation may be more closely coupled, with more substantial hindquarters, a stockier build, and a less elevated neck and head position. However, an extremely low head position with too much flexion is not desirable. Horses must be plain shod for all Western classes.

Horses are shown at a flat walk, jog-trot, lope, halt, and back. The reins should be loose, showing that the horse is not being restrained by the rider, and must be held in one hand. The horse should appear to be a pleasure to ride, with prompt, effortless transitions and easy-to-ride gaits.

Western Pleasure Saddlebred

- The ASB Western Pleasure horse is plain shod without with pads, bands, or any device between hoof and shoe.

- Horse is shown with natural mane and tail, both long and full.

- Hooves should be clean and dark hooves blackened. White hooves will be washed and left natural or painted with a clear coat.

- White legs should be sparkling clean.

Head

- The mane should be long, full, and natural, without braids.

- Forelocks are usually long and full, but sometimes the forelock is thinned down.

- Closely clip the ears, muzzle, and a 6- to 8-inch bridle path. Ears will have the diamond tips (see page 85).

- Apply highlighting gel, baby oil, or similar grooming product to the muzzle and above the eyes.

Western classes for American Saddlebreds include Western Country Pleasure, Western Show Pleasure, Working Western Pleasure (which includes a rail portion and an obstacles portion), Western Trail (an obstacles class), Western Pairs, and Versatility (in which the horse is shown under both English and Western tack). Grooming, tack, and attire are essentially the same for all types of classes.

Tail

- The tail should be washed and hand picked.

- The addition of a switch is allowed for the ASB Western horse, as it is for all ASB Country Pleasure horses. It should match and blend with the natural tail.

- The tail may need to be shorter, not dragging on the ground, if the horse shows in a class calling for pattern work.

- Tail sets, bustles, braces, or any other alteration of the tail carriage is not allowed.

Tack

- Use a Western saddle and bridle with a snaffle or curb bit, depending on your horse's level of training and the requirements of the class. Tack should fit well and coordinate with the color of the horse.

- The saddle blanket should match the rider's attire; Amateur and Youth exhibitors can select brighter colors and designs.

- Boots and wraps are not worn in the show ring.

CARE OF WESTERN TACK
Follow these simple steps to get your tack clean and ready for show

If you ask ten horse people for the best way to clean tack, you will hear ten different answers. The truth is there is no one single method for cleaning tack. There is a variety of products on the market, from glycerine soap to leather conditioner. You will learn what works best for you, but here is a simple set of instructions that will certainly get your tack clean.

In addition to your cleaning product, you'll need a bucket of warm water, a washcloth or sponge, and a soft brush, such as an old toothbrush. Dust off the surface of the saddle or bridle with a dry cloth. Dampen the cloth (or sponge) and wipe down the leather to remove surface dirt and dust. Apply a small amount of glycerine soap or saddle cleaner to a damp sponge and rub the leather. Rinse and squeeze out the sponge often for a better clean. Then rinse your tack with a

Keeping Light Leather Light

- Very light oil leather can be darkened by cleaning or conditioning products, so it's best to use them very sparingly and as infrequently as possible.

- Use a cleaning product designed for use on light oil, such as Lexol Cleaner

NF, which contains neat's-foot oil.

- Use only 100 percent pure neat's-foot oil. If the oil contains any additives, you run the risk of darkening the leather.

Cleaning and Care of Tooled Leather

- First dust off the saddle with a clean, dry cloth.

- Wipe the surface with a cloth or tack sponge dampened with pure water, no cleaning products, to remove as much dirt as possible. Rinse and squeeze out the sponge often.

- Using a small amount of cleaner and a bit of water, use a very soft toothbrush to gently scrub the tooled areas.

- Wipe again with a damp sponge or cloth, and finish with a light coat of conditioner if needed.

GROOMING HORSES

damp sponge and a small amount of clean warm water.

Next condition the saddle with oil or a conditioner. Brush a thin layer of oil onto the saddle with a washcloth, and work it in using your bare hands, which will help the oil absorb as your skin warms it. (You can also warm the oil slightly in the microwave.) If using a conditioner, rub in a sparing amount on one section of tack at a time. Do not over-oil or over-condition, which can weaken the leather, leave a sticky film, or cause stitching to rot.

If you use your tack every day in dusty, sweaty conditions, give it a light cleaning each day, plus a more thorough cleaning and conditioning once a month. If it is high-quality show tack that you use only for shows, keep it covered and stored in a cool, dry place, and you may have only to dust it off before each show.

Care of Silver Accessories

- Keep your silver conchos and accents sparkling by cleaning and polishing them regularly.

- Use a product made for cleaning silver.

- One good choice is Nevr-Dull, which is sold as pre-soaked cotton wadding. Tear off a small piece and use it to rub the silver, being careful to avoid contacting the leather. Use a new piece when it becomes dirty.

- Finish by buffing the silver with a soft cloth to bring out the shine.

Care of Navajo Blankets

- Wool Navajo saddle blankets require some special attention.

- Use a damp cloth or a clean stiff brush to remove surface hair and dirt after each use, and allow it to air-dry thoroughly before storing.

- For periodic cleanings, rinse the pad with clean water.

- Some blankets can be laundered with detergents made for wool (use only half the recommended amount to avoid residue). Read the manufacturer's care instructions to be sure this is safe for your blanket.

THE RIDER
Appropriate attire and equipment for the saddle seat pleasure rider

Saddle seat is an American style of riding that highlights the horse's animation, high head carriage, and brilliance in the show ring. Breeds well suited for this include the American Saddlebred, Arabian, Half-Arabian, Morgan, National Show Horse, and Tennessee Walking Horse. Some shows are breed-specific, while others have classes for particular breeds as well as open classes where different breeds show together. Classes are offered for beginning to advanced riders. They are

also divided by the age and ability of the horse.

The saddle seat pleasure horse, regardless of breed, is judged on manners and should look like it is a "pleasure" to ride. These horses are expected to do a flat-foot (four-beat) walk and make transitions between gaits in an "agreeable" manner. That being said, each of these breeds has a different set of stipulations governing its pleasure divisions. Do not assume that the specifications for Arabian English pleasure

Pleasure Suit with Saddle Seat Derby

- This attire is proper for any saddle seat class. (Younger riders can wear lighter, less conservative colors.)

- Coat and jodhpurs are made of matching material of a conservative color. The vest may match or be of a complementary color. Jodhpurs must have tie-downs.

- Wear a collared shirt, buttoned down or secured with a tie-bar, and complementary tie.

- Women and girls wear a felt saddle seat derby. Male riders wear a felt snap brim hat, which may be straw in summer.

Day Coat with Saddle Seat Derby

- A day coat with compatible appointments is proper attire for any class except for saddle seat equitation. The day coat is not the same color as the jodhpurs, vest, and derby, although the colors should work well together.

- Day coat usually has a shawl collar, not the notched lapels of the pleasure suit.

- Jodhpurs need to have tie-downs.

- Wear a collared shirt, as with the pleasure suit.

- The felt saddle seat derby is proper for women and girls.

are the same as Morgan English pleasure.

Attention to details in the turnout, whether of horse or rider, is important. Specific points on clothing include having your suit clean and well fitted. Even an "off the rack" saddle suit can have the coat/vest fitted and jodhpurs taken in to make a professional look. For all types of apparel, the rider should wear gloves, jodhpur boots, and spurs and carry a gaited whip. Women with long hair should wear their hair up in an appropriate bun with hair net.

Day Coat with Homburg

- The difference in this ensemble is the homburg, a felt hat that is shaped differently than the traditional saddle seat derby in both its crown and brim. It is more common with Arabian and TWH exhibitors than in the ASB or Morgan show rings. It is correct in all pleasure classes.

- The felt saddle seat homburg is proper for women and girls.

- All other clothing should be the same as the day coat with saddle seat derby.

Saddle Suit, Male Rider

- A men's pleasure or informal saddle suit is proper attire for any saddle seat class.

- Coat and jodhpurs are made of matching material of a conservative color (with collars and lapels of same color). The vest may be matching or can be of a complementary color.

- Jodhpurs need to have tie-downs.

- Wear a collared shirt with tie, as for the women's suits.

- Men and boys should wear a felt snap brim hat, which may be straw in summer.

THE AMERICAN SADDLEBRED
English show pleasure and English country pleasure

The American Saddlebred Pleasure divisions are where ASB enthusiasts show their horses without the extra responsibilities that come with the ASB performance horse (see page 196). The ASB pleasure horse still exhibits the show horse charisma so important in the performance divisions but is judged on manners first and performance second. The pleasure divisions often boast the largest classes at a Saddlebred show.

This division is restricted to amateurs and junior exhibitors. There are two types of ASB saddle seat pleasure horses: show pleasure and country pleasure. The specifications on which each is judged differ slightly, although manners are paramount for both. Horses cross-entering between show pleasure and country pleasure, between Three-Gaited and Five-Gaited, and between pleasure and any other division (other

American Saddlebred Pleasure

Head and Mane

- Horses must be well groomed and clipped, with bright white markings.

- Polish the hoof with fine sandpaper and wipe off. If the hoof is dark, paint it with hoof black. If the hoof is white, leave it uncovered. Any white stripes on a hoof should be painted black.

- ASB show pleasure horses may have shoe bands and pads on their feet.

- ASB country pleasure horses must be plain shod, with the sole and the entire frog of the foot visible. Shoe bands and full pads are not permitted.

- All ASB pleasure horses show with a full, clean, tangle-free mane.

- The show pleasure horse shows with a single braid and can have a forelock braid.

- The country pleasure horse is never braided, and artificial manes are prohibited.

- Trim the muzzle and lower jaw. Trim the inside of the ears clean, leaving diamond tips. Trimming the long eye feelers is optional.

- Highlight the muzzle, above eyes, and the bridle path with baby oil or other product to creates shine. Wipe ears with a damp cloth.

than in-hand) are not allowed at the same show. Stallions are not allowed in any ASB pleasure class.

A four-beat walk is required of both show and country pleasure horses. Suitability as a pleasure mount, with smooth transitions and an agreeable attitude, is a must. Show pleasure horses are asked to walk, trot, and canter. Country pleasure horses walk, trot, extend the trot, canter, and stop and stand quietly both ways of the ring. All horses must stand quietly and back readily in the line-up.

Tail

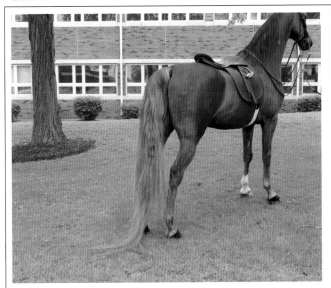

- All ASB pleasure horses show with natural, full, clean, tangle-free tails. The tail may not be set or braced during a class. The fact that a tail was once set does not disqualify that horse from competition.

- Both the show pleasure and the country pleasure horse

are allowed to wear tail switches (see page 140).

- The show pleasure horse may wear a tail set or bustle while on show grounds, but the country pleasure horse may not.

Tack

- The ASB saddle seat pleasure horse shows in a full double bridle or a Pelham. The browband is red or maroon patent leather. The cavesson may match the browband or the bridle.

- Clean and shine all leather. Tuck extra length of stirrup leathers behind the leg.

- Use a cutback saddle with a white girth, with or without a dark-colored saddle shaped pad.

- White bell boots are permitted on the front feet of the Five-gaited horse in both the show pleasure and country pleasure divisions.

ARABIANS
English pleasure and country English pleasure

All Arabian English and country pleasure horses show at the walk, normal trot, and canter both ways of the ring. Some classes, such as Arabian open English pleasure or Arabian open country pleasure, also require the strong trot and hand gallop. The country pleasure horse will halt on the rail, stand quietly, back, and walk off on a loose rein at least one direction of the ring. The rulebook specifically states that posting is required at any speed of trot.

It is imperative that the horses shown in the Arabian English pleasure divisions give the appearance of being a pleasure to ride. They must perform all gaits willingly. Horses may be asked to change from one gait to any other gait as listed in the class specifications. They should come into the line-up at the gait requested. Cross-entering between the Arabian Eng-

Arabian English and Country English Pleasure

Head and Mane

- The Arabian English or country pleasure horse shows with a full, clean mane and tail with white markings shining.

- Clip legs and pasterns clean.

- Hooves should be clean. Lightly sand dry hooves, then wipe off and paint with hoof black or a clear hoof product. (Horses shown in breeding or in-hand classes can have only transparent products on their hooves.)

- The Arabian English or country pleasure horse should have its head trimmed with the detailed show trim.

- The bridle path on the Arabian is longer than those of the other saddle seat breeds to accentuate the refinement of the throatlatch.

The Arabian is shown with a natural forelock.

- Grease the muzzle, above the eyes, and bridle path with baby oil or a highlighting product to give a polished look.

- Clean ears with rubbing alcohol before class.

lish pleasure and country pleasure divisions is not allowed at the same show. Stallions are allowed in all divisions.

Arabians cannot be shown with a tail switch or false tail.

Tail

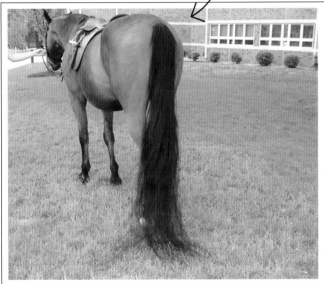

- The Arabian English or country pleasure horse should have its tail long, very clean, and well picked out so that it is as full as possible.

- Wipe out under the tail with a towel or damp rag, especially because of the

Arabian's naturally high tail carriage.

- Under USEF breed rules, Arabians cannot be shown in any division with a tail switch or false tail.

- Other governing bodies allow the use of tail switches.

Tack

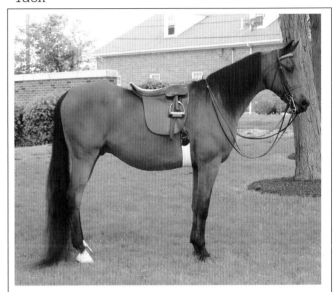

- Show with a full bridle. A Pelham bit is allowed.

- A junior horse may wear either a single curb or single snaffle instead of the full bridle.

- No martingales or tiedowns are allowed.

- The patent leather browband can be a single color or multicolored. The cavesson may match the browband or be of flat, dark leather matching the rest of the bridle.

- Use a cutback saddle and patent leather or vinyl dark or white girth.

189

MORGANS
English pleasure and classic English pleasure

The Morgan English pleasure horse shows at the walk, pleasure trot, road trot, and canter both ways of the ring. Pleasure horses, while still expected to be showy, are judged primarily on manners and the ability to give a good pleasure ride. There should be an observable increase in speed for the road trot. When lined up, the Morgan English pleasure horse may be asked to back, whereas the classic English pleasure horse must be asked to back.

Many shows offer multiple classes in the pleasure divisions such as open, junior horse, junior exhibitor, and ladies. Each class has slightly different specifications for the judge to take into consideration. In the Morgan English pleasure divisions, these are manners, performance, quality, presence, and the ability to give a good pleasure ride. The order in which these terms are written in the class specs is the order in which they are taken into consideration by the judge.

Morgan English and Classic English Pleasure

- Morgans show with a full, clean mane and tail with white markings shining.

- Legs should be clipped and pasterns clean of feathers.

- Hooves should be clean. Lightly sand dry feet, then wipe off and paint with hoof black or a clear polish.

- The hoof length allowed is 5 inches at the toe, including the shoe and pad in Morgan English pleasure classes and 4 1/2 inches in classic pleasure. Rim pads are the only pads allowed on a classic horse.

Head and Mane

- Trim the Morgan English or classic pleasure horse's head with the detailed show trim.

- The bridle path should be 8 inches long. Braid the forelock or secure it with a band to keep the hair from tickling the horse's ears. Tuck the forelock under the browband and cheekpiece on the mane side of the bridle.

- Rub the muzzle, above the eyes, and bridle path with baby oil or a highlighting product for a polished look.

- Clean inside ears with rubbing alcohol.

In the Morgan division, type and conformation are taken into consideration in all classes. A performance class is judged 60 percent on performance and 40 percent on type and conformation. In all Morgan under-saddle championship classes, the horses must be stripped and are judged 50 percent on performance and 50 percent on type and conformation. Some shows offer a stake class rather than a championship in a division. Stake classes are not stripped and are judged with the percentages of 60/40 percent.

Check your division's rules when considering using a tail switch.

Tail

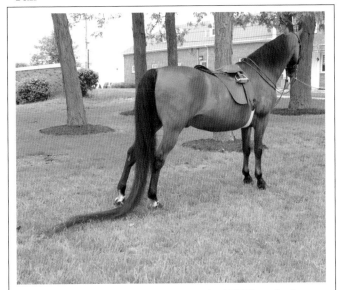

- For the show ring, wash and pick out the tail. The Morgan shows with an elevated tail, but it should not be up and over the horse's back.

- Under USEF breed rules, Morgans are not allowed to show in any division with a tail switch or any supplemental hair.

- Other governing bodies may allow the use of tail switches.

Tack

- Show with a full bridle and show browband and cavesson. A Pelham bit is not allowed. The show cavesson may match the browband or be of flat, dark leather matching the rest of the bridle.

- The patent leather browband can be a single color or multicolored. If multicolored, the design should be discreet.

- The cutback saddle and white girth are the standard appointments for any saddle seat class. An optional dark pad may be used under the saddle.

191

TENNESSEE WALKING HORSES
Plantation or Flat Shod divisions

The Tennessee Walking Horse showing in the Plantation division performs the flat walk, running walk, and canter. In this division, the use of action devices, such as light chains around the pasterns, is prohibited. These horses also show with a natural tail; bracing or setting the tail is prohibited.

The flat walk is a brisk four-beat gait with the back foot gliding over the hoof print left by the front foot on the same side:

right rear over right front, left rear over left front. This action is known as overstride and is a noted characteristic of the breed. The running walk is a similar four-beat gliding gait like the flat walk, only performed with more speed and overstep. Both the flat and running walks are amazingly smooth. Another unique trait of the breed is that the horse nods its head in rhythm with the cadence of the flat and running walks.

Tennessee Walking Horse Plantation Pleasure

Head and Mane

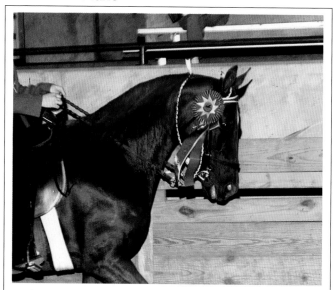

- The TWH is shown with a full, clean mane and tail with white markings shining.

- Legs should be clipped and pasterns clean of feathers.

- Hooves should be clean. Lightly sand dry feet, then wipe off and paint with hoof black or a clear polish.

- In the Plantation division, the shoe may be attached to the hoof only by nails; bands are not allowed. A maximum limit of two pounds is set for the shoes worn by all horses shown in the Plantation division.

- Clip the head with the detailed show trim.

- The bridle path should be 8 inches long.

- Rub the muzzle, above eyes, and bridle path with baby oil or a highlighting product. Clean inside ears with rubbing alcohol.

- Braid both the forelock and the first 1/2-inch of mane with ribbon (see page 114).

- Tuck the forelock braid under the browband and under the cheekpiece on the mane side of the bridle, and then wrap it a few times around the throatlatch.

The canter has "lift and drop" action of the front end and is referred to as the rocking chair gait.

There are four categories in the Plantation division, each with different shoeing regulations. These categories are Plantation, Country Plantation, Traditional Plantation, and Trail Plantation. Trail Plantation is for amateurs only. In Plantation, Country, and Traditional Plantation classes may be offered in each category, such as Open and Amateur, or divided by age of horse or rider. Many of the classes do not call for the canter, so be sure to check the class requirements.

The Tennessee Walking Horse showing in the plantation division must show with a natural tail.

Tail

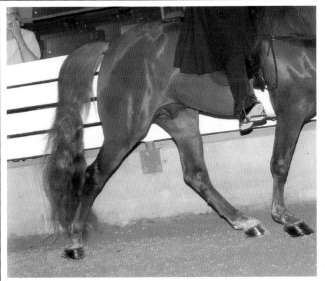

- For the show ring, wash and pick out the tail so it is as long and full as possible.

- The tail must be natural, with no tail extensions, braces, or other artificial tail-setting devices.

Tack

- The TWH show bridle features a single shanked bit, single rein, and the show browband and cavesson. The show cavesson may match the browband or be of flat, dark leather matching the rest of the bridle.

- The show browband is patent leather and can be a single color or multicolored. Sometimes metallic piping, such as gold or silver, is used for the accent.

- The cutback saddle, breaststraps, and patent leather or vinyl dark or white show girth are standard appointments, with an optional dark pad.

THE RIDER

Exhibiting at the pinnacle of the saddle seat divisions

The conservative saddle seat pleasure suit with a saddle seat derby (see page 184) is considered acceptable attire for any saddle seat class, including the elite performance divisions discussed in this chapter. There is, however, other show attire that may be more correct for riders in these classes, especially when showing in the evening and/or in championships.

At large shows, formal attire is correct in certain divisions after six p.m. With formal suits, solid conservative colors, such as black, navy, dark brown, or dark gray, are proper (and depending on the division, may be required). Suits with a pin stripe or herringbone pattern are acceptable as long as they appear to be solid in color. The most formal saddle seat attire includes a tuxedo-type jacket with matching silk collar and lapels; Kentucky jodhpurs with a satin stripe down the leg;

Pleasure Suit with Saddle Seat Derby

Formal Saddle Suit with Top Hat

- This attire is proper for any saddle seat class. (Younger riders can wear lighter, less conservative colors.)

- Coat and jodhpurs are made of matching material of a conservative color. The vest may match or be of a complementary color. Jodhpurs must have tie-downs.

- Wear a collared shirt, either buttoned down or secured with a tie-bar, and complementary tie.

- Women and girls wear a felt saddle seat derby. Male riders wear a felt snap brim hat, which may be straw in summer.

- Wear a formal coat and jodhpurs made of matching material; the coat should have satin lapels of the same color.

- Wear formal jods with a satin stripe down the outside of the leg and a pleated formal shirt, usually white, with a wing collar.

- A satin vest or a cummerbund matching the lapels with a matching satin bow tie (or a white pique shirt, vest, and bow tie) is appropriate.

- Wear patent jodhpur boots and a top hat with brim shaped like the saddle seat derbies.

GROOMING HORSES

formal bow tie with cummerbund or formal vest; gloves; and a top hat.

When to wear this most elegant of formal attire, however, varies between the breeds and divisions. Certain guidelines are uniform, such as the dark conservative colors and evening use only. On the ASB, the classic formal is worn only on horses with trimmed manes (Three-Gaited/saddle seat equitation) and horses in the Park division. Arabians, Morgans, and TWH use the formal in their English pleasure and park divisions.

ZOOM

Evening classes officially begin at six p.m. If the class is scheduled to begin at or after six o'clock., it is officially in the evening. A class starting before six o'clock could feasibly finish after six, such as in a saddle seat equitation championship with all riders performing individual workouts. The class technically began before six, however, so day apparel is correct.

Day Coat with Formal Accessories

- The day coat with formal accessories is proper for any class where a formal saddle suit would be worn, except for equitation (where it is mandatory that the coat and jodhpurs be of the same material).

- Wear a day coat with shawl lapels in a conservative color, formal jodhpurs with satin stripe down legs and pleated formal shirt with a wing collar.

- A satin cummerbund and matching bow tie and patent leather boots are appropriate. Wear a top hat with a shaped brim.

Men's Formal Suit and Dark Felt Riding Hat

- Men wear a formal suit (with collars and lapels of the same color and a formal shirt, bow tie, and vest. Conservative accessories are appropriate for evening.

- Alternatively, wear a dark-colored habit (with collars and lapels of the same color). The vest may match or be a very conservative complementary color. A shirt with collar (buttoned down or secured with a tie-bar) is appropriate.

- Men wear a complementary tie with or without tie tack. Conservative accessories are appropriate for evening.

ASB, THREE-GAITED
Elegance and expression

A Three-Gaited American Saddlebred is also referred to as a Walk/Trot Horse, although in the show ring it will perform the walk, trot, and canter. The Three-Gaited ASB is to be the embodiment of brilliance, elegance, and expression. Although the Three-Gaited ASB horse has two fewer gaits to execute than his Five-Gaited counterpart, he expends just as much energy during his performance in the ring.

The Three-Gaited ASB shows with a roached mane and a set tail. It performs an animated walk, park trot, and canter in the ring. The animated walk is a highly collected gait with action and style. The park trot is highly collected. Extreme speed is penalized. Rather than speed, the horse's energy should be directed toward animation and expression. The canter should be collected, relatively slow, lofty, and fluid

Three-Gaited American Saddlebred

- The Three-Gaited ASB shows with a roached mane and a set tail. White markings should be shining.

- Legs should be clipped and pasterns clean of feathers.

- Hooves should be clean. Lightly sand dry, dark feet, then wipe off and paint with hoof black. Lightly sand white feet. Black stripes on white feet should be hoof-blacked.

Head and Mane

- The Three-Gaited ASB should have its head trimmed with the detailed show trim.

- The mane should be freshly roached off including the forelock.

- Rub the muzzle, above eyes, and roached mane with baby oil or a highlighting product, such as Highlighter by Ultra, to give a polished look.

- Clean the inside of ears with rubbing alcohol a few hours before class.

with a definite three-beat cadence. The Three-Gaited ASB will not be asked to back.

The ASB saddle seat equitation mount is turned out exactly like that of the Three-Gaited ASB. The saddle seat equitation division is not interchangeable with ASB saddle seat pleasure equitation where the horses show with full manes and natural tails. Equitation riders may not show in both divisions during the same calendar year and show together only if the show does not offer both saddle seat equitation divisions.

Tail

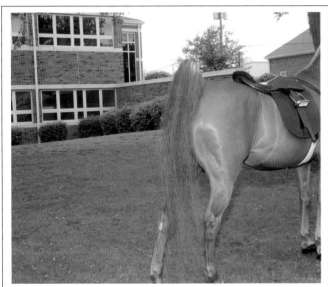

- The Three-Gaited ASB wears a tail-set throughout the show season, resulting in a flexible tail without any discomfort to the horse.

- For the show ring, wash and pick out the tail. Tail switches are allowed.

- To get the tail up and forward over the horse's back, tie it with dark shoestring or brace it. See page 2 for more information on tail braces.

- Take off the shoestring or brace and switch immediately after the class.

Tack

- Show with a full bridle and show browband and cavesson. The cavesson may match the browband or be of flat, dark leather matching the rest of the bridle.

- The show browband is patent leather and can be a single color or multicolored.

If multicolored, the design should be discreet.

- The cutback saddle and white girth are the standard appointments for any saddle seat class. An optional dark pad may be used under the saddle.

PERFORMANCE

ASB, FIVE-GAITED
Animation, brilliance, collection, and speed

The Five-Gaited American Saddlebred is an elite individual in this ultimate of show horse breeds. The signature gaits that set the gaited horse apart are the slow gait and rack. Both of these gaits have four beats, meaning that at any given step there is only one of the horse's feet on the ground at a time. The ASB can trace its ability to perform these gaits back to various ancestors that comprised the "easy-gaited"

breeds of the European Middle Ages. The Five-Gaited horse walks, trots, and canters but will not be asked to back.

Not all Saddlebreds will be Five-Gaited, but those individuals that have the ability may eventually become contenders in this exclusive division. The slow gait and rack begin with the horse's rear and front feet of the same side stepping forward almost together, but the hind foot contacts the ground

Five-Gaited American Saddlebred

- The Five-Gaited ASB shows with a clean, full mane and a set tail; white markings must be shining.

- Legs should be clipped and pasterns clean of feathers.

- Hooves should be clean. They should be presented

as with the Three-Gaited ASB (see page 196).

- The Five-Gaited ASB can wear protective boots on his front feet (see Zoom sidebar). Since the boots may cover so much of the hoof wall, often the hidden area on a dark hoof is not blackened.

Head and Mane

- Clip the head with the detailed show trim.

- Rub the muzzle, eyelids, and bridle path with baby oil or a highlighting product.

- The bridle path should be 8 inches long; leave 1 inch width or less for the forelock.

- Braid the first 1/2-inch of mane with ribbon (see page 114).

- Tuck the forelock braid under the browband in front of the ear and under the cheekpiece of the bridle on the same side as the mane, then wrap a few times around the throatlatch.

before the front foot does. The perfected slow gait is highly collected, animated, and slow. The rack is also collected and animated but done at speed, a fast four-beat gait, each foot meeting the ground at equal and separate intervals. It is breathtaking to watch, exhilarating to ride, and difficult to execute.

The ASB has been referred to as the peacock of the show ring and for good reason. The breed has been thrilling spectators since the early 1800s, long before there was an American Saddlebred Association!

ZOOM

The Five-Gaited American Saddlebred can wear protective boots in front in the show ring. Types include bell, trotting, hinged-quarter, and scalping boots. Boots should be white. If a horse performs better without boots, apply white electrical tape around the top of the hoof wall but not overlapping the coronary band.

Tail

- The Five-Gaited ASB wears a tail-set throughout the show season, resulting in a flexible tail without any discomfort to the horse.

- For the show ring, wash and pick out the tail.

- To get the tail up and forward over the horse's back, tie it with shoestring or brace it.

- A tail switch is allowed. Remove it as soon as possible after the class.

Tack

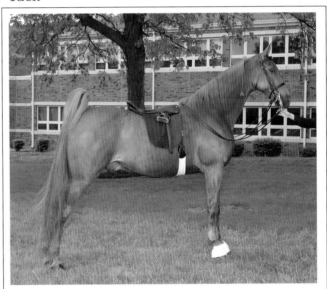

- Show with a full bridle and show browband and cavesson.

- The show cavesson may match the browband or be of flat, dark leather matching the rest of the bridle.

- The cutback saddle and white girth are the standard appointments. An optional dark pad may be used under the saddle.

- The white show girth is usually vinyl and shaped, narrowing slightly at the horse's elbows to allow complete freedom of movement.

199

ARABIAN PARK HORSE

The Arabian Park is powerful but refined

The Arabian Park horse performs at the walk, park trot, and canter. The park trot is a two-beat diagonal gait executed with brilliance and style. This same description is given for many a "park trot," but don't be misled. The Arabian Park horse's signature gait is truly extraordinary.

Correct execution of the Arabian Park trot is a study in contrasts—the hind end exhibiting impulsion and power,

the front end airy and light. It is characterized by extreme shoulder movement and animation, but action alone is not enough. The front legs should have elevation and extension, meaning that when a front leg is at its highest level the forelimb should extend fully forward as well. The hind legs must step well underneath the horse's body to deliver the impulsion required but also exhibit extreme hock action

Arabian Park Horse

- The Arabian Park horse shows with a clean, full mane and tail; white markings must be shining.

- Legs should be clipped and pasterns clean of feathers.

- Hooves should be clean. Lightly sand dry feet, then wipe off and paint with

hoof black or a clear hoof product. Horses that show in breeding or in-hand classes are allowed to have only clear or transparent products on their hooves while in these specific divisions.

Head and Mane

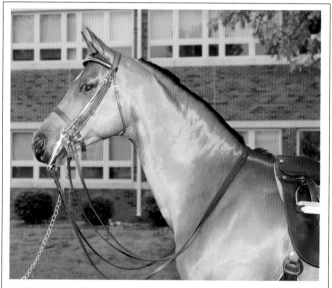

- Clip the head with the detailed show trim. During show season, touch up with #40 blades to keep stubble away.

- The bridle path on the Arabian is longer than on other saddle seat breeds to accentuate the refinement of the throatlatch. The Ara-

bian shows with a natural forelock.

- Grease muzzle, above eyes, and bridle path with baby oil or a highlighting product.

- Clean inside ears with rubbing alcohol a few hours before class.

when flexed to balance with the front. The trot should seem effortless.

The Arabian Park horse must perform a true, four-beat walk, although it may be animated and brisk. The canter should be collected, elevated, slow, and straight on both leads. Judges take all required gaits into consideration but at the same time favor the horse with the most brilliant performance, presence, and quality. It is no wonder that superior Arabian Park horses are really something special.

Tail

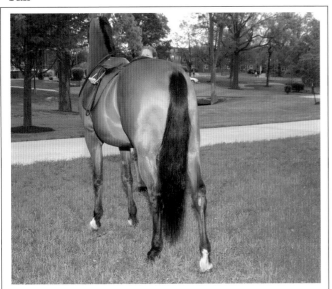

- The Arabian Park horse should have its tail long, very clean, and well picked out so that it is as full as possible.

- Wipe out under the tail with a towel or damp rag, especially because of the Arabian's naturally high tail carriage.

- Arabians are not allowed to be shown in any division with a tail switch or false tail.

Tack

- Show with a full bridle or Pelham bit.

- A junior horse (five years or younger) may use a single curb or snaffle instead of the full bridle.

- The patent leather browband can be a single color or multicolored. The

cavesson may match the browband or match the rest of the bridle.

- No martingales or tie-downs are allowed.

- Use a cutback saddle and patent leather or vinyl white or dark show girth with an optional dark pad.

PERFORMANCE

201

MORGAN PARK HORSE

The Morgan Park shows animation with attitude

All breeds of horses take conformation and quality into consideration when defining their champions. Morgans go one step further and also identify "type" as a factor. The Morgan Park horse performs at the walk, trot, and canter, and Morgan type, as well as performance, is considered in every class.

Entering at the trot, the Morgan Park horse should be highly collected, animated, and distinctly energetic. Attitude is im-

portant; the Park horse should give the impression that he "owns the arena." The Morgan Park needs to have a balanced trot, meaning that he will be able to flex his hocks as well as he can flex in front. Going above level (when the horse's knee reaches a point higher than its elbow when lifted) is highly desired, but the hocks need to be equally engaged. Unbalanced action front-to-back and/or leaving the hocks behind

Morgan Park Horse

- Show with a clean, full mane and tail; white markings must be shining.

- Clip legs and pasterns clean of feathers.

- Hooves should be clean. Lightly sand dry feet, then wipe off and paint with hoof black or a clear polish.

- Black stripes on white feet should be hoof blacked (Q-Tips work well).

- The hoof length allowed is 5 3/4 inches at the toe, including the pad and shoe.

Head and Mane

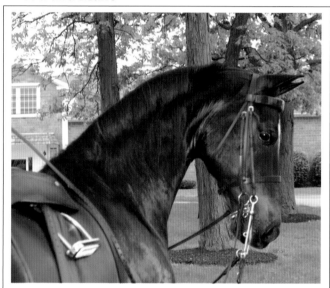

- Clip the head with the detailed show trim.

- The bridle path should be 8 inches long. Secure the forelock with a band, tape, or braid. Tuck it under the browband and cheekpiece on the mane side of the bridle.

- The mane should be freshly washed, picked, or combed out.

- Rub muzzle, above eyes, and bridle path with baby oil or a highlighting product.

- Clean inside ears with rubbing alcohol before class.

(not having the horse step under its body with the hind legs) are considered faults.

The Park walk is collected and animated and may be executed as a two- or four-beat gait. The canter is also collected and straight on both leads. It can be stronger than the canter of the English pleasure horse but not out of control. The Morgan Park horse will not be asked to back.

Tail

- The Morgan may wear a bustle throughout the show season to encourage the horse to carry its tail in an arched manner. A bustle is similar to a tail set; however, the tail lies over a padded support.

- For the show ring, wash and pick out the tail. The Morgan shows with an elevated tail, but it should not be up and over the horse's back like the set tail seen on an ASB.

Tack

- The Morgan Park horse shows with a full bridle and show browband and cavesson. Pelham bits are not allowed. The cavesson may match the browband or be of flat, dark leather matching the rest of the bridle.

- The show browband is patent leather and can be a single color or multicolored. If multicolored, the design should be discreet.

- The cutback saddle and white girth are the standard appointments for the Morgan Park horse. An optional dark pad may be used under the saddle.

TENNESSEE WALKING HORSE
Performance, show performance, and park performance

The highest level of animation for the TWH is found in the Performance division. It features four categories—performance, show performance, park performance, and park. They are all saddle seat classes, and the horses show with set tails unless otherwise specified. Horses showing in performance exhibit the natural gaits of the breed (flat walk, running walk, and canter) but with accentuated form.

The signature gait of the TWH is its running walk. It is a smooth gliding gait, with animation in front and an amazing overstep behind. Many horses step up well underneath themselves when engaged, but none like the TWH in performance at its running walk! As the speed of the running walk increases, the horse oversteps the hoofprint of the front foot with the back (on the same side) by a distance of 6 to 18

Tennessee Walking Horse

Head and Mane

- The TWH is shown with a clean, full mane and tail; white markings must be shining.

- Legs should be clipped and pasterns clean of feathers.

- Hooves should be clean. Lightly sand dry, dark feet, then wipe off and paint with hoof black. Lightly sand white feet; covering them with a clear polish is optional.

- Depending on the division, the TWH may wear a lightweight chain (no more than six ounces) on its front pasterns to enhance its gait.

- Clip the head with the detailed show trim.

- The bridle path should be 8 inches long, with the forelock shaved or left long.

- Rub muzzle, above eyes, and bridle path with baby oil. Clean inside ears with rubbing alcohol.

- Braid the forelock and the first 1/2 inch of mane with ribbon.

- Tuck the forelock braid under the browband and under the cheekpiece of the bridle on the side with the mane. Then wrap it a few times around the throatlatch.

inches. The more stride the horse has, the more exciting the performance. The walker nods his head in cadence with his step. The gait is powerful, exciting, and amazingly smooth for the rider.

The TWH canter is executed with an elevated up beat featuring both spring and rhythm that is surprisingly smooth for the rider. It is sometimes referred to as the rocking-chair canter because of the definite "lift and drop" motion. The flat walk is a four-beat gait with the horse nodding his head with every stride.

Tail

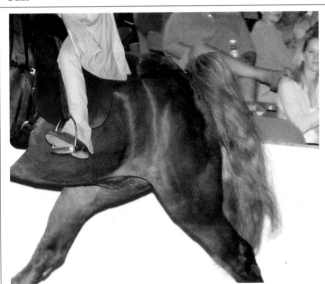

- The TWH wears a tail-set throughout the show season, resulting in a flexible tail without any discomfort to the horse.

- For the show ring, wash and pick out the tail.

- Brace the tail to get it up and forward over the horse's back.

- A tail switch is allowed. Remove it as soon as possible after the class.

There are detailed rules regarding the shoeing of all divisions of the TWH for the show ring. Performance Walkers wear pads in front to increase the overall length of the hoof and accentuate the running walk. The shoeing rules for these "Big Lick" horses cover the width of pads, the size of the shoe, hoof bands, action devices, and how the measurements of heel/toe and pad to natural hoof are taken. Shoeing style determines what class a TWH can be shown in.

Tack

- The show bridle features a single shanked bit and single rein.

- The patent leather show browband can be a single color or multicolored.

- The show cavesson may match the browband or be of flat, dark leather matching the rest of the bridle.

- Use a cutback saddle, breaststraps, and a patent leather or vinyl white or dark show girth with an optional dark pad.

PERFORMANCE

AQHA/STOCK TYPE HALTER

Conformation, breeding, and handling classes for Quarter Horses, Appaloosas, and Paints

A halter class is a class in which the horse is judged based upon its conformation. Horses are shown in hand, wearing only a halter, and are led before the judge at a walk, trot, and halt. The judge assesses conformation, temperament, and gait.

Stock-type horses are the traditional Western working breeds and include American Quarter Horses (AQHA), Paint horses (APHA), Appaloosas (ApHA), Palominos, and Buckskins, among others. Breed standards vary, but generally halter horses are stocky and muscular, with powerful hindquarters, attractive heads, and graceful necks. According to the AQHA rulebook, "the purpose of the class is to preserve American Quarter Horse type by selecting well-mannered individu-

GROOMING HORSES

Halter Horse

- The halter horse should have a short, slick, shiny coat to accent his muscular structure.

- To this end, the horse may be kept under lights and blanketed in cooler seasons.

- The tail should be as long and full as possible.

- White legs should be booted up (see page 66).

- The handler must wear Western attire, including pants (either slacks or jeans).

- Wear a long-sleeved shirt with a collar, a Western hat, and cowboy boots. Male handlers may wear suits.

Halter Horse, Head and Mane

- Horses are shown with manes pulled to 3 1/2 to 4 1/2 inches, with a bridle path of 4 to 8 inches long.

- Braiding is not allowed, but the mane may be banded.

- Heads are fully clipped and accented with highlighter gel on the muzzle and around the eyes.

- Halters are leather, often embellished with silver.

als in the order of their resemblance to the breed ideal and that are the most positive combination of balance, structural correctness, and movement with appropriate breed and sex characteristics and adequate muscling."

Showmanship classes, also conducted with the horse in hand, judge the handler's ability and the horse's level of training, rather than the horse's conformation and type. The handler leads the horse through a predetermined pattern, which may include working around cones at the walk and trot, halting, turning, and backing.

Showmanship

- The horse should be well groomed, shiny, and clean.

- Tails are long, full, and well picked out.

- The handler must wear Western attire, including pants (either slacks or jeans).

- Wear a long-sleeved shirt with a collar, a Western hat, and cowboy boots. A jacket or vest is also usually worn. Pants often match the color of the jacket or shirt. Bright colors and elaborate decoration are typical.

Showmanship, Head and Mane

- Horses are shown with manes pulled to 3 1/2 to 4 1/2 inches, with a bridle path of 4 to 8 inches long.

- The mane may be banded.

- Halters are leather, often embellished with silver.

ARABIAN, HALF-ARABIAN HALTER

Conformation, breeding, and suitability classes are offered for Arabians

Arabian and Half-Arabian halter horses are shown with a long, natural, unbraided mane and typically have a bridle path of up to 8 inches long to accentuate the curve of the neck. The tail must be natural, unset, and ungingered.

Horses shown as sport horses may have a pulled and braided mane appropriate to their discipline (dressage, hunter, or jumper). These horses should also be shown in a bridle appropriate to the discipline.

Various grooming infractions can be cause for elimination from competition, including gingering, removal of the eyelashes, dying of the mane or tail, use of excessive amounts of grease or oil around the muzzle or eyes, and use of any

Arabian Halter Horse

- Clip the lower legs. If body clipping, clip the horse well in advance of the show so there is time for the bloom to return to the coat.

- Tails must be natural, with no hair extensions or setting devices.

- No substances may be applied to the horse to alter its color (such as powder on white markings).

Arabian Head and Mane

- The head should be closely clipped and rubbed with baby oil or highlighter gel.

- Ears should be fully clipped out.

- Bridle path should be 6 to 8 inches long and rubbed with baby oil.

- The mane should be long, full, and natural.

- The horse may wear a bridle or halter appropriate to its discipline.

product that conceals or disguises the hooves. (However, clear hoof polish is acceptable.)

Gingering is the practice of applying an irritant, such as ginger, capsaicin (red pepper), or caustic chemicals, under the horse's tail to cause him to carry it in a more elevated manner. Gingering is strictly prohibited under USEF Arabian breed show rules. Any person who is involved in gingering a horse can be subjected to suspensions and fines.

Tail

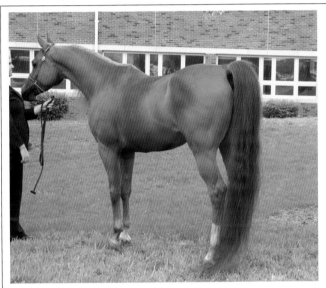

- Tails should be full, long, natural, and well picked out.

- Tail extensions are not allowed, and altered or crooked tails will be penalized.

- Gingering is strictly prohibited.

- Wipe out under the tail with a towel or damp rag, especially because of the Arabian's naturally high tail carriage.

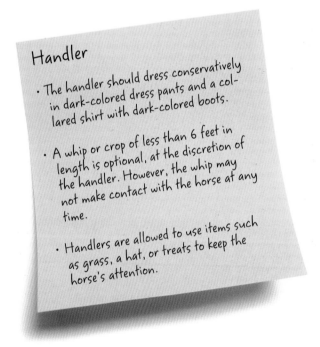

Handler

- The handler should dress conservatively in dark-colored dress pants and a collared shirt with dark-colored boots.

- A whip or crop of less than 6 feet in length is optional, at the discretion of the handler. However, the whip may not make contact with the horse at any time.

- Handlers are allowed to use items such as grass, a hat, or treats to keep the horse's attention.

BREEDING CLASSES

MORGAN, AMERICAN SADDLEBRED

In-hand and "strip" classes are an important part of showing these breeds

Morgan horses should be shown with a long, full, unbraided mane, forelock, and tail. A small rubberband or tape in the forelock is allowed to more clearly show the set of the ears. Morgan horses must exhibit natural tail carriage, uninfluenced by irritants or equipment. As with Arabians, horses being presented as a sport horse—that is, dressage, hunters, or jumpers—may have their manes pulled and braided as appropriate to their disciplines. False tails or false hair of any type is not allowed.

The American Saddlebred is the epitome of the show horse. He exudes an air of refinement, class, and brilliance. He should be in good weight, with good muscle tone and a

Morgan

- Clip the lower legs. If body clipping, clip the horse well in advance of the show so there is time for the bloom to return to the coat.

- Tails must be natural, with no hair extensions or setting devices.

- No substances may be applied to the horse to alter its color (such as powder on white markings).

Morgan Head and Mane

- The head should be closely clipped and rubbed with baby oil or highlighter gel.

- Bridle path should be 6 to 8 inches long and rubbed with baby oil.

- Use an inconspicuous band to contain the forelock.

- The mane should be long, full, and natural.

- The horse may wear a bridle or halter appropriate to its discipline.

smooth, shiny coat. The mane should be long, with a bridle path of 6 to 8 inches. Weanlings and yearlings shown in hand must have natural (that is, uncut and unset) tails.

Saddlebreds are shown in a bridle or leather halter, with no boots, wraps, or any other tack. Both Saddlebreds and Morgans are presented to the judge in a "parked out" stance, with the hind legs stretched out behind. Boots, wraps, or any other leg coverings are not allowed in halter or in-hand classes for either breed.

American Saddlebred

- American Saddlebreds showing in in-hand, breeding, or stripped classes should be turned out according to their specific discipline.

- Pleasure horses should have unset tails, but performance horses may show with set tails.

- Tail extensions or switches are allowed.

- The color and markings of the horse may not be altered by artificial means.

American Saddlebred Head and Mane

- Three-Gaited horses have roached manes, while Five-Gaited performance horses and pleasure horses show with a long mane, braided with the Saddlebred braid (see page 114).

- Horses are shown in hand in a full bridle appropriate to their discipline.

BAROQUE BREEDS

Friesian, Andalusian, and Lusitano horses are in a category of their own

The Baroque breeds are known for their uphill conformation, high and vertical neck carriage, noble bearing, and ability to collect the gaits. They are often used in classical dressage or traditional Iberian disciplines.

The Andalusian (also known as the PRE, or Pura Raza Española) and Lusitano originate from Spain and Portugal, respec-

tively. In the United States their official breed registry is the International Andalusian Lusitano Horse Association (IALHA). Friesians are a Dutch breed originally developed for warfare and later used for carriage driving. They are now being developed into a sport horse breed suitable for dressage. Friesians are virtually always black.

Friesian

Head and Mane

- The horse should wear a halter or bridle appropriate to its discipline. Figure-8 and flash nosebands and gag or twisted bits are not allowed.

- Either reins or a chain lead (not exceeding 12 feet long) may be used.

- Never clip or shorten the feathers of a Friesian. The feathers should be bathed, conditioned, and combed.

- Bandages and leg wraps of any kind are not allowed.

- Clip the muzzle, jaw, cheek-bones, and ears. Bridle paths are a maximum of 2 inches for Friesians and 4 inches for Andalusians and Lusitanos.

- The bridle for a Friesian being shown in hand is made of white leather.

- Horses being presented as sport horses should be shown in a dressage bridle with snaffle bit and may have their manes braided in dressage-appropriate style.

Baroque horses show with a full, flowing mane and tail. False tails, false hair, gingering, or artificial coloring of any type is not allowed. Braiding the mane in a French or Continental braid is optional (see pages 110 and 112). Feathering on the legs of Friesians should not be clipped or shortened.

The exception is young Andalusians, which may be presented in the "Andalusian style" with mane roached, tailbone shaved, and tail hair banged up to age two. There are slight variations in the style to reflect the age and gender of the horse. (See the USEF rulebook for specifics.)

ZOOM

Doma Vaquera is a riding style developed from the maneuvers needed in bullfighting and working cattle on Portuguese and Spanish ranches. It resembles reining and dressage, requiring such movements as explosive gallops from a standing start, skid stops, canter pirouettes, spins, piaffe, lateral movements, and collected gaits. Riders and horses dress in traditional Iberian tack and attire.

Tail

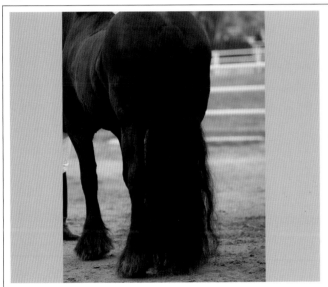

- The tail should be very long, full, and thick.

- The tail may be banged, but this is rarely done for Friesians. It is more common for Andalusians to have a banged tail.

- Weanling and yearling Andalusians are traditionally shown with the tail completely shaved off.

The Handler

- The handler may carry a whip up to 6 feet long.

- Andalusian or Lusitano handlers wear jumpsuits or dress pants and long-sleeve shirts with a tie or pin.

- Friesian handlers wear white pants and shirts with a dark-colored tie.

- Jeans are not allowed. For Andalusians and Lusitanos, traditional Spanish or Portuguese attire is optional. Tuxedos may be worn for evening classes.

BREEDING CLASSES

WARMBLOOD INSPECTIONS

Turnout and grooming for warmblood inspections and sport-horse breeding classes

Warmblood is actually a type of horse rather than a breed. These are the traditional sport horses, which excel at dressage and jumping. What we often think of as "breeds" of warmbloods (Oldenburg, Hanoverian, Westfalen, Dutch Warmblood, etc.) are the various European registries for sport horses. Horses can be (and often are) accepted into more than one of these registries for breeding purposes. There are also two American warmblood registries: the American Warmblood Registry (AWR) and the American Warmblood Society (AWS). See Resources for more information on the warmblood registries.

Each of the warmblood registries has demanding breed in-

Warmblood In-Hand

- Groom the horse thoroughly as if going to a show.

- Body clipping is not usually needed, since the inspections generally take place during the summer months.

- Clip the lower legs, muzzle, and edges of the ears to offer a more refined look. Ears

do not need to be clipped out.

- Tails are not braided. Adult horses may be presented with pulled tails.

- Do not use leg boots, except on stallions in the free-jumping test.

Head and Mane

- Braid the mane and forelock as for dressage or hunters. Stallions may have the forelock unbraided.

- Larger dressage-type braids may help a thin neck look more developed.

- Horses age two and over should wear a bridle with a snaffle bit.

- Weanlings, yearlings, and broodmares with foals should be shown in a halter.

214

spections (also known as keurings) to qualify horses for inclusion in their stud and mare books. Horses cannot be used for breeding in these registries unless they have been approved at an inspection. In addition, foals and young horses may be presented for scoring. Inspections may include in-hand gait evaluation, ridden tests for potential in dressage or jumping, conformation analysis, and temperament evaluation.

Generally speaking, turnout for warmblood inspections is similar to turnout for dressage or hunters. All horses should have their manes pulled and braided and should be neatly clipped and impeccably groomed to present a professional image. Foals and weanlings can be tricky since their baby coats may be shedding, causing them to look a bit rough. Inspectors understand this and will not let it affect the baby's score. Despite a scruffy coat, it's best not to clip the foal. Daily grooming in advance of the inspection will produce the best possible coat. Similarly, a foal's mane may be too sparse to braid, in which case it is fine to leave it unbraided. However, the mane should be tidy to show off the neck.

Mare and Foal or Weanling

- Young foals are presented alongside their mothers. The dam wears a leather halter and is led by a handler, while the foal follows.

- Foals and weanlings may have a rough, shedding coat, which is to be expected. It does not need to be clipped.

- Weanlings and yearlings should have braided manes like older horses, but a very young foal does not need to be braided.

The Handler

Although there are no actual rules governing dress, most handlers stick to the following wardrobe:

- The handler should wear khakis or light-colored dress pants or may choose to wear dark pants for contrast when showing a dark-colored horse.

- Wear a solid-colored collared shirt. Polo shirts are common, or men may wear white dress shirts and ties.

- Most importantly, wear shoes, such as paddock boots or tennis shoes, that will allow you to run to keep up with those big-strided horses.

RESOURCES

Paperwork Needed for Showing

Coggins
Health Certificate
Brand Inspection

Horse Care and Grooming

Books

Harris, Susan, *Grooming to Win,* Howell Book House, 1991
Harris, Susan, *The US Pony Club Manual of Horsemanship,* Howell Book House, 1994
Shiers, Jessie, *101 Horsekeeping Tips,* The Lyons Press, 2005

Magazines

Equus
Horse Illustrated
Practical Horseman

Websites

Horse City: www.horsecity.com
EquiSearch: www.equisearch.com

Hunter/Jumper

Books

Kursinski, Anne, *Anne Kursinski's Riding and Jumping Clinic.* Doubleday, 1995
Morris, George H., *George H. Morris Teaches Beginners to Ride,* The Lyons Press, 2006
Morris, George H., *Hunter Seat Equitation,* Doubleday, 1990
Shiers, Jessie, *101 Hunter/Jumper Tips,* The Lyons Press, 2005

White-Mullin, Anna Jane, *Judging Hunters and Hunter-Seat Equitation,* Trafalgar Square, 2006

Magazines

Practical Horseman
Hunter & Sport Horse
The Chronicle of the Horse

Websites

The United States Equestrian Federation: www.usef.org
The United States Hunter/Jumper Association: www.ushja.org
Results and News: www.towerheads.com

Dressage

Books

Bryant, Jennifer, *The USDF Guide to Dressage,* USDF, 2006
Burn, Barbara, *101 Dressage Tips,* The Lyons Press, 2005
Collins, David, *Dressage Masters,* The Lyons Press, 2006

Eventing

Books

O'Connor, Sally, *Practical Eventing,* Half Halt Press, 1998

Wofford, Jim, *101 Eventing Tips,* The Lyons Press, 2007

Magazines

Eventing USA

The Chronicle of the Horse

Websites

United States Eventing Association: www.useventing.com

The United States Equestrian Federation: www.usef.org

The Fédération Equestre Internationale (FEI): www.fei.org

Results and News: www.eventingetc.com

Magazines

Dressage Today

USDF Connection

The Chronicle of the Horse

Websites

USEF: www.usef.org

The United States Dressage Federation: www.usdf.org

The Fédération Equestre Internationale (FEI): www.fei.org

Results and News: www.dressagedaily.com

Western Performance

Books

Dunning, Al, *Reining,* Western Horseman Books, 2002

Harrel, Leon, *Cutting,* Western Horseman Books, 2002

James, Charmayne, *Charmayne James on Barrel Racing,* Western Horseman Books, 2005

McRae, Marlene, *Barrel Racing 101,* The Lyons Press, 2006

Sellers, Laren, *101 Reining Tips,* The Lyons Press, 2006

Magazines

Western Horseman

Barrel Horse World

NRHA Reiner

Cutting Horse Chatter

America's Cutter

Websites

American Quarter Horse Association: www.aqha.org

American Cutting Horse Association: www.achacutting.com

National Reining Horse Association: www.nrha.org

National Cutting Horse Association: www.nchacutting.com

National Barrel Horse Association: www.nbha.com

Horse City: www.horsecity.com

Saddle Seat

Books

Coleman, Lori, *The American Saddlebred Horse,* Edge Books, 2006

Lutring, Cheryl, *The American Saddlebred,* J. A. Allen, 2005

Oetonger, Judy Fisher, *The Saddlebred: America's Horse of Distinction,* Harmony House, 1991

Magazines

The National Horseman

Saddle and Bridle

Websites

Results and News: www.saddlehorsereport.com

Information and Online Community: www.trot.org

Driving

Books

Bean, Heike, Sarah Blanchard, and Joan Muller, *Carriage Driving,* Howell Book House, 2004

Walrond, Sallie, *Breaking a Horse to Harness,* J. A. Allen, 2000

Walrond, Sallie, *Driving a Harness Horse,* J. A. Allen, 2002

Magazines

The Whip (quarterly journal of the ADS)

The Wheelhorse

The Carriage Journal (publication of the CAA)

Websites

The Carriage Association of America (CAA): www.caaonline.com

American Driving Society (ADS): www.americandrivingsociety.org

Information and Online Community: www.carriagedriving.net

Breeds

Each breed registry maintains a website that provides useful information on breed standards, history, breeders and farms, registration, show schedules and regulations, and other topics. Most organizations have rulebooks available online as well. Rulebooks are an invaluable source of information on breed standards and grooming and equipment expectations for shows. Some breeds run their competitions under USEF regulations, in which case the rulebooks can be found on www.usef.org.

Breeds Shown under USEF Rules (see www.usef.org)
- Andalusian/Lusitano
- Arabian/Half-Arabian/Anglo-Arabian
- Connemara
- Friesian
- Hackney
- Morgan
- National Show Horse
- Paso Fino
- Saddlebred
- Shetland
- Welsh

American Warmblood Registry (AWR)
www.americanwarmblood.com
P.O. Box 197
Carter, MT 59420
(406) 734-5499
Warmblood News (AWR publication)

American Warmblood Society
www.americanwarmblood.org
2 Buffalo Run Road
Center Ridge, AR 72027
(501) 893-2777

International Andalusian & Lusitano Horse Association (IALHA)
www.ialha.org
101 Carnoustie North
Box 200
Birmingham, AL 35242
(205) 995–8900

Appaloosa Horse Club (ApHC)
www.appaloosa.com
2720 West Pullman Road
Moscow, ID 83843
(208) 882-5578
Appaloosa Journal

Arabian Horse Association (AHA)
www.arabianhorses.org
0805 E. Bethany Drive
Aurora, CO 80014
(303) 696-4500
Modern Arabian Horse magazine

Dutch Warmblood: North American Department of the
Royal Warmblood Studbook of the Netherlands (KWPN-
North America)
www.nawpn.org
P.O. Box 0
Sutherlin, OR 97479
(541) 459-3232

Friesian Horse Association of North America (FHANA)
www.fhana.com
4037 Iron Works Parkway, Suite 160
Lexington, KY 40511-8483
(859) 455-7430

American Haflinger Registry
www.haflingerhorse.com
1686 East Waterloo Road
Akron, OH 44306-4103
(330) 784-0000
Haflinger Horse magazine

American Hanoverian Society
www.hanoverian.org
4067 Iron Works Parkway
Lexington, KY 40511
(859) 255-4141

American Holsteiner Horse Association
www.holsteiner.com
222 E. Main Street, Suite 1
Georgetown, KY 40324-1712
(502) 863-4239
Holsteiner magazine

American Miniature Horse Association
www.amha.org
5601 South Interstate 35W
Alvarado, TX, 76009
(817) 783-5600
Miniature Horse World magazine

Missouri Fox Trotter Horse Breed Association
www.mfthba.com
P.O. Box 1027
Ava, MO 65608
(417) 683-2468

American Morgan Horse Association (AMHA)
www.morganhorse.com
American Morgan Horse Association
122 Bostwick Road
Shelburne, VT 05482-4417
(802) 985-4944
The Morgan Horse magazine

Norwegian Fjord Horse Registry
www.nfhr.com
1203 Appian Drive
Webster, NY 14580
(585) 872–4114

Oldenburg Horse Breeders' Society
www.oldenburghorse.com
150 Hammocks Drive
West Palm Beach, FL 33413
(561) 969-0709

American Paint Horse Association (APHA)
www.apha.com
P.O. Box 961023
Fort Worth, TX 76161-0023
(817) 834-APHA (2742)
Paint Horse Journal

Paso Fino Horse Association
www.pfha.org
101 North Collins
Plant City, FL 33563-3311
(813) 719-7777
Paso Fino Horse World magazine

Peruvian Paso: North American Peruvian Horse Association (NAPHA)
www.pphrna.org
3095 Burleson Retta Road, Suite B
Burleson, TX 76028
(817) 447-7574

Pony of the Americas Club (POAC)
www.poac.org
3828 South Emerson Avenue
Indianapolis, IN 46203
(317) 788-0107
POA magazine

American Quarter Horse Association (AQHA)
www.aqha.org
American Quarter Horse Association
1600 Quarter Horse Drive
Amarillo, TX 79104
(806) 376-4811
America's Horse magazine

Rheinland Pfalz-Saar International (RhPSI)
www.rhpsi.com
6349 Daylily Court
Alta Loma, CA 91737
(909) 948-2934

Rocky Mountain Horse Association
www.rmhorse.com
P.O. Box 129
Mt. Olivet, KY 41064
(606) 724-2354
The Rocky Mountain Horse magazine

American Saddlebred Horse Association (ASHA)
www.asha.net
4083 Iron Works Parkway
Lexington, KY 40511
(859) 259-2742

American Shetland Pony Club
www.shetlandminiature.com
81 B Queenwood Road
Morton, IL 61550
(309) 263–4044
The Journal magazine

Tennessee Walking Horse Breeders and Exhibitors Association
www.twhbea.com
250 N. Ellington Parkway
Lewisburg, TN 37091
(931) 359-1574
Voice magazine
www.nationalhorseshowcommission.com

American Trakehner Association (ATA)
www.americantrakehner.com
1536 West Church Street
Newark, OH 43055
(740) 344-1111

Welsh Pony and Cob Society of America
www.welshponies.com
720 Green Street
Stephens City, VA 22655
(540) 868-PONY (7669)
Welsh Review magazine

SHOW DAY CHECKLIST

For the Horse

- ❑ grooming kit
- ❑ braiding or banding kit
- ❑ first-aid kit for horses
- ❑ cordless touch-up clippers
- ❑ bridles and bits
- ❑ saddle
- ❑ girth or cinch
- ❑ other tack (martingale, breastplate, etc.)
- ❑ saddle pad
- ❑ extra saddle pad
- ❑ cooler
- ❑ stable sheet, rain sheet, or blanket (depending on weather)
- ❑ boots or wraps for warmup or showing, if needed
- ❑ leather halter and lead
- ❑ extra halter and lead
- ❑ longe line and longe whip
- ❑ buckets
- ❑ hay nets and hay
- ❑ fly spray
- ❑ ear net, if needed
- ❑ sponge and sweat scraper
- ❑ towels and rags
- ❑ baby wipes for muzzle and ears
- ❑ treats
- ❑ head bumper, shipping boots, and tail wrap
- ❑ manure fork and muck bucket
- ❑ drinking water

Ringside Groom's Kit

- ❑ tote
- ❑ rags or towels
- ❑ soft brush
- ❑ fly spray
- ❑ baby wipes
- ❑ hoof pick
- ❑ hoof polish
- ❑ water bottle and snack for rider
- ❑ lead line

For the Rider

- ❏ boots
- ❏ boot socks
- ❏ helmet or hat
- ❏ riding pants or jeans
- ❏ show shirt
- ❏ show jacket or vest
- ❏ riding gloves
- ❏ belt
- ❏ street clothes and shoes
- ❏ sweatshirt or fleece jacket big enough to wear over your show clothes
- ❏ boot polish
- ❏ rags
- ❏ hair brush, hair net, bobby pins, hair elastic, hair spray
- ❏ string or pins for your number
- ❏ whip or crop
- ❏ spurs
- ❏ chaps

- ❏ healthy snack (Granola bars, fruit, sandwiches)
- ❏ drinks (water, juice, sports drinks)
- ❏ baby wipes and/or hand sanitizer
- ❏ first-aid kit for humans
- ❏ boot pulls and boot jack
- ❏ baseball cap or sun hat
- ❏ sunglasses
- ❏ rain gear if needed
- ❏ sunscreen
- ❏ camera
- ❏ cell phone
- ❏ checkbook and wallet
- ❏ extra cash for tolls and food
- ❏ prize list
- ❏ directions to show
- ❏ rulebook and tests or patterns
- ❏ folding chairs

FIRST-AID KIT CHECKLIST

For the Horse

Cleansers, Ointments, and Other Products

- ❏ Betadine Solution or other diluted iodine solution
- ❏ Betadine Scrub or other antibacterial shampoo
- ❏ Hydrogen peroxide
- ❏ Antibacterial ointment
- ❏ Antibacterial powder spray
- ❏ Icthammol
- ❏ Saline solution or other eye cleanser
- ❏ Antifungal product
- ❏ Witch hazel, calamine lotion, or other anti-itch product
- ❏ Epsom salt for soaking abscessed hooves
- ❏ Poultice
- ❏ Electrolytes
- ❏ Mineral oil

Medications Provided by Your Vet

- ❏ Bute (phenylbutazone)
- ❏ Banamine
- ❏ Ace (Acepromazine, a sedative)

Bandaging Materials

- ❏ Sterile gauze sponges
- ❏ Rolled cotton
- ❏ Self-adhesive bandage
- ❏ Four pillow wraps and four standing bandages
- ❏ Instant cold pack
- ❏ Duct tape
- ❏ Hoof boot

Tools

- ❏ Rectal thermometer and petroleum jelly
- ❏ Blunt-tipped bandage scissors
- ❏ Stethoscope
- ❏ Flashlight
- ❏ Twitch
- ❏ Hoof pick
- ❏ Wire cutters
- ❏ Mini cordless clippers
- ❏ Latex medical gloves
- ❏ Tweezers
- ❏ Syringe for dosing or for flushing out a wound
- ❏ Small, clean towels
- ❏ Extra lead rope with chain
- ❏ List of emergency phone numbers

For the Human

- ❏ Latex medical gloves
- ❏ Sterile gauze
- ❏ Bandage tape
- ❏ Alcohol pads
- ❏ Hydrogen peroxide
- ❏ Waterless hand sanitizer
- ❏ Triple antibiotic ointment
- ❏ Burn ointment
- ❏ Hydrocortisone ointment
- ❏ Adhesive bandages in a variety of sizes (Band-Aids or similar)
- ❏ Saline solution for flushing eyes
- ❏ Thermometer
- ❏ Epi-Pen
- ❏ Aspirin or other oral painkiller/anti-inflammatory
- ❏ Scissors
- ❏ Tweezers
- ❏ Instant cold pack
- ❏ Ace bandage
- ❏ List of emergency phone numbers

Horse and Human Mini Kit for the Trailer

- ❏ Adhesive bandages
- ❏ Aspirin or other oral painkiller/anti-inflammatory
- ❏ Alcohol pads
- ❏ Hand sanitizer
- ❏ Hydrogen peroxide
- ❏ Gauze pads
- ❏ Triple-antibiotic ointment (for humans)
- ❏ Scissors
- ❏ Equine rectal thermometer
- ❏ Vet-Rap
- ❏ One pillow wrap and one standing bandage
- ❏ Duct tape
- ❏ Banamine
- ❏ Bute
- ❏ Equine antibacterial ointment
- ❏ Bottle of water

GLOSSARY

Bandage bow: Swelling of the tendon sheath caused by an incorrectly applied leg wrap or boot.

Banding: The process of dividing a horse's mane into many tiny sections, each secured by a rubberband, for Western showing.

Banged tail: A tail that has been cut straight across the bottom.

Bean: A waxy gray ball of smegma that builds up within the tip of the urethra of a male horse.

Bell boots: Horse boots that fit around the pastern and hang down to protect the coronary bands and the bulbs of the heel.

Betadine: The trade name of a antibacterial product with povidone iodine as the active ingredient. It is available as either a scrub (shampoo) or a solution.

Bib clip: A clipping style that includes clipping the front of the throat and neck, the chest, and the belly to just behind the girth.

Biotin: A nutrient that aids in healthy hoof and hair growth.

Body clip: A clipping style in which the horse's entire body is clipped short, including the head and legs.

Booting up: Closely clipping the white markings on a horse's lower legs to make them stand out.

Borium: Small droplets of metal added to the bottom of a horseshoe to give the horse extra traction on ice.

Bots: Bot fly eggs look like tiny yellow or white specks stuck to the horse's hair. If the horse ingests these eggs, they will hatch and develop into larvae in his intestines.

Brace: A liquid or gel that is rubbed briskly into the muscles or tendons and joints of the legs, usually after a hard workout, to reduce inflammation, reduce pain or stiffness, and encourage circulation to the area.

Braid Aid: A four-pronged comb that divides the hair into three equal sections to be braided.

Breeding class: An in-hand horse show class in which the horse's conformation is judged.

Bridle path: A short section at the top of the mane, just behind the ears, that is clipped short to provide a space for the crownpiece of the bridle to rest. The length of the bridle path varies by breed and discipline.

Bustle: A padded support used under the tail to enhance its upright carriage.

Button braids: Large, round, sewn-in braids along the crest of the neck used on dressage horses.

Cactus cloth: A thick, rough cloth used to rub the coat and remove sweat marks.

Chinks: Western chaps that cover the upper parts of the legs and end at the knees.

Cold hosing: Running cold water from a hose over an injured leg to reduce inflammation.

Conditioning: The system of feeding and exercise used to develop a horse physically to prepare it for a particular task, such as showing.

Continental braid: A method of dividing and banding the mane into sections to create a pattern that looks like macramé.

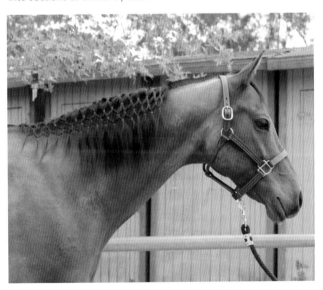

Cooler: A wool or synthetic fleece sheet used to keep the horse warm as it wicks away sweat or moisture from the coat.

Coronary band: The top part of the hoof, between the hoof wall and the pastern, from which the hoof wall grows.

Curry: A round, rubber brush used in a circular motion to loosen dirt and dander from the horse's coat.

Dandy brush: Also called a hard brush or a body brush, this stiff-bristled brush is used to remove the majority of loose dirt from the coat.

Denier: The thread count of blanket material. A higher denier generally means a more durable blanket.

Derby: A small, felt hat with a narrow brim. Different styles of derby are worn in upper-level dressage and in saddle seat showing.

Dock: The bony top part of the tail, as opposed to the skirt, which consists only of hair.

Ear twitch: A method of restraining a horse by twisting an ear. This is painful for the horse and causes him to become headshy of anyone working around his ears.

Equitation: The art of riding. The term is used in showing to designate classes in which the rider, not the horse, is being judged.

Feathers: This can refer to either the long, coarse hairs on a horse's fetlocks and pasterns (especially on a draft horse) or to the short hairs at the top of the tail.

Finger combing: The process of carefully separating each hair in a tail or long mane by hand to produce a full look with minimal hair breakage.

Finishing brush: Also called a soft brush. Used to remove the last bits of dust from the coat as well as to set and polish the hair.

Fly predators: Tiny wasplike insects that feed on the larvae of flies, available through mail order.

Forelock: The very front part of a horse's mane, which falls forward between his ears onto his forehead.

French braid: A single thick braid that runs the length of the crest on a long-maned horse. Also, a braid in the tail that incorporates the hair along the tailbone.

Galloping boots: Horse boots that have a padded area that protects the inner tendons of the lower legs during work. Also called brushing boots or splint boots (since they protect the splint bones from brushing against the opposite hoof).

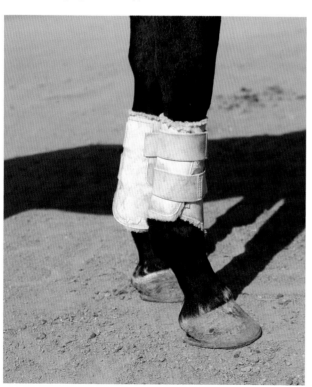

Halter: A horse show division in which the horse's conformation is judged. Also may refer to a horse bred to be shown in halter classes, such as a halter-type Quarter Horse.

Hives: Itchy welts on the skin that are usually a symptom of an allergic reaction.

Homburg: A felt hat that is shaped differently than the traditional saddle seat derby in both its crown and brim. Common with Arabian and Tennessee Walking Horse exhibitors.

Hoof boots: Hard rubber boots that fit over the horse's entire hoof, protecting the sole and frog against hard or rocky ground.

Hot toweling: A method of using very hot, damp towels to clean the coat when bathing is impractical.

Humane twitch: A twitch that uses a rounded clamp rather than a twisted chain.

Hunter braids: Small, neat, knoblike braids along the crest of the horse's neck. These braids are appropriate for all English disciplines.

Hunter clip: A clipping style that involves clipping the body, including the head, except for a small patch of hair in the saddle area for protection against the cold as well as saddle rubs. The legs are also left unclipped.

Interference: When a horse accidentally contacts any part of his hoof or leg with any other part of another hoof or leg while in movement, potentially causing injury.

Irish clip: A clipping style that involves clipping a triangle of hair from the throat to the midpoint of the belly.

Irish knit: A loosely woven netlike sheet used to wick away sweat.

Jelly scrubber: A very soft rubber curry with small, gentle knobs. Ideal for sensitive-skinned horses who don't tolerate traditional curries.

Liniment: A liquid or gel that is rubbed briskly into the muscles or tendons and joints of the legs, usually after a hard workout, to reduce inflammation, reduce pain or stiffness, and encourage circulation to the area.

Mud knot: A method of braiding or tying up the tail to keep it clean in muddy conditions.

Omega-3 fatty acids: A nutrient found in certain fat sources such as flax seeds and fish oil. It aids in skin, coat, and hoof health and helps produce a shiny coat.

Open-front boots: Boots that have protective backs and sides but only thin straps across the fronts of the cannon bones.

Panic snap: A safety snap used on cross ties and trailer ties. The design allows the snap to be released when it is under tension.

Pleasure: A term used in showing to designate a class in which the horse, not the rider, is being judged.

Polo wraps: Thick, stretchy fleece wraps used to protect and support the tendons of the lower leg during work.

Poultice: A thick, sticky, claylike material used to reduce inflammation, reduce pain or stiffness, and encourage circulation to the area.

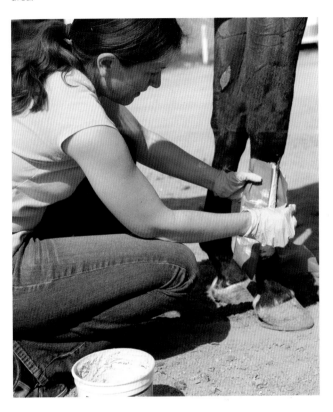

Pulled mane: A mane that has been thinned and shortened by the use of a pulling comb to a uniform length of 3 1/2 to 4 1/2 inches.

Pulled tail: A tail that has had the short hairs along the sides of the tailbone pulled out to result in a smoother appearance.

Pulling comb: A specialized metal comb used to pull out mane or tail hairs.

Pull-through: A hooked instrument used to pull the end of a braid up through the base of the braid.

231

Quarter boots: Horse boots that are firmly attached on the horse's hoof below the coronary band. They protect the bulbs of the horse's heel and are typically used on horses that perform at the rack, such as the Five-Gaited Saddlebred.

Quarter marks: A checkerboard pattern made on the hindquarters by combing the hair in different directions.

Rain rot: A bacterial infection caused by the Dermatophilus bacteria that develops on the skin of the back, neck, and hindquarters when the horse has been wet.

Ratcatcher: An English show shirt with a stiff, circular choker.

Ringworm: A highly contagious fungal skin condition that causes small, round patches of scaly skin with missing hair.

Roached mane: A mane that has been completely clipped off.

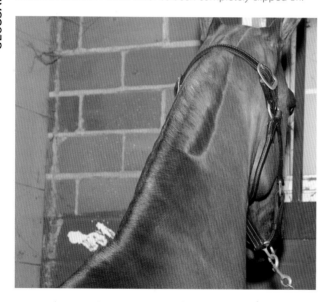

Rub rag: A small towel used after grooming to rub the horse's coat, polishing it to a high shine.

Scratches: A fungal infection of the pastern and fetlock that causes painful, scaly scabs, hair loss, and inflammation.

Set tail: A tail that has been altered by cutting the muscle on the underside of the dock and held in place with a tail set (a harnesslike device that supports the tail in the upright position).

Sheath: The outer portion of a male horse's genitalia, which covers the penis. It needs to be cleaned periodically to prevent itching or possible infection or urinary obstruction.

Shedding blade: A flexible metal implement with small teeth and a handle, used during shedding season to rake the long, loose hairs from the coat.

Shipping boots: Tall, thick, durable boots used only when trailering a horse.

Skid boots: Horse boots that protect the backs of the horse's legs during sliding stops in reining and cattle work.

Skirt: The long hair of the tail, as opposed to the dock.

Smegma: Waxy black material that builds up inside the sheath of a male horse and must be removed by periodic cleaning.

Snow balls: The hooves of a shod horse can build up a thick, rounded layer of ice and snow, making it difficult to balance.

Sport boots: Neoprene full-coverage horse boots that protect the tendons of the lower leg, including a suspensory strap that wraps under the fetlock to cover and support the suspensory tendon.

Standing wraps: Two-part wraps consisting of a thick, cushioning underlayer and a tight, thin wrap as a top layer. Used to reduce or prevent inflammation, protect the legs, and cover wounds.

Stock tie: A type of tie worn by English riders, especially in dressage.

Stud chain: A short piece of chain on the end of a lead rope that can be passed over the horse's nose for added control.

Sweat: A waterproof covering, possibly used over a mild liniment, to reduce inflammation (as in an injured leg) or to refine a body part for showing (as in a neck sweat).

Sweat scraper: A plastic or wooden implement used to squeegee water (usually not sweat) from the horse's coat for faster drying time after a bath.

Sweet itch: An extremely irritating condition caused by an allergy to biting Culicoides midges.

Tail bag: A protective sleeve worn over the tail that prevents breakage.

Tail extension or switch: A so-called fake tail (made of real horsehair) used to enhance the thickness and length of the horse's natural tail.

Tail set: A harnesslike device worn by some saddle seat show horses to enhance their upright tail carriage.

Tail wrap: A bandage wrapped around the tailbone either to protect it while traveling or to smooth down the hairs for a polished look in the show ring.

Tea tree oil: A natural essential oil known for its healing and anti-bacterial properties.

Thrush: A bacterial infection of the clefts of the hoof that produces a soft, black substance and a distinctive foul odor.

Toweling: The process of rubbing a horse by hand with a small towel after grooming. A ten-minute daily toweling session helps produce a shine on the coat.

Trace clip: A clipping style that involves the underside of the throat and neck, the chest, belly, and a strip across the stifle and flank.

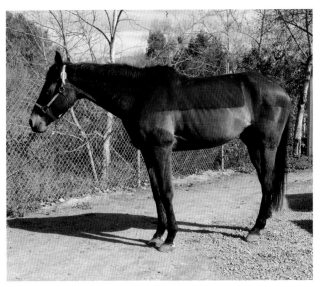

Training braids: Simple braids that "teach" an unruly mane to lie down flat on one side of the neck.

Twitch: A method of restraining a horse by looping and twisting a short rope or chain around the upper lip.

Witch's knots: Dreadlock-like tangles in a long mane or tail.

INDEX

INDEX

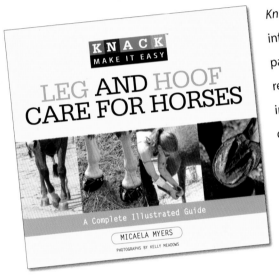